THE DIRTY DOZEN

N. Sundaresha Subramanian is a business journalist and newsroom leader. With his rich experience in hard-hitting journalism and a keen focus on public interest, he has driven award-winning coverage in critical areas including corporate and regulatory affairs, corporate governance and wrongdoing, policy, geopolitics and emerging areas of ESG and energy transition. Currently the Executive Editor at *Economic Times' ET Prime*, Sundaresha began his journey in journalism as part of the team that launched the Mumbai edition of *Hindustan Times* in the early 2000s and has since worked with *DNA Money*, *Mint* and *Business Standard*. He lives and works in Delhi.

THE DIRTY DOZEN

INDIA'S TWELVE BIGGEST CORPORATE DEFAULTERS

N. SUNDARESHA SUBRAMANIAN

PAN

First published 2024 by Pan
an imprint of Pan Macmillan Publishing India Private Limited
707 Kailash Building
26 K. G. Marg, New Delhi 110001
www.panmacmillan.co.in

Pan Macmillan, The Smithson, 6 Briset Street, Farringdon, London EC1M 5NR
Associated companies throughout the world
www.panmacmillan.com

ISBN 978-93-89109-17-7

Copyright © N. Sundaresha Subramanian 2024

The moral rights of the author have been asserted.

All rights reserved. No part of this publication may be reproduced, stored in or introduced into a retrieval system, or transmitted, in any form, or by any means (electronic, mechanical, photocopying, recording or otherwise) without the prior written permission of the publisher. Any person who does any unauthorized act in relation to this publication may be liable to criminal prosecution and civil claims for damages.

The views expressed in this book are the author's own and the facts reported by him have been verified by the publisher to the extent possible. The publisher hereby disclaims any liability to any party for loss, damages or disruptions caused by the same.

1 3 5 7 9 8 6 4 2

This book is sold subject to the condition that it shall not, by way of trade or otherwise, be lent, re-sold, hired out, or otherwise circulated without the publisher's prior consent in any form of binding or cover other than that in which it is published and without a similar condition including this condition being imposed on the subsequent purchaser.

Typeset in Bembo Std by Manmohan Kumar
Printed in India by Gopsons Papers Pvt. Ltd., Noida

To the three Meenakshis of my life – my mother, my daughter and She who rules our beloved Madurai

Contents

Foreword by Dr M. S. Sahoo ... ix
Introduction ... xvii

PART I: SETTING THE SCENE

1. The Origins ... 3
2. Companies Cry, But Owners Party ... 14
3. Corruption and Political Involvement ... 38
4. Mallya and the Art of Leaving ... 52

PART II: THE DIRTY DOZEN

5. The Point of No Return? ... 73
6. Lanco Infratech ... 80
7. Amtek Auto ... 87
8. Jaypee Infratech ... 95
9. Alok Industries ... 104
10. Era Infra Engineering ... 112
11. Jyoti Structures ... 120
12. ABG Shipyard ... 128

13.	Essar Steel	136
14.	The Bhushan Twins: Bhushan Steel and Bhushan Power & Steel	146
15.	Monnet Ispat & Energy	160
16.	Electrosteel Steels	168

PART III: THE AFTERMATH

17.	Conquerors, Survivors and Hindustan Leavers	181
18.	The Central Bank's Response	214
19.	The Sell-off Struggle	234

Epilogue	261
Notes	265
Abbreviations	287
Acknowledgements	293

Foreword

The Dirty Dozen is an iconic 1967 American war film, adapted from E. M. Nathanson's gripping 1965 novel by the same title. Noted for its enthralling narrative, both novel and film brim with suspense, drama and pulse-pounding action. The plot, in both, centres around a military mission that trains a dozen hardened convicts into highly skilled commandos. This book, titled *The Dirty Dozen*, although unrelated to the works mentioned above, draws parallels with its cinematic counterpart, embarking on an economic mission to rejuvenate twelve beleaguered companies fighting for survival. With a narrative as gripping as its namesake film and novel, this book by N. Sundaresha Subramanian promises to enthral readers with its tale of failure and redemption amidst corporate chaos. My professional journey allowed me a glimpse of the run-up to the 'Dirty Dozen' and their life and our economy thereafter.

Kongo Gumi Co. Ltd., a Japanese firm revered for its temple construction expertise, ran for a record 1,429 years. On failing to repay its debts, the company filed for bankruptcy in 2006, underscoring the destructive powers of this double-edged leverage. For while on one hand, bankruptcy can increase returns, allowing debtors to grow faster than they would otherwise, on the other, it can equally aggravate losses, especially during economic downturns. The latter can lead to severe consequences such as insolvency and asset forfeiture.

In the best of times, it is difficult for an astute business entity to figure out its optimal leverage. Companies may be tempted to overleverage if the economy is booming, and debt is easily available. The situation gets exacerbated when the creditor, having no effective means to recover the debt, is obligated to extend a fresh round to avert the borrower from defaulting – a vicious cycle. A poignant caricature by Ravikanth succinctly captures this heady cocktail where a debtor jests with a banker: 'Your lending rates are okay! But the high NPA numbers, wow, that's what attracted me to your bank!'[1]

In early 2016, the inevitable happened. The Indian economy suffered from the 'twin balance sheet syndrome' (TBS). The balance sheets of both firms and banks were under severe stress, with half of the firms reporting an interest coverage ratio (a measure of how well a firm can pay the interest due on outstanding debt) of less than one, implying little room to service their debt obligations. Meanwhile, with non-performing assets (NPAs) exceeding 9 per cent by mid-2016, the profitability of banks was critically impacted and constrained fresh lending. The problem continued to aggravate. NPAs kept growing, while credit and investment kept falling. An effective insolvency law, one that could settle NPAs and improve credit availability by enabling swift and cost-effective resolution of stressed assets, became a necessity. Thus emerged the Insolvency and Bankruptcy Code (IBC) in May 2016, as an urgent response to the TBS.

A real sector company typically funds its operations through equity and debt. Ideally, this equity and debt should be safeguarded by their stakeholders – the shareholders and creditors, respectively. Sadly, this was not the case. The shareholders retained control over the company even after exhausting its equity. Failure to repay debt did not have any consequence on them, thereby incentivizing excessive leverage. With the introduction of the IBC, power now lay with the creditors, enabling them to take charge of debt-laden companies. While any stakeholder could initiate insolvency proceedings as soon as equity became depleted, the code placed financial creditors (FCs) in the driving seat, considering their commercial wisdom, allowing them to decide the company's fate. The IBC empowered these stakeholders to close an insolvency proceeding, decide to liquidate the company at any time or rescue it.

Armed with this unprecedented authority, the FCs could now orchestrate the rescue of distressed companies through a comprehensive resolution plan. With the IBC in place, they could: (a) scour the global market for the most viable resolution plan, in a significant departure from previous mechanisms that prevented existing promoters from resorting to them; (b) take and/or cause a haircut of any amount to any or all stakeholders as may be required for rescuing the company; and (c) undertake resolution plans that may entail any measure(s) – a change of management, technology, or product portfolio; acquisition or disposal of assets, businesses or undertakings; restructuring of organization, business model, ownership or balance sheet; strategies of turnaround, buyout, merger, amalgamation, acquisition or takeover, etc.[2]

Having said that, some companies were beyond repair and had to be closed. The IBC provided a structured framework for the closure of such companies.

There was an unprecedented urgency to implement the IBC in the face of the festering TBS. The Insolvency and

Bankruptcy Board of India (IBBI), which oversees insolvency matters, was created on 1 October 2016. It was tasked with enforcing the corporate insolvency resolution provisions in the code, starting from 1 December 2016. The IBBI set up the necessary ecosystem to handle insolvency, which included the creation of professional roles and agencies focused on insolvency. Additionally, they designed the guidelines that activated the mechanism for resolving corporate insolvency from the expected date. This fresh system has brought about a sea change in how insolvencies are managed in India, delivering on both efficiency and transparency.

Everything was arranged for the banks to take advantage of the IBC – like taking a horse to water. Unfortunately, like the proverbial horse, they refused to drink. Despite being the top victims of unpaid loans and possessing full control over the IBC proceedings, banks were reluctant to wield this power. In the first two quarters, 166 companies were admitted to the IBC process. About a quarter of them were initiated by FCs. The reluctance of banks to initiate IBC proceedings against defaulting companies, particularly those with substantial defaults, remains a conundrum.

A case was made to find solutions outside the IBC. The government's economic think tank echoed this in the Economic Survey for 2016–17:

> The problem is that the new bankruptcy system is not yet fully in place, and even when it is, the new procedures (and participants) will need to be tested first on smaller cases. Some considerable time will consequently elapse before the system will be ready to handle the large, complex cases.

It suggested an alternative:

> 'One possible strategy would be to create a "Public Sector Asset Rehabilitation Agency" (PARA), charged with working out the largest and most complex cases.'[3]

As banks waited for an alternative to the IBC, the IBBI found itself in an uneasy spot after expeditiously establishing the insolvency framework. The government, too, having invested a lot in the IBC, was wary about considering alternatives, believing the IBC to be suited for all cases, regardless of their size. Leaving aside its efficacy, the creation and implementation of the proposed PARA would take a few years. Faced with pressing growth imperatives, the government opted to push for IBC usage by enacting the Banking Regulation (Amendment) Ordinance, 2017, on 4 May 2017. This ordinance empowered the Reserve Bank of India to direct banks to use the IBC, ensuring timely resolution of default cases.

In June 2017, the RBI first told banks to start insolvency proceedings under the IBC. These proceedings, involving twelve accounts with significant Non-Performing Assets (NPAs) – around 25 per cent of the banking system's total NPAs – came to be widely known as the 'Dirty Dozen'. This phrase was popularized by Sanjeev Sanyal, the Senior Economic Adviser at the finance ministry at that time. This galvanized the FCs, who had been watching from the sidelines until then, to use the code for the resolution of their stressed assets. By the last quarter of 2023, over 60 per cent of insolvency proceedings were initiated by FCs, underscoring both their newfound assertiveness and the government's steadfast commitment to insolvency reform.

And so commenced the arduous odyssey. Shortly thereafter, on 23 November, the Swachhata Drive found its way to the IBC through section 29A, which prohibited unclean hands from taking over a company through a resolution plan. This brought about a shift in debtor–creditor relationships, leading to ownership changes in many large companies that were furiously contested up to the Supreme Court. As the dust settled, a remarkable transformation unfolded. Some of the 'Big Twelve' managed to recover convincingly, others had to be liquidated and a few are still in the middle of the process. By September 2023, the banks' NPAs had gone down to 3.2 per cent, from a peak of 11 per cent in September 2018. The banks reported a net profit of ₹2,63,214 crore in the financial year 2022–23, compared to a loss of ₹32,438 crore in 2017–18. Meanwhile, companies also improved their functioning, resulting in strong balance sheets, sensible borrowing levels, and an interest coverage ratio over 3.5. This shift from stress due to unpaid loans to having twin balance sheet benefits marked a significant turn of events.

A recent IIMA* study finds that post resolution, the companies have witnessed substantial improvements. Their turnover increased by 76 per cent, profitability ratios converged with benchmarks, and market capitalization tripled over three years. Corporate governance, too, witnessed improvement, as demonstrated by the decrease in transactions between related parties after the implementation of the IBC. In the first three years of the IBC, India's global ranking in resolving insolvency parameters jumped from the 136th place to the 52nd. The clear risk of losing their company caused debtors to take active steps to avoid the IBC process. This is evident from the fact that

---

* Indian Institute of Management Ahmedabad

insolvency applications for initiation of the IBC process against 27,514 companies, with an aggregate default of ₹9.74 trillion, were withdrawn before admission, reinforcing the maxim that the best use of the IBC is not using it at all.

The Dirty Dozen isn't merely a chronicle of corporate downfall and revival; it serves as a beacon of hope and inspiration amidst adversity. These narratives work as poignant reminders that even in the bleakest of circumstances, there exists a flicker of possibility waiting to be seized. May the cautionary tales contained within these pages ignite a flame of inspiration, encouraging companies to not only embrace change but also to navigate challenges with resilience and fortitude. Within the crucible of adversity lies the opportunity for growth and transformation, ultimately enabling companies to emerge stronger and more resilient than ever before.

Dr M. S. Sahoo
Former Distinguished Professor, National Law University Delhi & Former Chairperson, Insolvency and Bankruptcy Board of India

February 2024

Introduction

It was February 2016. The country's second-largest public sector lender, Punjab National Bank, put out a list of wilful defaulters from among its clients. Some of the names that featured prominently on the list were Vijay Mallya's Kingfisher Airlines, Jatin Mehta's Winsome Diamonds and Jewellery, and Vijay Choudhary's Zoom Developers. This was a group of accounts that had deliberately not repaid loans despite having the means to do so. They now comprised a kind of blacklist and were partly ostracized from the financial system that could put them, the defaulting borrower, in a difficult spot. Their credit lines, not only with the lenders on whom they had defaulted, but with others too, were cut off.

Although most of us often came across news reports about a so-and-so being declared a wilful defaulter from time to time, banks did not place this information in the public domain regularly. Against this backdrop, the list of wilful defaulters on PNB's website threw open – for the very first time – an opportunity for journalists like me to further analyze and explore the antecedents and public and private records of these unscrupulous borrowers.

As I went looking for these establishments after gathering some basic details, such as names of directors and registered addresses from the Registrar of Companies, some interesting stories emerged, many of which were documented in a *Business Standard* article entitled 'The mystery of PNB's vanishing loans'.[1]

One particular image etched in my memory is of a rickety first-floor chamber in North Delhi's Shahdara neighbourhood that displayed the nameplates of some seventeen companies of the Apple Industries group. These (obviously) asset-less, business-less shell entities had managed to procure loans of over ₹400 crore, on which they had promptly defaulted.

Compare this with the experience of an ordinary individual. It is unthinkable that the bank and its managers would even offer a few thousand rupees to such a borrower from Shahdara. Here, they not only lent ₹400 crore but were on their way to writing it off!

This was one in a string of humongous loans that were destined to default. It led me to ask many questions. How did the maker-checker architecture of authorization, fundamental to banking, fail to catch this gross bluff at its origin? Why did the whistles not blow? How did the penny not drop? These and similar questions that confounded me formed the genesis of this book.

As the Reserve Bank of India, then headed by the mercurial Raghuram Rajan, took steps to ringfence banks from the impact of looming defaults, the massive bad loans problem that extended to the wider banking system became apparent. It was around this time that a new regulator to deal with insolvency and bankruptcy was born – the Insolvency and Bankruptcy Board of India (IBBI).

However, Rajan's departure, coupled with the Narendra Modi-led central government's decision to demonetize ₹500 and ₹2,000 currency notes later that year significantly diverted public attention and, more importantly, consumed the bandwidth of the banks required to look after this huge volume of day-to-day work.

My idea for a book on bad loans also took a back seat. Six months later, in a major boost to the fledgling insolvency regime, the RBI decided to refer twelve large defaulters to the insolvency resolution process under a new law. Unlike the Shahdara shell entities, these were not fly-by-night operators. In fact, most of these companies had a long track record, reputed promoters, and each had bad loans of ₹5,000 crore or more.

With debt piles reaching as high as ₹56,000 crore in the case of Bhushan Steel alone, the total amount at stake in these twelve companies was a staggering ₹3.45 lakh crore. The new insolvency law or IBC, as it came to be known, intoduced something unprecedented. Until then, come what may, the promoter seldom lost control of his company. Often the lenders were left with the Hobson's choice of throwing more and more good money at the bad. But, under the IBC, they had the power to remove the management and take control of the borrower. The new law provided for the cover of a court-controlled, time-bound resolution process.

An entire ecosystem came alive around these twelve defaulting companies, their defaulting promoters, their employees, stakeholders, suitors and, above all, a new community of officials called resolution professionals. A lot of drama ensued both inside and outside the courtrooms. The legal proceedings also brought to light what was really going on in these marquee companies. The stigma of losing their family jewels, fear of investigative agencies and non-disclosure clauses pushed most stakeholders, especially the promoters, into a shell. Even though it became harder to get information, more and more facts trickled into the public domain.

It was also becoming clear just how difficult it would be to tell the story of India's bad loans without addressing the 'dirty dozen' – the moniker by which the twelve central characters of this book became known. Though about half of this book revolves around to these defaulters, with resolutions in several cases still awaiting completion a full six years after the process began, theirs are not the only stories recorded here.

The book, divided into three sections, begins by setting the context of the early 2000s leading up to the heady years of 2007–08, when the seeds of the Indian banking and financial crises were sown. It also explains how the concept of bad loans came into being and the regulatory aspects surrounding the phenomenon.

Then we move on to the crux of the bad loan issue – that, in many cases, the delinquent promoters remain wealthy and sometimes continue to enjoy ostentatious lives even as their companies turn defaulters. By examining some real-life case studies, like that of Nirav Modi, we try to scrutinize the various systemic problems surrounding this crisis, including the processes followed by lenders, the power equations at the time of recovery, along with an interesting first-person account from a retired public sector banker.

The third chapter touches upon the elephants in the room – corruption and political influence. Citing some prominent examples of senior bank officials' direct involvement in these cases, I argue that the default is often destined at the point of disbursal itself.

No case can better encapsulate all the aspects discussed above than that of Vijay Vittal Mallya. Be it the ostentation, the political connections or the big default, Mallya and his Kingfisher Airlines are right up there. Some lesser-known details about his UK court cases helps portray with more nuance the life and times of the Bengaluru baron turned favourite whipping boy of the government. Mallya's is also the one case that never reached the IBC, as he was declared a wilful defaulter and accused of fraud even before the IBC came into effect.

Then, we dive deep into the heart of this book – the 'dirty dozen' – ranging from a Telugu contractor, a Kolkata-based businessman, a third-generation scion to a first-generation entrepreneur, the steel and power industry to real estate and infrastructure. These twelve gripping stories are as much about financial misdemeanours as about plain bad luck.

Each one of these stories is unique, yet there is a common thread of bad decisions, greed and the tendency to take prudent financial principles for granted. The case studies also underline the destructive powers of excess leverage. A mountain of debt can rise with relative ease, consuming assets built over a lifetime, if not several.

Next, we talk about a few highly leveraged groups that have been living on the edge. Their fortunes have fluctuated. Some like the Reliance Anil Dhirubhai Ambani Group and Videocon have fallen into the clutches of insolvency courts, while others like Adani have embarked on a deleveraging exercise by selling the promoters' stake. Very few, like the JSW group and Reliance Industries, have thrived by managing their debts efficiently.

The last two chapters summarize the institutional response from policymakers and the incessant hiccups experienced while taking over and/or selling off the big twelve.

Just like the resolution process these nefarious borrowers and their companies went through, this book also experienced a chequered journey over the past six years. I remember when I completed the first draft in late 2018, only one of the twelve resolutions was close to completion. The draft had to be updated several times during the editing process, as resolution processes progressed and a few large accounts were settled.

Plus, the impact of Covid-19 was so profound that it stole away two long years. The final draft was put together in the period before the pandemic struck. I have tried to update the developments since then as far as possible. I hope that you find these pages worth your time.

N. Sundaresha Subramanian
January 2024

PART I

SETTING THE SCENE

1
The Origins

Economic growth is seen as a panacea for many social evils. In a country like India, where a large section of the population still struggles to fulfil its basic needs, economic growth is considered to be the only hope. However, capital – one of the key resources essential for this growth – is mostly in short supply. Successive governments at the centre have tried various methods to unlock growth, using limited capital in innovative ways.

Before diving deep into the cast of characters of the 2016 financial debacle, following their tumultuous journeys and making sense of the new bankruptcy law of 2017, it is important to not only understand the technicalities of the banking world, but also the build-up to the sudden downfall.

Government Initiatives

The Atal Behari Vajpayee government, which was in power from 1998 to 2004, embarked on the road to growth by selling their vision of world-class highways that would connect every nook and corner of the country. Many of these projects were compensated with development rights for the contractors. The Vajpayee government also triggered a retail housing boom by relaxing lending norms and doling out tax breaks to people who borrowed to buy houses. Thus, land and real estate development became the key drivers of growth.

The Manmohan Singh-led United Progressive Alliance (UPA), which followed in 2004, decided to fire up the energy and infrastructure boom even further by allotting hundreds of coal mines across the country to private players. These companies could then extract coal from them to set up power and steel plants.

Armed with winning bids and coal block allocations, promoters approached banks for funds to build long-gestation infrastructure, steel mills and thermal plants. Banks that were under pressure to grow their balance sheets in order to keep up with the booming stock market played ball.

Both these models looked good on paper. They would have delivered sturdy growth, generated employment and created a win-win situation if they had been executed transparently. Corruption, nepotism and crony capitalism crept in as middlemen and politicians sought to enrich themselves. The outcome is the story of the ₹10 lakh crore worth of bad assets in the Indian banking system. However, though the scale and spread were unprecedented, the defaults themselves were not new.

The Father of Banking Reforms in India

M. Narasimham was a diminutive, bespectacled man who briefly served as the thirteenth governor of the RBI in 1977 – so brief that currency notes bearing his signature are now selling on eBay for a premium as 'rare' collectibles.

Though he did not have any major impact on the central bank during his term, even as the country was in the midst of a major political churn following the Emergency, he more than made good this lacuna a decade later.

Narasimham, who had spent nearly four decades within and around the government, once famously quipped that in times of crises, the nation's approach was to tackle the problems by establishing a committee and creating a new institution. Often, Narasimham himself was part of these committees.

In the early 1990s, when India was steadily working towards liberalizing the economy, Narasimham headed two important committees on the financial system that focused largely on banking reforms. Some of their recommendations were implemented, while others – such as hiving off all bad loans into an asset reconstruction fund (ARF or bad bank) and creating three to four large banks by merging the two dozen in the public sector – did not see the light of day immediately. But they are in different stages of coming to fruition.

The first Narasimham-led panel (1991–92) proposed a system to recognize and provide against bad loans, also known as non-performing assets (NPA) in banking jargon. This was one of the recommendations that found favour with the government.

An NPA was defined by the panel as an advance where interest on term loans had not been repaid for over 180 days, overdrafts and cash-credit accounts remain out of order for over 180 days or bills purchased or discounted were not settled for over 180 days.

Narasimham's NPA system suggested a four-tier asset classification:[1]

1. **Standard assets:** These are loans which are being serviced properly by the borrowers, and therefore, are not NPAs.

2. **Sub-standard asset:** These are NPAs that have been past due for more than twelve months. They have a significantly higher risk level, combined with a borrower that has less-than-ideal credit. Banks usually assign a haircut (reduction in market value) to such NPAs because they are less certain that the borrower will eventually repay the full amount.
3. **Doubtful asset:** NPAs belonging to this category have been past due for at least eighteen months. Banks generally have serious doubts that the borrower will ever repay the full loan. This class of NPAs seriously affects the bank's own risk profile.
4. **Loss asset:** These are NPAs with an extended period of non-payment. So, essentially, loss has been identified but the amounts have not yet been written off. With this class, banks are forced to accept that the loan will never be repaid, and must record a loss on their balance sheet. The entire amount of the loan must be written off completely.

The framework has undergone several tweaks and changes over the years, including the halving of the repayment period from 180 to ninety days. More recently, under the governorship of Raghuram Rajan, the provisioning norms were further tightened to ensure that banks acknowledged the problem, which they were all too happy to sweep under the carpet earlier.

The three alphabets – N-P-A – have cast a ₹10 lakh crore shadow over the Indian banking system and, by extension, the whole economy. A significant portion of these loans was funded by deposits raised from the common public.

Macroeconomic factors, such as structural decline in commodity prices, land acquisition and coal allocation issues have badly hit certain highly leveraged industries, like steel, infrastructure and power. Companies and corporate groups engaged in these sectors form a greater part of the overall stressed assets (SAs)*.

The overhang has affected the public as it freezes credit, cripples good businesses that need money to expand, and steals the livelihoods of millions.

There is also a more direct impact on the common public. Since most of these bad loans have been advanced by public sector banks (PSBs), the onus is on the government to plug this hole. And the money must eventually come from the taxpayers.

This is not the first time large borrowers have backed their lenders into a corner. Months after the Narasimham Committee's put forth its recommendations on the treatment of NPAs, the P. V. Narasimha Rao government formed another panel, headed by another Indian economist named Omkar Goswami, comprising eminent economists and statisticians, to study industrial sickness and suggest measures for corporate restructuring. The Goswami Committee had estimated the amount of capital locked up in sick industrial units by the end of the 1980s to be ₹9,500 crore.[2]

Is the Situation Getting Better or Worse?

The NPA figures from the Goswami panel look quite benign today. Though numbers have improved slightly from the lows of mid-2018, there is still a long way to go. At its peak, the total bad loans in the banking system hovered around ₹10 lakh crore – over 100 times larger than the Goswami Committee's estimate. Over 90 per cent of these assets are in

---

* A sum of non-performing assets, restructured loans and written-off assets. SAs are a strong indicator of the Indian banking system.

the books of government-owned banks. In addition to this, there are restructured loans, technically not bad, but which many experts fear could add up to an equal, if not greater, sum. While each passing quarter contributer to this number, a significant jump was due to the Asset Quality Review (AQR) initiated by the RBI under Raghuram Rajan and implemented late 2015 onwards.

According to a reply in the Parliament by Union Finance Minister Nirmala Sitharaman on 24 June 2019, State Bank of India (SBI) – India's largest lender by assets – topped the bad loan chart.[3] The bank had ₹1.76 lakh crore of gross NPAs as on 31 March 2019. Punjab National Bank came second on the list with ₹78,031 crore gross NPAs, followed by Bank of India (₹59,117 crore), Bank of Baroda (₹53,383 crore) and Union Bank of India (₹49,995 crore).

Among private banks, ICICI Bank with ₹43,148 crore gross NPAs tops the list. In terms of ratios, Industrial Development Bank of India (IDBI), with 24.11 per cent, emerged as the winner. This means more than ₹24 out of every ₹100 lent by the bank had not come back. Indian Overseas Bank and UCO (United Commercial) Bank followed with 23.6 and 19.87 per cent gross NPAs, respectively. Of the twenty-one state-run banks, eight had gross NPAs of over 15 per cent.

The RBI often has the best view from its perch within the top of the ivory tower on Mumbai's Mint Street. Every quarter, it publishes a financial stability report, which tries to assess the financial sector as a whole and examine and evaluate risks to the system, among other things. The December 2017 edition did not paint a very enchanting picture.[4] Every parameter used by the central bank to track the health of banks was beeping red.

The gross non-performing assets (GNPA) ratio* of scheduled commercial banks (SCBs)** had increased from 9.6 to 10.2 per cent between March and September 2017, whereas their restructured standard assets (RSA) ratio† declined from 2.5 to 2 per cent. The stressed assets (SA) ratio rose marginally from 12.1 to 12.2 per cent during the same period.

The GNPA ratio of PSBs increased from 12.5 to 13.5 per cent while their SA ratio rose from 15.6 to 16.2 per cent during the same period. The net non-performing assets (NNPA) of all scheduled commercial banks as a percentage of total net assets increased from 5.5 to 5.7 per cent. PSBs, too, recorded a distinctly higher NNPA ratio of 7.9 per cent.

The GNPAs of all SCBs saw an increase of 18.5 per cent on a year-on-year (y-o-y) basis in September 2017. Private banks (PVBs) registered a higher increase (40.8 per cent) as compared to their public sector counterparts (17 per cent). The surge in the NNPAs of all SCBs was about 11.1 per cent on a y-o-y basis. The status of NPAs has been fluid since; it had worsened before slightly improving in the last quarter of 2019. In response to a question in the Parliament by Congress MP Rahul Gandhi, the union finance minister stated the following:

> The NPAs of scheduled commercial banks, after reaching a peak of ₹10,36,187 crore as on 31.3.2018, declined to ₹9,58,156 crore as on 31.12.2019 (provisional data as on

---

* The total gross NPAs divided by the total assets.

** Commercial banks that perform banking activities like accepting deposits, providing loans and other banking services.

† The relationship between restructured standard assets and gross non-performing assets.

31.12.2019). Further, SCBs have affected [the] recovery of ₹5,12,687 crore over the last four financial years and the third quarter of the current financial year, including record recovery of ₹1,56,692 crore during the financial year 2018–19.[5]

What this data does not capture is the number of people and corporations who have 'wilfully defaulted'. These are individuals and businesses who have the means but have not paid or have diverted money for purposes other than that for which it was lent. As of September 2017, there were over 9,000 such cases, totalling an outstanding debt of over ₹1.11 lakh crore.

There is a very high likelihood that many of these company promoters have illegally enriched themselves. This is often done with the connivance of bank officials and patronage of the political class.

The banks have filed criminal complaints in a number of these cases. While a few, such as those of Vijay Mallya of Kingfisher, Jatin Mehta of Winsome Diamonds and Nirav Modi of Firestar Diamonds, make headlines every now and then, not much is heard about the smaller and the less well-known defaulters.

Of these wilful defaulters, just fifty companies account for about ₹48,000 crore. Each of these firms has defaults amounting to ₹250 crore or more.[6] The central investigative agencies and economic offences wings of the state police, which are laden with these cases, are forced to choose and prioritize as their meagre resources are spread across multiple areas. The promoters know the limitations of the overburdened legal system all too well.

A mid-level banker once told me how a promoter of a small company quipped before a room full of bankers at the

Joint Lenders Forum* that he had stashed enough money to take care of himself if things went wrong. Bragging about his ability to pay off even jailors, he asked, 'What have you got?' to a shocked group of poorly remunerated public sector bankers.

This stark asymmetry in both the means and motivation between the lender and the borrower has ailed the Indian banking system for decades now. The issue is still relevant more than twenty years after the Goswami panel put these words on the first page of its report: 'There are sick companies, sick banks, ailing financial institutions and unpaid workers. But there are hardly any sick promoters. There lies the heart of the matter.'

The nearly three-decades-old report by the Goswami Committee describes the vicious cycle of bad lending practices that in turn draw the bank into a trap of evergreening:

> Until recently, poor financial sector practices have been barriers to early identification and treatment of industrial sickness. These have also forced a particular type of error – that of supporting doubtful rehabilitation cases when economic logic suggests otherwise. In the past, banks as well as financial institutions followed very unsatisfactory methods of detecting bad accounts and provisioning for them. The loans advanced to sick units were insufficiently written down in the books of the secured creditors. Inadequate provisioning meant that creditors could neither give part write-offs on old debt to assist a financially strained but operationally viable company, nor

---

* A group of lender banks formed to speed up decisions when an asset (loan) of ₹100 crore or more turns out to be a stressed asset.

demand winding up of unviable, terminally sick companies – in effect making it a bad debt that required immediate and full provisioning, which hurt the account books even further. In other words, there were strong managerial incentives to support very unhealthy, contaminated, as well as terminally sick accounts.[7]

The Narasimham Committee's suggestions nudged the banks in the right direction, inducing them to opt for better health codes to detect incipient sickness and provide for doubtful loans in a manner that approximated the Bank of International Settlements (BIS) standards.

The Goswami panel felt that a banking sector reform was the key to restructuring the industries.

> It is very important to closely monitor, indeed accelerate, the pace of financial sector reforms. The faster we implement reforms in the financial sector, the quicker will we be able to restructure the industrial sector. It is in India's interest to implement the Narasimham Committee reforms as early as possible. Given this, and the possibility that commercial banks as well as RBI might prefer to go slow on these reforms, the Ministry of Finance must force the pace, and ensure that the books are thoroughly cleaned by 1995.[8]

Almost a quarter-century later, after a major scam involving PNB broke out, the RBI formed another committee to study, among other things, the rampant under-reporting of NPAs by banks. What is surprising is that over these twenty-five years, while the number of NPAs has ballooned manifold, the reasons for industrial failure and the methods to revive them have not undergone any major conceptual change. However, the laws and framework have undergone a sea change.

Soon after coming to power with an overwhelming mandate in 2014, the Narendra Modi government formed a committee on reforms for bankruptcy laws. With the establishment of the Insolvency and Bankruptcy Board of India in 2016, a new framework came to life. Today, over 1,300 cases of defaults are in various stages of resolution across the country. Among these are twelve prominent ones that have been referred to the insolvency resolution process by the RBI, following a special ordinance of the government.

Although the number of defaulters is in the thousands and would take its own sweet time to be resolved – even under this time-bound process – the proceedings of these twelve cases can help us understand the efficacy of the exercise. As per a report from March 2022, financial lenders were expected to reclaim ₹1.16 lakh crore from eight out of the initial twelve large accounts after their resolution plans had been approved. This amount is over twice the liquidation value of ₹0.52 lakh crore. At the time of updating the final draft of this book, two were still undergoing insolvency proceedings and the remaining two were ordered for liquidation.[9]

2

Companies Cry, But Owners Party

One of the episodes of this the 'Sick Company, Wealthy Promoter' soap opera aired on Valentine's Day in 2018 when the country's second-largest state-owned lender, PNB, announced that it had suffered a fraud of ₹11,400 crore. The amount later swelled to ₹12,700 crore.

Even as their companies defaulted on their obligations to the bank, the promoters, celebrity jewellery designer Nirav Modi and his uncle Mehul Choksi, scooted off with their families to exotic locations like the Caribbean, New York or London. While Modi remains behind bars at London's Wandsworth Prison, Choksi is still at large. It is the sequence of events which led to his arrest that lends further credence to the belief about a nexus between the establishment and such defaulters.

The red flag raised by the Deloitte auditor Abhijit Damle about the possible overstatement of stocks and receivables of Modi's company, Firestar International, was in the public domain as early as February 2017. Somewhere in the middle of the year, Modi's wife withdrew their children from their schools in India and enrolled them in the US. Yet the bank continued to provide their facilities.

In early January 2018, the entire family moved out of the country, one by one. It was then that PNB woke up. In its complaint to the Central Bureau of Investigation (CBI), filed three weeks after Modi's exit from India and a week after his now-infamous photo op with the Indian prime minister at Davos, Switzerland, the bank blamed a low-level employee and offered an unconvincing theory about fraudulent messages sent through its SWIFT* system.

It is obvious to any lay person that the malaise runs deeper and people at the higher echelons have at least an indirect, if not a direct, role in such scams. The CBI has already questioned scores of top PNB executives, including its chief executive.

PNB's is not an isolated case. Close to 10,000 entities have been reported as wilful defaulters by several banks. Banks typically give two types of lending options to businesses. In the first, they fund the acquisition of fixed assets. This extends to land and buildings, as well as plants and machinery, which would then then be put to use. The income generated from these is used to service the loans. The second involves providing cash credit, or what is commonly known as working capital loans. These loans are issued based on stocks and receivables. Up to 75 per cent of working capital is financed and the borrower is required to bring in the remaining.

Usually, the problem is created at the time of sanctioning itself. Often, bankers lack the means of verifying the claims and projections provided by the borrowers. Ambitious projections

---

* The Society for Worldwide Interbank Financial Telecommunication, legally S.W.I.F.T. SC, is a Belgian cooperative society providing services related to the execution of financial transactions and payments between certain banks worldwide.

of revenue are quite common and such claims are taken at face value. In the case of fixed assets, the price is frequently inflated, sometimes even by 200–300 per cent.

When dealing with working capital loans, banks are required to verify stocks. Chartered accountants are appointed to issue a certificate of verification. Sometimes, the stocks don't exist but that hardly matters, owing to the connivance of the bank officials, the CA and the borrower.

Just like in investing, a sound exit strategy is the key to success in money lending. Therefore, the process of recovery begins from day one. It is the lender's responsibility to ensure that the borrower has enough skin in the game. This should be done by verifying whether the projections are realistic, ascertaining the presence of adequate collateral and continuously monitoring the use of such funds.

In reality, banks are able to enforce these principles more than efficiently in the case of small borrowers like farmers and small businesspersons, often by unleashing recovery agents on them without any hesitation. However, the same banks seem to develop cold feet when it comes to larger borrowers.

It is possible that this could be a class issue. For an average mid-level banker, who takes home about one lakh rupees a month, dictating terms to a small borrower comes easily. But how can he exhibit the same rigour for a person who gets photographed wining and dining with the political bosses and moving around in private jets?

A public interest litigation (PIL) filed in 2015 by non-profit Swaraj Abigyan before the Supreme Court of India (SC) laid out the fundamental problems in the lending process followed by the banks. Some of the issues brought forward by the PIL have been discussed in the sections that follow.

Faulty credit evaluation, monitoring and recovery processes at PSBs

The growing number of SAs endanger the very existence of PSBs, and a large amount of public money is being loaned every year without adequate disclosures, accountability and/or transparency. Loans are very often sanctioned, diverted or misused by scheming bankers, corporate houses and auditors. In many instances, public deposits with the banks are used to disburse loans to undeserving corporate borrowers due to various systematic failures, weak due diligence by the banks, lack of data sharing among banks and so on. Basic parameters, such as scientific and techno-economic evaluation of the projects, credibility of the borrowers, record in the execution of earlier projects, time taken in the servicing of earlier loans and adequate collateral security, are often ignored when loans are authorized.

One of the most crucial aspects of project finance that PSBs tend to overlook is the source and structure of the equity contributed by the promoters. Banks do not always ensure that promoters' contribution is funded through equity, and not debt, so that the promoter has a reasonable stake in the venture. Since adequate attention is not paid to the source of equity, many times the project is funded through structured borrowings by the promoters at the holding company level within the larger group, which is then downstreamed as equity in the subsidiaries. Such inherent weaknesses in credit evaluation lead to poor cash flows. As a result, loans are not serviced on time and run the risk of being classified as non-performing assets.

Speaking at BANCON* 2013, then deputy governor of the RBI, Dr K. C. Chakrabarty, criticized the lax credit evaluation,

---

* Bank of India's annual conference

monitoring and loan recovery systems, tendencies to window dress, the evergreening of loan accounts and misuse of RBI circulars and approvals by PSBs. However, little attention seems to have been paid to his reproach. Chakrabarty had also lamented, 'Even in cases of restructuring, there seems to be a distinct bias towards the large-ticket borrowers than the weaker segments of the economy (i.e., micro and small enterprises, agriculture and priority sectors). Statistics on restructured advances shows that the medium and large segments account for over 90 per cent of restructured accounts while the share of micro and small segments keeps dwindling over the years.'[1]

The classification of an account as an NPA affects the banks adversely. Income on such accounts cannot be accrued further and all earlier accruals have to be reversed, besides additional provisioning, all of which leads to stressed balance sheets, ultimately affecting the lender's profitability. As a result, PSBs conveniently fall prey to the temptation of evergreening loans – sanctioning additional funds to the same borrower to revive a loan on the verge of default – thereby falling deeper into the pit. Eventually, a significant portion of the loans disbursed by the PSBs become stressed, entering the bounds of NPAs.

Growing NPAs alone do not offer a complete picture

Out of the total NPAs in the banking system, the percentage of those belonging to PSBs increased alarmingly from 75 per cent in 2003 to 85 per cent in 2013. Yet the share of PSBs in the total bank credit increased only marginally, from 74 to 76 per cent. These figures demonstrate the deteriorating quality of management and the lack of corporate governance in PSBs compared to private banks. However, this growing ratio of NPAs alone did not represent the complete problem with the asset quality of PSBs.

At the same BANCON 2013, Dr K. C. Chakrabarty had also suggested the use of 'impaired assets ratio' – the ratio of gross NPAs, restructured accounts and cumulative write-offs to the total advances – which he believed to be a more robust indicator of the asset quality of banks. According to him, the impaired assets ratio of PSBs rose sharply from 6.8 to 12.1 per cent between 2009 and 2013. In contrast, the ratio fell for new private sector banks and foreign banks, standing at 5.3 and 6.4 per cent, respectively, in March 2013.

According to Chakrabarty, in the decade leading up to the gross delinquency, the asset quality of PSBs was on a southward journey and posed a serious threat to the safety of the deposits made by the general public as well as to the strength of the country's financial system. Though public money was being disbursed as loans to bribe-givers, promoters with dubious track records and for non-viable projects, the data relating to it all had not been made available in the public domain. The stringent measures adopted for disbursing and recovering agricultural or education loans are often forgotten when it comes to corporates.

As per a study conducted by global rating agency Fitch in February 2023, it was found that the banks' sustained improvement in financial performance would support creditworthiness and bode well for intrinsic risk profiles. While increased write-offs have been a key factor in this development, higher loan growth, supports by improved recoveries and lower slippages were seen as equally important and conducive.[2]

As for projected improvement in the gross non-performing assets (GNPA) ratio for banks: It is expected to be 3.3 per cent in the next financial year, down from 4.2 per cent in FY2023. For private banks, the GNPA is anticipated to improve from 2.5 per cent in FY2023 to 2 per cent in FY2024, while public sector banks are expected to improve from 5.2 to 4.1 per cent. This analysis considers the impact of the ongoing GNPA write-off trend in the banking system.[3]

Blatant misuse of RBI circulars/schemes

What further exacerbates the problem of stressed assets is that PSBs and public financial institutions do not adopt tighter restrictions to recover bad loans. Despite enough early warnings and a long track record of non-compliance and repayments, PSBs tend to shy away from declaring promoters as 'wilful defaulters'. Kingfisher Airlines, or KFA, (debt of ₹8,000 crore) is a classic example of a promoter being declared a wilful defaulter only after irretrievable damage had been done. A clear case of too little action too late.

In many cases, instead of focusing on recovery, they help corporations camouflage their actual position by restructuring or disbursing additional loans, under the RBI's schemes, like the 5/25 scheme of 'flexible structuring of long-term project loans to infrastructure and core industries'[4] or the corporate debt restructuring (CDR) scheme.[5] Some of these schemes are detailed below.

Flexible Structuring of Long-term Project Loans to Infrastructure and Core Industries

On 15 July 2014, the RBI issued a circular which is now commonly referred to as the 5/25 scheme. In effect, the circular allowed banks to extend loans to infrastructure projects and core industry sectors for up to twenty-five years, with periodic refinancing every five to seven years. The scheme was applicable only to new projects of over ₹1,000 crore.

However, a slew of large infrastructure companies with payment difficulties immediately misused this circular to restructure their loans. These included Bhushan Steel (outstanding debt of ₹35,000 crore), GMR Infrastructure (consolidated loans of over ₹42,000 crore) and Jaypee Infratech (combined debt of ₹57,000 crore in three infrastructure projects) – three of the twelve big defaulters. Additionally, Reliance Gas Transportation Infrastructure Ltd, an unlisted, loss-making company owned by Mukesh Ambani, with an outstanding debt of ₹16,010 crore, also got its loan restructured and the tenure of repayment extended to 2030–31 under this scheme.

Misuse of the Corporate Debt Restructuring Scheme

In August 2001, the RBI introduced the scheme of Corporate Debt Restructuring (CDR) for implementation by banks. A voluntary framework, CDR is a means for financial institutions to reorganize a distressed company's outstanding obligations so as to provide support, restore its liquidity and/or to keep it in business. The default risk can be avoided by either reducing interest rates, extending the time period of repayment or reducing the debt amount. Other arrangements, such as the occasional forgiveness on debt by creditors in exchange of an equity position in the company, might also help potential defaulters steer clear of bankruptcy.

Seeing this in light of Chakrabarty's criticism of 'evergreening' and restructuring loans at BANCON, the distinct bias towards 'large-ticket borrowers' as compared to the weaker sectors of our economy becomes even more apparent.

Further, large-ticket accounts hold a major share of CDR cases, with almost 90 per cent of restructured accounts belonging to the medium and large segments. This contradicts the spirit of allowing the restructuring facility, as the economic downturn is more likely to impact small borrowers who are more vulnerable to business cycles and hence may require restructuring to tide over temporary problems unlike large borrowers.

The ground reality is that advances to smaller borrowers with genuine needs get overlooked and they turn into NPAs, which enables a perception that the NPA share is higher among small borrowers. This consequently promotes a push towards large-ticket advances in complete ignorance of the basic fact that the lower NPAs among larger borrowers are primarily on account of extensive restructuring/write-offs in the first place. In their scramble to lend to large borrowers, banks tend to lose out on a massive business opportunity. There is enough evidence to suggest that the provisions of the CDR mechanism have not been used as judiciously or effectively as expected.

The PIL files by Swaraj Abhigyan in 2015 went on to list several individual cases of alleged fraudulent promoters, some of whom were politically connected.

Ironically, five years later in 2018, Chakrabarty, whose speech was quoted extensively by the PIL, himself came to be accused of some of these irregularities. The CBI issued a lookout circular against Chakrabarty in two cases, including one related to business tycoon Vijay Mallya that we will learn more about in a later chapter. Though Chakrabarty has denied these allegations, a special court refused to revoke the circular in 2018.[6]

Public–Private Partnerships

A study[7] by Professor Charan Singh, from Indian Institute of Management Bangalore (IIM-B), and Jagvinder Singh Brar, a partner at KPMG India, offers interesting details about how banks do not always ensure that the promoters' contribution is funded through equity and not debt so that the promoter has sufficient skin in the game. As we've already seen, not enough focus is given to where the money comes in from for a project. Projects could be funded through intricate borrowings at the holding or main company level, with the money being treated as smaller investments. Overlooking this critical aspect weakens the project's financial health. This makes it difficult to pay back loans on time, putting them at risk of turning into NPAs. A major source of stressed assets is infrastructure projects, such as roads, bridges and other public utilities, taken up under the public-private partnership (PPP) model, which essentially enables large-scale government projects to be completed with private funding. The IIM-B study details how banks are conned by the concessionaires to fund these projects.

A procuring authority (PA) and PSBs are usually the fundamental constituents of the public sector partner in India. Sometimes PVBs may also be part of the lender consortium and these private players may commit to bring in common equity. The project entity is often a special purpose vehicle (SPV), that is, the concessionaire. The PPP delivery model, which was developed during the last two decades, and was officially introduced in India in 2011, has offered ambivalent results, given our limited experience with it.

The large value loans sanctioned by many PSBs in relation to PPP infrastructure assets have been classified as SAs. At least three of the dozen major companies discussed later in this book – Lanco Infratech, Jyoti Structures and Era Infra Engineering – were involved in such projects. Singh and Brar's analysis showed that several concessionaires misused the PPP model. In most such cases, the SPVs borrowed huge sums from PSBs and either diverted these funds to their other businesses or siphoned them off (both within India and overseas) while bringing in little or no equity. This flies in the face of the original intent of the PPP delivery model which was meant to harness funds and expertise from the private sector but was instead manipulated by some private players, causing disservice to the public.

The IIM-B study argued that this unchecked plundering of public funds underscores the apparent gaps in the existing legal, policy and regulatory frameworks. It simultaneously pointed towards a dire need to revisit the provisions of the model concession agreements (MCA), which enable private firms to get in business with the government. The study further claims that the PSBs hesitate to restructure the loans of such PPP borrowers owing to the legal and operational challenges of removing delinquent promoters. Additionally, it argued, the banks may not possess the wherewithal to run the businesses after overtaking them from these errant borrowers.

There is an immediate need to address these gaps and issues before more new public infrastructure projects are financed through the PPP model. Some of the key issues highlighted by Singh and Brar are summarized below:

1. Fake equity

A duping mechanism frequently employed by some concessionaires involves appointing an engineering-procurement-construction subcontractor or an EPC contractor along with some other suppliers who usually belong to the same promoter group.

Grant and loan funds that the PA or PSBs provide are used to make interim payments or offer advances to suppliers, who in turn circulate the sum back to the concessionaire as the promoter's required 'equity' on paper. In some cases, 'phantom payables' are created by mis-invoicing or over-invoicing goods and services. Fictitious items could also be added to the same. These phantom payables are then converted into or floated as equity using fake bills.

The monitoring and supervision carried out by PSBs after disbursing loans are often inadequate or non-existent, frequently failing to identify the equity's real source.

2. Inflated project construction costs

Some project owners use a deceptive tactic of exaggerating the total project cost (TPC) by it two or three times the original estimate prepared by the Project Authority (PA). This inflated TPC is aimed at securing higher grants and loans, which puts stress on the bank loans. When the public sector banks question these increased costs, the project owner may provide documents, like contracts or bills, from companies within the promoter group. These documents artificially inflate construction costs, making them seem much higher.

This results in the entire construction cost being funded mostly by public funds, allowing the project owner to contribute little or nothing, even going into negative equity. The funds from the Project Authority and PSBs are then redirected, either through diversion or by charging unusually high margins for work done by entities in the promoter group. The inflated project cost estimate might even be used to seek more loans from the banks.

3. Conversion of secured funds into unsecured assets

The funds that the PSBs extend to concessionaires/project owners are often secured assets usually kept in special escrow accounts. However, these sums are disbursed by the concessionaires to the EPC contractors and suppliers as unsecured loans or inter-corporate deposits (ICDs). This way, when the concessionaire defaults, PSBs fail to enforce their security interest (under the Debts Recovery Tribunals [DRTs] or Recovery of Debt Due to Banks and Financial Institutions Act of 1993), leaving them without a solid legal option to get their money back.

4. Lack of personal and corporate guarantees from the promoter group

Sometimes PSBs advance the funds secured from PSBs to other promoter group entities or related parties, which in turn may have stashed the monies in foreign accounts. Another possibility is that the claims of secured or unsecured creditors will outrank that of PSBs to the concessionaire.

PSBs may face another legal issue – the interpretation of the promoter group. The loan amount may be diverted to legal entities which, on paper, are owned by relatives of the promoter. Even when evidence of this is present, PSBs often encounter substantial legal hurdles in trying.

In the absence of personal guarantees from promoters, holding companies or other group entities of the concessionaires, seeking legal recourse against them as well as their personal assets becomes challenging for PSBs.

5. No right to audit and inspect other promoter group entities

A majority of loan agreements do not explicitly spell out legal rights for accessing the books or financial records of the related parties that may have received significant funds from the concessionaire at the expense of PSBs. With these rights being missing, crucial for determining the end use of funds and gathering evidence against the diversion, siphoning or round-tripping of funds, PSBs have no way of determining whether a promoter group is a wilful defaulter or not.

6. Foreign minority shareholder

Employing a foreign, passive entity, usually a shell company that is shown to be holding a minority equity stake in the concessionaire or promoter group's structure, is quite commonplace. Often, the foreign entity contributes neither equity nor technical expertise during the construction phase. However, once the concession period begins and revenues start pouring in from tolls, this passive entity becomes entitled to receiving a proportionate profit share. This legal loophole makes it possible for the concessionaires or promoter groups to remit money abroad and create foreign wealth.

A Bank Official's Perspective

Many bank officials who handle loan books worth hundreds of crores are from humble service-class backgrounds, where values are held above valuation. Most of them think of themselves as honest employees and say so. Since I do not have any specific evidence to prove otherwise, I will believe this. During my research, most of these officials relayed anecdotes of how they had caught people trying to fool their respective banks, how their sharp mind and eye for detail helped save the day for their bosses and so on. In a consortium lending arrangement, where multiple banks come together to lend to a borrower, these officials claimed to have detected some red flags and quietly pulled out of the arrangement. But the system did not make provisions for a reliable communication mechanism, where a fraud detected early by one bank could be reported safely for the benefit of everybody. Thus, everyone tried to protect their own interests.

Post-nationalization, when nationalized banks were expected to start lending to small-scale industries and businesses in a big way, many banks hired engineers upon realizing that these professionals would be better able to understand the production cycle of the prospective borrowers. This would ensure that the banks were well-placed to lend need-based working capital facilities to potential borrowers. A large number of term loans for the acquisition of fixed assets, viz. land, building, plant and machinery, were to be mainly funded by state-level financial corporations or industrial development corporations.

A few years ago, I met a retired official of Syndicate Bank who had worked as the manager post-nationalization and was one of the eighty engineers recruited to enable better appraisals of lendings. During his long years there, he had dealt with many loan accounts at the Mumbai and Delhi branches. The group of engineers was posted at the bank's offices in several metropolitan cities, state capitals and districts to assess and evaluate credit proposals from these sectors. Although it was a good and timely step and the outcome was beneficial to both banks and the growth of small-scale units, the former lost their way somewhere in the middle.

Post liberalization, with the entry of the private sector into the banking scene, the emphasis shifted from purpose-based to security-based lending, which – coupled with the provision of multiple banking arrangements instead of a consortium – changed the entire landscape of financing. Under the arrangements of security-based lending, many banks loaned out long-term funds against existing fixed assets, which were further leveraged and treated as net working capital to raise operational funding from different sets of lenders. In the practice of multiple banking, though not procedurally, lending banks did not share information with each other. Banks lent money to the same business entities and assessed them individually, and borrowers provided different projections to different banks to suit their lendor's requirements.

The monitoring of lent money thus became a major casualty and bank officials at all levels of hierarchy, either to dilute or divide their own responsibility and accountability, started outsourcing functions like stock verification, inspection and valuation of securities to CAs, cost accountants and certified valuers for a fee. Based on these subsequent assessments, banks began to make lending decisions, without first ensuring the accountability of the professionals sharing such reports with them. The empanelment of these professionals created another opportunity for favouritism, mostly on a quid pro quo basis. Soon after, credit rating agencies (CRAs) also jumped into the fray and started assessing borrowers for a fee directly negotiated by the CRAs and borrowers. These agencies were backed by prominent figures, and they even succeeded in getting their ratings listed as an important pre-requisite under the risk management regulations themselves.

With banks going public, necessitating regular reporting on performance, misreporting or non-recognition of NPAs became the norm. Defaults in PSU banks had to be mandatorily investigated to make sure that were due to genuine business failure rather than corruption. This led to yet another opening for lending as banks started to significantly restructure advances based on future business projections, which were mostly unrealistic ab initio. The restructuring happened to such a degree that a new mechanism called corporate debt restructuring (CDR) was enabled through a separate entity, CDR Cell. All major lenders were encouraged to participate. It suited both the bank officials who escaped accountability and scrutiny by the CBI or the vigilance department and the borrowers who got additional funds, often on liberal terms or waivers.

Then came a large number of infrastructure projects – in the road, power, port and airport sectors, which every bank saw as a huge business opportunity. Several private sector banks immediately put their syndication teams in place and started doing rounds of PSU banks, meeting their top officials with project reports, investment memorandums, showing fancy projections and large lending opportunities. PSU banks, too, fell for the bait and began undertaking significant financial exposures in infrastructure lending, in line with their herd mentality, without an adequate understanding of the issues or risks involved. Since these projects were mostly based on the PPP model and were being developed by the biggest names in the Indian business world, lenders perceived them as the safest.

Project monitoring was discouraged because asking questions was considered bad and seen as an obstruction to business, more so in times of positive business cycles when there was severe competition amongst banks to secure a lending opportunity.

In the nineties and early 2000s, anything above ₹10 crore was labelled a large corporate account, and a separate office dealt with them. While the loan appraisal and administrative work would take place at this special branch, the funds would be disbursed at the home branch, which was commonly located where the company operated from. The retired Syndicate Bank official I spoke to recalled a meeting with a Gujarati borrower who told the bankers, quite candidly, that it was the bank officials who should be afraid of investigations and regulatory processes. The man, whose dues fell in the range of ₹400 crore, bragged that the offences were civil in nature and that he had the means and the contacts to 'handle it'. The borrower said his maximum punishment could be a jail sentence for a maximum of six months, for which he was prepared. He even boasted about having connections who'd ensure that he slept in a hotel at night and went to the jail during the day to sign his attendance. The cost would be as low as ₹10,000 per night. 'I can endure it for months. You guys wouldn't last even a day,' the promoter had apparently said to the bankers, who earned a few thousand rupees as their monthly salary.

The banker also recalled an experience of consortium lending, led by the SBI, while working at another state-owned bank's large corporate branch at Cuffe Parade.

The banker's engineering background helped him gauge what the borrower was trying to do by looking at the papers they had filed. The company was seeking funds to set up a new manufacturing unit for metal sheets used to pack boxes. They sought a ₹150 crore facility to set up plants in the Kutch region of Gujarat. The manager understood that it was a four-stage production process – melting steel, creating sheets, softening them and then cutting them to preferred sizes. The loan request included a fixed assets advance (required to meet the costs of the business' long-term needs, like infrastructure), a working capital advance (for maintaining the business' current liabilities, like cash, inventories, etc.) and a letter of credit (LC) discounting (that serves as a guarantee provided by banks to pay sellers on behalf of defaulting buyers). There was no way to verify the submitted quotations, and the state-owned bank played along with the consortium, which had, as previously discussed, no provisions for reliable communication.

After a year or so, the borrower came back with a request for an additional loan of ₹40 crore. The pretext was expansion. Upon looking at the documents, the manager was not convinced. 'He wanted to buy machinery for stages 1 and 3 (of the production process), and he mentioned these as expansion.' The question then became, how had the business been operating and orders been executed all this while without the use of machinery for these two stages? Receiving no convincing answers, the banker informed his general manager (GM) that the facts were not adding up.

The consortium wanted to go ahead with the assignment of the loan. The state-owned bank had to take a call, so the GM decided to visit the factory in Kutch and asked our banker friend to come along. So the GM, the banker and the facilitator went to Gujarat.

It being a weekend, the promoter and senior staff were not present at the site. After walking around the facility for a few hours, the three of them realized that there were neither assets commensurate with the loans nor any real stocks. The bank decided not to participate further and tried to recover as much of the amount they had disbursed as possible. When the manager at SBI questioned this move, the banker told him what they had found. Immediately, his counterpart at SBI wanted to know if the vigilance department was investigating. The banker replied that the matter had not gone that far yet. However, a couple of years later, the same borrower opted for CDR under the same consortium. A CDR Cell representative looking into the matter had asked the banker what had happened. '[The money] has been siphoned off,' he replied, adding that he did not want to bring this on record, probably out of fear of inquiry.

The salaries of public sector bank officials are governed by a system of scales and grades that does not take into account the salaries earned by similarly placed executives in the private sector. To add to this, appointments at senior levels are heavily compromised by corrupt processes and favouritism. Bankers fear inquiries. Not everybody is corrupt and there are going to be business failures. As this now retired bank manager put it: 'The system itself promotes incompetency by disincentivizing competency. As you grow up, you are taught to say "yes". And it is these people who move up and get plum postings. At the end of the day, even a banker who is not corrupt wants to enjoy a good posting and timely promotions.'

Financing of infrastructure projects is another area where banks do not possess any expertise whatsoever. 'We were not financing the project. We were financing the promoter,' the retired official added.

There were instances when the banks would get funding offers from powerful groups on a take-it-or-leave-it basis. The banker recalled an instance where there was a proposal for a ₹300 crore funding made on behalf of the Anil Ambani group. This was before the 2008 Global Financial Crisis (GFC) which was triggered by the collapse of Wall Street investment banks and further deepened by the collapse of the Lehman Brothers Inc. When the official went through the proposal, he found hardly any details regarding the end use of the loan being sought.

Those were better times and so his superior asked, '*Kya ji,* Anil Ambani *ko bhi nahi denge toh kisko* loan *denge?*' (If we don't lend to Anil Ambani, who else will we give a loan to?)

'*Nahi* (No) sir, we don't know the purpose. Tomorrow, based on these funds, the company might create an asset and take out further loans on it. And, just like that ₹1,200 crore *ka* account *khada ho jaayega* (it will become a loan amounting to ₹1,200 crores) without any contribution from the promoter.'

Despite this warning, the loan was granted and, fortunately, the loan amount was repaid in time.

But there are corporate groups that have used loan write-offs as a business model. Many bankers say that the Essar Group has had seventeen write-offs in the past three decades and continues to get significantly big loans to undertake large-scale projects.

Another structural issue some investigators bring up is how the Securitisation and Reconstruction of Financial Assets and Enforcement of Security Interest Act, 2000 (SARFAESI Act), formulated for empowering banks to recover NPAs without a court's intervention, allows a thirty-day window for reporting charges created on assets. In several cases, this has allowed borrowers to use the same assets to borrow funds multiple times from different banks.

The unions, which represent millions of foot soldiers of the banking industry, blame the endemic favouritism and corruption at the top of the banking tree for continuing fraudulent borrowing and bad loans. C. H. Venkatachalam, former president of the All India Bank Employees Association (AIBEA), believes that a criminal probe into the nexus between bankers and borrowers needs to be launched. According to him, the absence of stringent laws to recover funds from wilful defaulters is one of the main reasons behind these extensive bad loans.

Another problem is that the procedure for getting a verdict in favour of the bank for a loan default takes an inordinate amount of time. Also, there are no fast-track special courts for trying bank loan defaults, and the toothless DRTs further complicate the situation. The striking down of the clause which required the deposit of loaned money in court before appealing against the verdict of the DRTs has come in handy for the wilful defaulter. 'The connivance of some of the top executives of banks, politicians and big corporates for the sanction of huge loans also plays its role,' said Venkatachalam. According to him, the RBI should publish a list of defaulters seeking bank loans of ₹1 crore and above periodically – say, once in six months. Wilful default of bank loans should be made a criminal offence, and such defaulters should be prohibited from holding public office and contesting in general or assembly elections. Laws governing the recovery of funds also need amendment. Legislations should be introduced to attach the personal properties of the managing directors, their dependents and the directors of the companies who wilfully default, in order to help with the recovery of bad loans. Before appealing against the verdicts of the DRTs or fast-track special courts, defaulting companies and borrowers should be made to deposit the entire amount due to the lenders in the court.

The efforts made by banks so far have not been fruitful because of the insincere nature of these attempts to recover the huge corporate bad loans. Instead, banks have been managing the bad loans portfolio through writing-off, restructuring – for instance, via corporate debt restructuring (CDR), strategic debt restructuring (SDR), scheme for sustainable structuring of stressed assets (S4A) – or transferring the loans to assets reconstruction companies (ARCs) at a discount and so on. As of 30 August 2017, the total number of cases submitted for CDR was 656 and the amount involved was ₹4,74,351 crore.[8] CDR, SDR and S4A do nothing but camouflage the bad loans, preventing them from being shown as NPAs. Eventually, they will all fall into the bad loan category, as Venkatachalam explained in December 2018, broadly echoing the sentiments expressed in Bhushan's PIL.

In February 2018, days before the Nirav Modi–PNB scam surfaced, the RBI wound up all these restructuring schemes in favour of the new corporate insolvency regime under the IBBI. The bankruptcy law committee, which conceptualized the entire framework, had a slightly different view on the stereotype of 'rich promoters of defaulting entities'. The committee felt that this stereotype led to two schools of thinking: '(i) the idea that all default involves malfeasance and (ii) the idea that promoters should be held personally, financially responsible for defaults of the firms they control.'[9]

It also offered certain interesting perspectives that are key to understanding why everything is not black-and-white.

1. In a growing economy with a weak insolvency regime, certain business plans can and will go wrong. This is simply because firms will devise risky plans, some of which might fail and cause default. If this is equated with malfeasance, it can hinder firms from taking risks, which is an undesirable outcome, as an enterprising spirit is the fountainhead of economic growth.
2. Historically, the concept of limited liability corporations was created for the very objective of risk-taking. Limited liability gives shareholders the option of walking away and exploring alternative business models, their exploration ultimately

benefitting society through risk-taking, which, as per the committee, bankruptcy laws must make room for in order to safeguard the interests of limited liability corporations.
3. When a borrower defaults on its debt, bankruptcy laws must ensure that control of the firm is transferred to the creditors. In case there is a dearth of prompt and decisive mechanisms for achieving this shift, the firm's control should be retained with shareholders and management teams in case of a default.
4. The committee further defines malfeasance as 'the illegitimate transfer of wealth out of companies by controlling shareholders'. While a firm is sound and creditworthy, corporate governance will ensure that benefits procured through each and every share are equal. However, when a borrower starts losing steam and approaches default, the management may, out of anticipation, conduct cash transfers illegally. Bankruptcy processes must therefore be designed with a special focus on preventing such illicit behaviour.

In essence, bankruptcy laws must equip honest debtors with a second chance and penalize all those who act disingenuously.

We shall see how this new framework dealt with these existing complexities, especially in the twelve cases discussed in subsequent chapters.

3

Corruption and Political Involvement

Occasion Silver was a trader of silver jewellery and articles, gold and imitation jewellery, diamond, gift items and crockery. Through its accounts at the Kamla Nagar branch in New Delhi, the company promoted by Kapil Gupta and Raj Kumar Gupta allegedly cheated Canara Bank to the extent of ₹68.38 crore. In an FIR registered in January 2016, the CBI alleged that the loan sanctioned by the bank in December 2013 was disbursed within the next three months and became an NPA on 29 September 2014, within a year of its opening. The funds were siphoned off through a chain of alleged bogus transactions facilitated by fake sister concerns, family members and bank officials, including the top executives. The CBI further alleged that the promoters knew the bank's then chairman-cum-managing director (CMD) R. K. Dubey and used the connection for procuring the loans. The investigating body found text messages sent by Dubey to subordinate officers of Canara Bank telling them to favour Occasion Silver with regard to disbursing loans.[1] Dubey and Gupta's are not isolated cases.

A few years ago, in August 2014, the CBI had arrested S. K. Jain, the CMD of Syndicate Bank. Jain's arrest was significant back then as it confirmed that the rot in the Indian banking system began right at the top. At the time, the CBI also arrested Vineet Godha, a Congress politician. Godha, Jain's brother-in-law, was said to have handled a ₹50 lakh bribe meant for Jain. In exchange for this money, favourable terms were to be granted to some borrowers. The CBI seized ₹21 lakh in cash and gold worth ₹1.68 crore from the premises of the CMD's residence apart from fixed deposit receipts of about ₹63 lakh.[2] People in the industry point out that Jain, in his early fifties, had become the CMD too soon.

Fast forward to early 2018: the CBI booked Arun Kaul, who was the CMD of Kolkata-based UCO Bank. It was alleged that under Kaul's watch, a company had fraudulently diverted ₹621 crore worth of loan funds to purposes not mentioned in the sanctioned loan document, which caused the bank a loss of over ₹737 crore.[3]

A banker once told me how some middlemen specialize in the transfer and posting details of senior and mid-level bankers and maintain a laundry list of the same. They are also aware of the movement of people who are in the headquarters, which post they are lobbying for and what the going rate is.

Another reason behind this ubiquitous corruption is the disparity in the pay structure of the public and the private sector bankers. While the chairman of SBI, the country's largest bank, earns a paltry ₹31 lakh a year, their private sector counterparts earn roughly twenty to thirty times more. This gap further widens the room for corruption and inefficiency.

This culture of cuts and commissions runs deep through the ranks and files of the banking sector. While Jain's methods were probably crude, many other bankers use sophisticated methods to reap the rewards of their decisions. For example, the swindling by Dubey and Kaul came to light years later, only after forensic audits of the companies they had struck deals with were performed.

One of the common methods of inducement are post-retirement postings. Several former bank chairmen and top officials can today be found on the boards of various companies, earning much more in sitting fees for a few board meets than what they had managed to during their many years of service.

The human resources framework and policies of banks, especially the state-run ones, have been a major cause for worry as there is a widespread feeling that these do not reward competence. While honest career bankers wait till the age of fifty-seven or fifty-eight to get to the executive director level, many officials at the lower rungs, typically from small PSBs banks, get fast-tracked because of their political connections to the union finance ministry. These connections then come back to extract their pound of flesh in the form of demands for loan sanctions to undeserving companies, restructuring on favourable terms and so on.

A curious case was that of Dena Bank, whose officials were ahead of their peers at larger banks in making it to coveted positions. Dena Bank, despite being one of the smallest public sector banks with low rankings in various aspects, stood out in promoting its general managers to executive director positions. In the five years leading to Jain's arrest, eight Dena Bank general managers advanced to executive director roles, surpassing larger banks like PNB. Dena Bank became the third-largest contributor to board members for PSBs, trailing only Bank of Baroda and Allahabad Bank, with thirteen and nine of their GMs being promoted to the Directorate of Enforcement (ED) level respectively. This small bank's officers outperformed their counterparts, with some even reaching top positions in more prominent lenders, including the now-jailed CMD of Syndicate Bank, S. K. Jain.[4]

Critics of the current method of selecting bank managers for PSB boards say it lacks clear guidelines, making the process controversial and prone to favouritism and corruption.* The issue was even referred to the RBI by the finance minister at that time. Bankers argue that it's challenging for someone from a smaller bank to succeed in a merit-based selection due to the exposure offered by larger banks. Dena Bank's officers stood out for five years, prompting questions. Allegations suggest that an influential politician and bureaucrat created a special route, benefitting Dena Bank officers in the national selection process. Incidentally, Dena Bank lead the State Level Bankers' Committee (SLBC) for Gujarat, which is now led by Bank of Baroda. Successive Dena board aspirants were said to have used this channel effectively.

A former CMD of a PSB told me that the process was not transparent and that the criteria kept changing. 'People are shortlisted by the ministry on seniority and merit and called for an interaction – they don't call it an interview.'

Recognizing that several smaller banks have been prominent in appointing executives to board positions such as ED and CMD recently, former Bank of Baroda chief Anil Khandelwal, who also led the committee on HR issues of PSBs, remarked, 'I would only say the selection process and grooming process of board members and CMDs needs reforms. It appears the system

---

*The Bank Boards Bureau was introduced in 2016 by the central government followed by the Financial Services Institutions Bureau in 2022 for the purpose of recommendations and appointments.

has a number of flaws. The selection of a chairman cannot be only a departmental process. A lot of due diligence has to go into [examining the] experience and leadership qualities of candidates.' He also mentioned that the suggestions made by the Khandelwal Committee in 2009 regarding the appointment process for CMDs and EDs should be put into action.* He argued that a group of skilled GMs and deputy GMs should be identified and made to undergo a thorough leadership development programme. He added, 'The scheme of board nominations dates back to the time of bank nationalization; it is forty-five years old. Board reforms are long overdue and are unpostponable in the current context.'[5]

He further referred to the P. J. Nayak Committee's report from May 2014 that reviewed the governance of boards of banks in India and highlighted many pitfalls in the nomination of people on the board of PSBs.

The Nayak Committee report had stated: 'It is unclear that the boards of most of these banks have the required sense of purpose, in terms of their focus on business strategy and risk management, in being able to provide oversight to steer the banks through their present difficult position. The boards are disempowered and the selection process for directors is increasingly compromised. Board governance is, consequently, weak.'[6]

While the government abuses the appointment process for EDs and top officials, it also has a disproportionate say in the appointment of non-executive and shareholder directors.

---

* Anil Khandelwal has been a key advocate for modernizing HR policies in public sector banks. He chaired the influential Khandelwal Committee in 2009, making impactful recommendations for HR reforms in these banks. Later, in 2011–12, he led the advisory group on HRD for the Ministry of Finance, showcasing his ongoing contribution to HR development.

Going back to the committee headed by former Bank of Baroda CMD Anil Khandelwal, who was appointed in 2009 to study the human resources issues in banks, the panel had submitted a comprehensive report containing about 105 recommendations. About a half of these were forwarded to banks for formulating an HR policy, while the other half were held back as they involved 'deliberations'.

With a view to ensure that human resource development (HRD) is built into the system, the Khandelwal Committee had recommended the following:

1. Large banks with a business mix of over ₹300,000 crore and staff strength of over 30,000 should be provided to ED (HR) to drive the HR agenda from the top.
2. Every CMD should take HRD on his agenda. A Steering Committee for the HR Board should be constituted in each bank, with a government director and two outstanding HR professionals (having knowledge of HR tools like 360-degree feedback, assessment centre and others) apart from the CMD and the ED, as members, to discuss critical issues in HR every quarter.
3. Banks should recruit HR professionals at both senior and junior levels to undertake HR activities. Lateral recruitment should be encouraged for getting top talent in HR. All HRD staff should be trained before they are posted to HR roles.
4. All PSBs should automate HR administration through a web-based system for efficiency, cost reduction and transparency in HR management.
5. Banks should introduce and carry out an HR audit once in two years.

6. A Monitoring Group comprising of the Secretary (financial services), Joint Secretary (also for financial services) and two HR professionals, preferably with exposure to the banking industry, should be constituted in the Ministry of Finance to monitor the introduction of HRD, best practices and the transformation agenda of different banks.
7. An award should be instituted for best HR practices.
8. PSBs should have the freedom to negotiate wages and service conditions to create a better fit between compensation and performance. PSB boards should decide bank-specific wage and compensation structures in relation to capacity to pay, profitability, productivity and the like, strictly within the overall guidelines of the government in this regard.
9. Banks should consider variable pay as a major component of wages. In such an arrangement, banks must have the discretion to opt for a cost-to-company (CTC) concept.
10. The ceiling for staff welfare could be revised in relation to the business size of the banks and the employee strength, within the existing cap of 3 per cent of the net profit of each bank.

The Nayak Committee also aimed at studying governance issues at the banks. The committee suggested a three-phase reform process. Upon the committee's recommendation, and to address HR and governance issues, the government formed the Banks Boards Bureau (BBB), a self-governing autonomous body of the Central Government. Former Comptroller and Auditor General of India, Vinod Rai, was appointed the first chairman of the body and Anil Khandelwal was inducted as one of the members. The BBB began work in April 2016, with a two-year mandate.

The functions of the BBB were as follows:

1. To be responsible for the selection and appointment of the board of directors for financial institutions (FIs) and PSBs (full-time directors and non-executive chairman).
2. To advise the government on matters relating to appointments, confirmations or extensions of tenure and termination of services of the board of directors of the above-mentioned levels.
3. To advise the government on the desired structure at the board level and for senior management personnel, for each PSB and FI.
4. To advise the government on evolving suitable training and development programmes for management personnel at PSBs and FIs.
5. To advise the government on the formulation and enforcement of a code of conduct and ethics for the managerial personnel at PSBs and FIs.
6. To build a data bank containing data relating to the performance of PSBs and FIs, their senior management and the board of directors and share the same with the government.
7. To help banks develop a robust leadership succession plan for critical positions that would arise in the future through appropriate HR processes, including performance management systems.
8. To help banks with developing business strategies, capital raising plan and new business plans.

9. Any other work assigned by the government in consultation with RBI.[7]

Although the body was appointed with much fanfare, it soon found out that there were vast swathes of government bank management issues that would be out of bounds for it. For instance, the following case that occurred in September 2016 comes to mind.[8]

On Life Insurance Corporation (LIC) chief S. K. Roy's last day at Yogakshema, the opulent Nariman Point central office, 1,077 shareholders of Syndicate Bank had gathered for an extraordinary general meeting. They had an important task at hand – the selection of a shareholder director. Non-promoter shareholders were set to vote, with two candidates contending for the position.

The first was S. Rajagopalan, a professor at IIM-Bangalore. As per his official profile, he possessed 'extensive experience of working with technology and innovation systems' both within and outside government organizations. He had served as the chief executive officer of the Karnataka State Council for Science and Technology from 1982 to 1993 and had been actively 'involved in managing innovations that addressed the problems of Karnataka'.

The other contender was Sunil Vashisht, a Delhi-based CA. According to one of his public profiles, he held the position of the national co-convenor of the Commerce Cell of the Bhartiya Janata Party (BJP) and 'has been active and zealous in promoting the ideology and principles of the BJP ever since his early childhood. In view of his dedication and efforts for the party while holding several important positions and his outstanding performance, he has been entrusted with the responsibility of co-convener at Commerce Cell.' BJP publications dating back to 2010–11 confirm this. Though these cells officially stand dissolved, the BJP's website continued to refer to him as convenor of the Chartered Accountants Cell.

No prizes for guessing who won. Vashisht emerged as the winner with 80.01 million votes (votes cast per share), surpassing Rajagopalan's 20.05 million votes. A substantial portion of Vashisht's votes, precisely 79.84 million, originated from a single public institution. The only shareholder that had that such a significant number of votes was LIC. Though LIC held 101.98 million shares, its voting power was restricted to 10 per cent. In Syndicate Bank, with a total of 798,499,537 outstanding shares, 10 per cent amounted to 79.84 million.

The story does not end there. In October 2015, when Vashisht competed for the shareholder director role, he was defeated by Kamal Kishore Singhal, a Mumbai-based CA with a substantial history with LIC. As per *Bloomberg* data, Singhal held the position of Chief Risk Officer at LIC. What had changed within the span of a year? Why was Vashisht shunned in 2015 and favoured so heavily the subsequent year?[9] What parameters did LIC consider before backing a candidate? Did the most qualified candidate emerge victorious?

More openness in LIC's voting policy would benefit everyone involved, including policyholders, shareholders and the public. Despite seeking comments on this matter via email, LIC did not respond. At the bank level, the new framework's implementation seems questionable, as the government already had full control over top management appointments and government-nominated directors. It was alleged by some that by influencing the selection of shareholder directors through LIC, the government was extending its monopoly in this area. This could be disheartening for institutions that cast nearly 19.93 million votes for the unsuccessful candidate. Vashisht is not the first BJP member on a bank's board. In July 2015, Rajinder Mohan Singh Chhina, the BJP's Punjab unit vice-president, became a shareholder director at PNB. The government nominee route also has BJP representation, as seen with Gopal Krishna Agarwal's appointment as a non-executive, part-time director at Bank of Baroda in July 2016. Despite individual performance, the contentious history of chartered accountant-turned-directors associated with the ruling party remains noteworthy.

More instances of the BBB being sidelined by the finance ministry have been reported since. The sudden, surprise changes in the top management of two large PSBs eventually led to the resignation of veteran banker and invaluable BBB member H. N. Sinor in May 2017.[10] Though he was later convinced to withdraw his resignation by Vinod Rai and reinstated, the bureau could not deliver anything substantial till the end of his tenure in March 2018. And weeks before the two-year mandated term came to an end, one of the biggest scandals in the history of public sector banks – the ₹13,000 crore Nirav Modi scam – came to the fore.

In a letter to the finance minister, after the scam broke out, the All India Bank Officers' Association (AIBOA) wrote about other checks and balances in the system that had been compromised.

There is a strong audit system in banks, such as daily concurrent audits by an external chartered accountant, periodical internal audit, revenue audit, external audit, statutory audit, RBI audit, Long Form audit and so on. If an audit cannot help with detecting fraudulent transactions of such huge proportions, it loses value. Earlier, the RBI would appoint auditors to audit banks after a lot of scrutiny. After liberalization, though, the top management of each bank was allowed to appoint external/foreign auditors of their choice. Bank trade unions have objected to this practice.

Sensitive transactions like the reconciliation of nostro accounts (a bank account held in another country by a domestic bank, denominated in the currency of the foreign country) are always on the priority radar of the banks as well as the RBI. If they have been overlooked, then the question that naturally arises is by whom and why? The RBI cannot escape its accountability in this episode.

There is another aspect that should be brought to attention. The role of the board of directors of PSBs has been grossly diluted in recent years – another effect of the post-liberalization era. The powers of the board are concentrated in the hands of a few in the name of committees now. Many important aspects of control and monitoring are relegated as routine agenda. Here also repeated submissions from AIBEA have been ignored.

In 2018, in a letter addressed to then finance minister Arun Jaitley, the AIBEA General Secretary C. H. Venkatachalam wrote, '… under the Banking Companies (Acquisition and Transfer of Undertakings) Act 1970 and 1980, the Scheme of Management of Banks includes appointment of Workman Employee Director and Officer Employee Director on the Boards of each public sector Bank. Right from 1970/1980, these appointments were being made. These Employee Directors have been playing the role of a watchdog. Unfortunately, after the National Democratic Alliance (NDA) Government came to power in May 2014, not a single appointment for these posts have been made.'[11]

As per the bank employee union, the posts of Workman Employee Director and Officer Employee Director in all of the twenty public sector banks back then were, as a result, vacant. They further provided a list of the unoccupied Workman Employee Director post:

1. Union Bank of India: since April 2014
2. Canara Bank: since October 2014
3. Corporate Bank: since December 2014
4. Punjab and Sind Bank: since November 2014
5. Bank of India: since July 2015
6. Oriental Bank of Commerce: since January 2016
7. UCO Bank: since February 2016
8. PNB: since March 2016
9. Indian Bank and United Bank of India: since May 2016
10. Vijaya Bank: since July 2016
11. Bank of Maharashtra: since June 2016
12. Allahabad Bank and Central Bank of India: since July 2016
13. Syndicate Bank: since August 2016
14. Andhra Bank: since November 2016
15. Dena Bank since September 2017

In all these banks, AIBEA is the recognized and verified majority union and they have submitted the panel of names as per the scheme. At SBI, Bank of Baroda and Indian Overseas Bank, too these posts had been lying vacant. Similarly, the post of Officer Employee Director in all the twenty PSBs had not been filled either, even though a panel of names had been recommended to the government by the respective banks. Venkatachalam further added: 'We know not why, but the fact remains that till today, the appointments have not been cleared.'

As per a recent research study conducted in January 2023, using publicly available data reports, around 35 per cent of director board positions are still lying vacant in public sector banks. The research was conducted by the Commonwealth Human Rights Initiative (CHRI), an independent non-governmental, non-profit organization headquartered in New Delhi. None of the current twelve PSBs have a full complement of directors, as is legally required.[12] In fact, among the twelve PSBs, SBI, Bank of Maharashtra and Central Bank of India have seven vacancies each in their respective boards. The oldest vacancy, at Punjab and Sind Bank, dates back to 2009. As for the others, seven posts fell vacant in 2014, five in 2015, thirteen in 2016, five in 2017, three in 2018, eight in 2019, twelve in 2020, four in 2021 and two in 2022.[13]

But it is not just the PSBs that are stuck with governance problems. Stakeholders of ICICI Bank, the country's largest private sector lender, found to their horror that Chief Executive Chanda Kochhar and her relatives – including her husband Deepak Kochhar and brother-in-law Rajiv Kochhar – were being probed by the CBI, following revelations of alleged conflict of interest. Videocon Industries and several other top contributors to the ₹8.5-lakh crore NPAs list were among the 'friends with benefits' under investigation. In December 2022, the ex-ICICI Bank CEO and her husband were finally arrested by the CBI.[14]

4

Mallya and the Art of Leaving

At the peak of his prowess, Vijay Vittal Mallya was easily among the best-known business faces around the world. Stylish and flamboyant, he was not afraid to live the good life of luxury yachts, celebrity-filled parties, having good-looking models in tow and, of course, lots of booze. He revelled in the limelight, loved the media and was the self-anointed 'King of Good Times'. In a 1998 interview at the Mumbai's Mahalaxmi Race Course, Mallya was asked how he felt about often being compared to Donald Trump or called the 'Donald Trump of India'. He responded, 'Well, I don't know Mr Trump. I read a lot about him. He obviously likes to live his life as I indeed do, but I am not yet anywhere near bankruptcy [like Trump].'[1]

Two decades later, his fortune could not have reversed more dramatically. Trump reached the pinnacle of political power in the US and Mallya, who loved making poster girls out of top models for his much-followed Kingfisher calendar, had become the poster boy of the Indian bad debt problem. On 2 March 2016, the day a clutch of PSBs moved the DRT against him, Mallya fled the country.[2] On 10 December 2018, after he was declared a fugitive economic offender under the Fugitive Economic Offenders Act, the Metropolitan Court in London ordered the extradition of Mallya who had fled to the UK two years ago when IDBI Bank accused him of money laundering. The appeals process is still not complete, and Mallya is still in the UK as of August 2023. While the UK High Court has upheld the decision of the Metropolitan Court in April 2020, and cleared his extradition, it has been held up for two and a half years now due to 'secret proceedings' of an unknown nature. Indian law enforcement officials have asked their UK counterparts to expedite the extradition of the fugitive businessman.[3]

In March 2016, the King of Good Times had to leave the country of his birth on a Jet Airways flight, famously with eleven items (though later some accounts suggested three hundred bags and a load of cargo)[4] of personal luggage, perhaps never to return again.

Banks took the flak for being lax in their follow-up when the news of his departure broke.[5] But larger powers were at work. A. K. Sharma, a Gujarat-cadre officer at the CBI, is alleged to have played a crucial role.[6] He diluted the lookout notice against Mallya. While the earlier notice issued required airport authorities to stop his movement out of the country, Sharma turned it into an alert notice, wherein the airport staff were just required to inform the investigators about his departure. Mallya's destination that night was London, a favourite of political fugitives from across the globe.

In September 2018, Mallya hurled a bombshell before the English media. In a single-line comment that resonated several thousand kilometres away in New Delhi, he dragged to his defence the very top of the Indian political establishment. He invoked the name of the then finance minister, the late Arun Jaitley, arguably the second-most powerful person in Narendra Modi's cabinet.[7]

Speaking to reporters after his extradition hearing at the Westminster Magistrates' Court, Mallya claimed that he had met the finance minister before leaving the country in 2016. 'I left because I had a scheduled meeting in Geneva. I met the finance minister before I left, repeated my offer to settle with the banks. That is the truth.'

Political rivals were quick to pounce on Mallya's comment. Jaitley scrambled to put out a quick statement and was on TV in no time to clarify. But the damage had already been done.

Jaitley's version was slightly different. He first claimed that Mallya's statement was factually false. But then, he added: 'He paced up to catch up with me and while walking, uttered a sentence that "I am making an offer of settlement". Having been fully briefed about his earlier bluff offers, without allowing him to proceed with the conversation, I curtly told him, "There was no point talking to me and he must make offers to his bankers".'[8]

Two Congress members accused PM Modi and Finance Minister Arun Jaitley of 'helping' Vijay Mallya flee the country after defaulting on bank loans. The Congress even demanded Arun Jaitley's resignation over the issue and asked for a probe into how Mallya had escaped.

Meanwhile, as critics started making fun of Jaitley's explanation, which appeared contradictory in parts, his own party members were gunning for him. BJP Member of Parliament Subramanian Swamy said it was an 'undeniable fact' that Mallya told the minister about his travel plans. Swamy tweeted: 'We have now two undeniable facts on the Mallya escape issue: 1. Look Out Notice was diluted on Oct 24, 2015 from "Block" to "Report" departure enabling Mallya to depart with 54 checked luggage items. 2. Mallya told FM in Central Hall of Parliament that he was leaving for London.'[9]

Swamy might have been asking difficult questions after Mallya's exit. But in another life, he had worked closely with

Mallya. In the early 2000s, he had appointed Mallya as the national working president of Janata Party, which the then MP was running at the time. Even the Congress has been his fair-weather friend. Mallya had first entered the Rajya Sabha in 2002, riding on Congress and Janata Dal votes.

At the time, the NDA government, led by Atal Behari Vajpayee, was in power. Ramakrishna Hegde, the man Mallya calls his political mentor, was a minister in the Vajpayee cabinet. An ailing Hegde wanted to bring together various factions of the Janata Dal which had split after the I. K. Gujral government had fallen in 1998. Hegde's party and Samata Party joined hands in 1999 and formed the All India Praja Janata Dal. Since this outfit had not contested elections, they did not have an official symbol and were on the lookout for one. Swamy's Janata Party had the iconic farmer-with-the-plough symbol, which had taken the party to power in the 1977 general elections. Hegde asked Mallya to help him convince Swamy to patch up and 'forget the past'. Their feud goes back to 1989, when Hegde had filed a suit for defamation against Swamy in the Bombay High Court.[10] While talks were on, Hegde passed away in early 2004. As the elections were going to be announced soon, Mallya decided that the symbol was more important than the party and joined the Janata Party. He fielded numerous candidates and did extensive campaigning.

When asked if his ostentatious lifestyle could put off voters, Mallya had a different theory. He felt people would see that he was rich already and therefore would not try to loot them. 'I land my Boeing. Take the helicopter and go to them in my Mercedes. People can see I am rich. So, they trust me,' he said in an NDTV interview.[11] He then went off for a private party with Spanish singer superstar Enrique Iglesias and his then girlfriend, tennis star Anna Kournikova. Iglesias and Indi pop singer Sonu Nigam had been regulars at Mallya's extravagant parties, often held at his signature villas.

But Mallya was completely wrong about people's perception, as the deposits forfeited by his partymen stood testimony. He also probably did not realize then that the same lifestyle would become a millstone around his neck when his business calls turned bad.[12]

Mallya's parties were usually attended by more than two hundred guests and went on for a couple of nights. His annual birthday bashes in December were shows that everybody wanted invites to. However, his sixtieth birthday party in 2015, at the Kingfisher Villa in Goa, complete with designer fireworks and celebrity singers, did not go down well with the bankers, government or the public, as his companies had started facing financial problems. Both Iglesias and Nigam were part of this bash, which is said to have cost over $2 million.

'If you flaunt your birthday bashes even while owing the system a lot of money, it does seem to suggest to the public that you don't care. I think that is the wrong message to send. If you are in trouble, you should be cutting down your expenses,' RBI governor Raghuram Rajan said in a TV interview.[13] Taking cues from the RBI governor, the bankers began to turn on the heat, eventually leading to his exit from the country in early March 2016. Out of sight, out of mind, Mallya would have hoped. But that was not to be.

As the local media turned up their criticism, the Indian government intensified its legal measures in London and Mallya was briefly arrested in 2017 before being released on bail.

For most of his four decades of corporate life, Mallya lived on the edge. Though the last couple of years might have been the lowest in terms of reputation and public opinion, he has seen worse. His London arrest was not the first time Mallya had found himself in custody. Thirty-two years earlier, Mallya had been picked up for a Foreign Exchange Regulations Act (FERA) violation. This was before FERA was replaced by the less draconian Foreign Exchange Management Act, 1999 (FEMA). On 5 June 1985, he was apprehended at the Bangalore airport, while returning from Calcutta.[14]

Unlike in April 2017, when he was granted bail within three hours after being picked up by Scotland Yard in London, in 1985, the then thirty-year-old Mallya had to spend the entire night at the police commissioner's office on Infantry Road in Bangalore. Not many newspapers found out about the incident immediately. By the time the papers were out the next morning, Mallya had already been released with a surety from one of his managers. But the arrest drew national media interest in Mallya and ultimately led to the Shaw Wallace takeover story, which would play out over the next two decades. The non-resident Indian status that he uses efficiently in more ways than one can be traced back to that deal.

The allegations for his 1985 arrest were linked to his takeover battle for Shaw Wallace with the Dubai-based Sindhi businessman, Manohar Rajaram Chhabria. When Mallya found out that the coveted company's foreign shareholding was up for sale, he asked his friend Brijesh Mathur to rope in an NRI businessman who would be willing to buy it. The plan was to transfer the shareholding to himself once he was granted NRI status, since domestic laws back then did not allow Indian citizens to acquire a company based abroad. However, his best-laid plans went horribly wrong, and Chhabria won control of Shaw Wallace. Mallya was able to buy the company for 1,300 crores in 2005, only after his rival's death.[15]

Over these years, he would mount several other acquisition moves, some friendly and some not. Best and Crompton and Malabar Chemicals were among the companies he picked up in the late 1980s and early 1990s.

These buyouts were funded by the abundant cash generated by his late father Vittal Mallya's prized acquisitions, including United Breweries (UB), which he had bought from its British owners. However, the flashy Kingfisher Airlines (KFA) and its doomed acquisition of low-cost carrier Air Deccan would prove too much even for such a cash cow.

Kingfisher: The flight to doom

Kingfisher is a beer brand with a strong following across India and around the world. Its tag line, 'King of Good Times', became a moniker for the owner himself. Mallya often says that owing to the media-dark environment his liquor brands operated in, he took up the mantle of brand ambassador and stood for the good life his customers desired. For Mallya, who modelled himself on Virgin Group's Richard Branson,[16] Kingfisher was a natural choice when he wanted to float an airline à la Branson. He also chose red and white, the colours of Branson's Virgin Atlantic. Another reason Mallya gave at that time for starting Kingfisher Airlines was that he wanted to gift his son an airline on his eighteenth birthday.

A running joke is that if you want to become a millionaire, first become a billionaire and then float an airline.

When Mallya started the airline without much experience in 2005, after forming the company in 2003, he did not hire a professional CEO. He instead brought on S. R. Gupte, a former Air India executive, to the board of directors, and that was pretty much it. When things went sour, the conflict of interest among the directors also came to light.

He may have goofed around with his board, but Mallya focused on getting good-looking stewardesses, nice food and great service. His airline was described as a five-star hotel in the sky. But a majority of Indian fliers were cost-conscious, so other airlines had already tasted blood with the cheaper options offered by low-cost carriers such as Air Deccan. Mallya saw that Air Deccan was badly undercutting his market and wanted to put a stop to it. Further, though the service standards set by KFA were world-class, it could not fly on international routes because of an Indian rule that required a minimum five years of operation on domestic routes before an airline could turn international.

Mallya launched an aggressive takeover of Air Deccan. Captain Gopinath, the founder of Air Deccan, later revealed to K. Giriprakash, for his book *The Vijay Mallya Story*, that neither Mallya nor his lieutenants were keen to see or understand the balance sheet and financials. They just wanted to complete the transaction quickly.[17]

Gopinath had once joked, 'He [Mallya] is from Mars and I am from Venus.' But within months, they were in bed. The Serious Fraud Investigation Office (SFIO) would later find several irregularities in the manner in which the swap ratio was arrived at for the deal. 'The valuers did not use all four methods used in valuation and arrive at the average value of shares for determining the swap ratio. Two methods, namely, the net asset method and capitalized earning method were not used.' The explanation given by the valuers for this lapse was not convincing, the SFIO noted.[18] The valuers ignored a crucial deal in Kingfisher shares with Linkupsys (India)*, a third-party non-promoter entity, a few months before the deal with Air Deccan. It was also found that the boards of Kingfisher and Air Deccan did not have the factual memorandum and valuation report at the time they cleared and announced the swap ratio.

The deal to buy Air Deccan was closed in June 2007. For a few months, the flying was smooth. By the time the deal became effective on 1 April 2008, the subprime mortgage crisis in the US had begun rocking the global markets. Crude oil prices had hit an all-time high of $151 a barrel in May 2008. The cost of aviation fuel rose, and the value of the rupee declined against the dollar. By late 2008 and into early 2009, KFA decided to seek substantial loans from banks. On 15 January 2009, the airline ratified a business plan for financial years 2009 to 2015, including a plan to seek loans totalling ₹2,000 crore.

Between April and November 2009, five banks extended loans to KFA. These included: Bank of India, Bank of Baroda, United Bank of India, UCO Bank and SBI. The loans totalled ₹1,250 crore. Kingfisher needed another ₹750 crore to get to the desired levels.

In late 2009, KFA approached another bank – IDBI – to make up for the shortfall. A loan of ₹750 crore was sanctioned in a letter and agreement on 1 December 2009. An advance of ₹200 crore was also disbursed.

It is this IDBI loan that became the subject of the ongoing CBI case and the reason for the extradition request by the Government of India, which is still being contested in the UK courts.

---

* Now renamed Deccan Emerging Business Ventures.

The IDBI case

The CBI has, in its chargesheet and affidavits before the UK courts, alleged that the loans were obtained though fraudulent misrepresentation and a conspiracy to defraud. It further argued that Mallya had engaged in laundering some of the proceeds of the loans.

The UK court documents showed that troubles in Mallya's paradise began somewhere in mid-2009.[19]

Ravi Nedungadi, a CA from Kerala, was the key finance man for Mallya. His association with the UB group dates back to 1990, and he had been its CFO since 1998.

In an email exchange with Nedungadi, which was also marked to Kingfisher CFO A. Raghunathan in the first week of May 2009, Mallya said that 'the ₹500 crores from SBI was not enough to make seriously overdue operational payments and the more we use to meet banking commitments as against operational commitments, we are sure to hit a brick wall'. He added: 'Besides, SBI are virtually auditing every payment and have told Raghu that they will only release operational payments.' He was unsure as to whether SBI would agree to release funds to Yes Bank and complete the pending miniscule repayment of a loan that was pending.[20] He also revealed that out of the ₹500 crore that they were seeking, ₹48.6 crore had to be paid in interest to SBI and ₹35 crore to Indian Oil Corporation (IOC) 'under duress', since Kingfisher owed IOC around ₹160 crore and a cheque issued by the carrier to the oil company towards fuel dues had bounced.[21]

On 7 May 2009, Raghunathan replied saying that he had just returned from a meeting with SBI. Having collected the appraisal and covering notes, he had submitted them to various banks.

Later that night, the email exchange between Nedungadi and Mallya continued.

Nedungadi said he had not suggested shutting down KFA, rather simply highlighted that they were in fact long overdue on operational payments which had been paid on their behalf by the banks to several operating creditors.

By this time, IOC had also turned aggressive in their approach and wouldn't hold back from initiating penal prosecutions. This led Nedungadi to question the effective running of the company at a time its directors were trying to avoid arrest. Five minutes later, Mallya asked Raghunathan about the number of post-dated cheques outstanding with IOC.

By September of 2009, the executives at KFA had indicated concerns about the company's finances, for the year-end losses tabulated in March 2009 were considerable and the financial position of the airline had not improved, unlike what had been projected, between April and September.

At the hearing in the UK court, the CBI produced other email exchanges between Kingfisher executives and some external consultants regarding the financial condition of the airline.

On 3 September 2009 at 7:02 p.m., Nedungadi sent Mallya another email, thereby enclosing the latest financial projections that Mallya had asked ahead of a 'kick-off meeting' scheduled on 8 September 2009 with lawyers and bankers to discuss KFA's GDR* issue.

He informed Mallya that at the time they had submitted the loan proposal to SBI, the projection for FY 2009 presented

---

* Global depositary receipt: a negotiable certificate issued by a bank that represents shares in a foreign company traded on a local stock exchange

an EBITDA (earnings before interest, tax, depreciation and amortization) loss of ₹768 crore and a PBT (profit before tax) loss of ₹1,594 crore. The actuals EBITDA loss was of ₹1,326 crore and the PBT loss ₹2,155 crore.

The projection for FY 2010 presented an EBITDA of ₹969 crore and a net loss of ₹174 crore. He further reported that the loss in the first quarter was in fact more than ₹300 crores, and more recent projections showed an EBITDA at ₹74 crore and a net loss of ₹931 crore.

But Nedungadi was not sure if even that was accurate. That same year, load factors dropped from more than 70 in July to 'a mere' 62 per cent in August and 'that too with a lower yield (from ₹4,200 crore to ₹3,875 crore). At that rate, chances were that the actual loss for current year would far exceed current projections.'

The accumulated losses at the end of FY 2009 were to the tune of ₹2,250 crores Another ₹1,000 crore was estimated to be further added to this figure. Based on that projection, it was easy to ascertain that such significant losses could 'not be recouped even in the next five years'. Investors, equipped with this new-found knowledge, would be hard-pressed to put money into the company. He also mentioned in the email that if 'the underwriters insisted on the financials being adjusted for audit notes, the deferred tax of ₹2,200 crores and Maintenance Reserve Treatment of about ₹900 crores will be added to the accumulated losses.'

The 'third point' in his email was that given the high leverages that were common in their industry in, incurring high losses in extraordinary circumstances was normal, as was their ability to quickly make profits when times were good. But that did not seem to be happening with KFA, which had additionally, as public records would show, lost ground to other carriers in July and August. Nedungadi ended his email to Mallya with: 'I urgently seek your guidance as the reality of operations, particularly the sales performance seems to be very different from what was anticipated.'

Within six minutes of receiving this email, Mallya emailed Raghunathan, pushing him for answers to the questions Nedungadi had raised.

Later that same day, Nedungadi emailed Rajat Agarwal, the MD of Accenture, the consulting firm that was advising the KFA–Deccan Airlines merger, worried that bankers and lawyers would soon begin their due diligence on the company's operations, including financial projections.

His email said that ATVs* across all classes had dropped. Despite the discounting of tickets, the load factor had also significantly declined. He asked for Agarwal's urgent input on both domestic and international operations ahead of speaking with the underwriters the next morning.

Also looped into this email was S. R. Gupte (the additional director of KFA), as he had been closely monitoring operations of late. The CA outlined KFA's position, highlighting that the company would have accumulated losses of ₹3,500 crore by the end of FY 2010, which could further increase if 'certain accounting methods are changed'. All trends were downwards.

Encapsulating and summarizing all details, Nedungadi requested for Gupte's 'guidance' the following afternoon.

Four days later, on 7 September 2009, Anurag Mathur of Accenture forwarded an attachment to Nedungadi, which contained a comparison of the performance of KFA in the

---

* Average transaction values

first quarter against the business plan provided to SBI. The actual numbers were based on KFA's management information system (MIS). Another attachment contained a comparison of KFA's performance in the first quarter to that of Spice Jet, on a per aircraft basis, and a separate analysis of KFA's ATR* operations. Nedungadi then sent this forward to Harish Bhat, an employee of UB Group, and asked to discuss the material with him. On 9 September 2009, Bhat forwarded the attachments to Raghunathan.

In its loan application submitted to IDBI, KFA had relied on the previous information presented to SBI, even though they were clearly aware of the significantly deteriorated situation of the company. The true position of KFA was thus not set out in a letter dated 1 October 2009 through which the CFO Raghunathan had applied for a loan of ₹950 crore from IDBI. He told Bal Krishna Batra, the then deputy managing director of IDBI, that 'the impact of the loss for the previous financial year (FY 2009) [was] around ₹1,600 crore'. This despite the fact that just the previous month Mallya and Raghunathan had both been informed by their CA about the actual loss of ₹2,155 crore, misrepresenting the data.

The application seemed to blame KFA's situation on the price of fuel. It created an impression that KFA's problems were shared by the entire Indian aviation industry and would soon be alleviated, what with the falling oil prices and the government's plan to abolish import duty on fuel. Raghunathan described KFA's 'huge brand pull' and cost-cutting measures in the letter. Further, KFA also told IDBI later that the reason behind the poor numbers in the first half of the year was engine failure in

---

* A Franco-Italian aircraft manufacturer.

twenty aircrafts, a point that was never mentioned in the KFA's internal emails.

Whatever may have been KFA's position in early 2009, when it had secured a loan of ₹1,050 crore via the consortium of banks, by 1 October 2009, it had become significantly worse. To add to that, out-of-date information was shared with IDBI. The business plan sent along with the letter was dated January 2009 and the brand valuation was from November 2008, both reviewed by Grant Thornton.

In reality, the steep rises in fuel prices had caused KFA losses of nearly ₹1,600 crore in FY 2009 and, as a result, the carrier had been forced to defer payment to creditors. KFA needed ₹2,000 crore, of which they had already raised ₹1,050 crore, to clear out dues and raise more working capital.

As for the question of security, a corporate guarantee from UB Group and a personal guarantee from Vijay Mallya himself would be secured and the loan would be 'repaid in instalments by January 2014'. Raghunathan also assured IDBI that SBI would gladly share their appraisal note with them.

Meanwhile, KFA's finances did not improve, and by 2010 the airline was in deeper trouble. SBI took the lead in preparing a 'Master Debt Recast Agreement ' (MDRA), to restructure the borrower's debt. Twelve other lenders joined the SBI-led consortium comprised of six institutions that had lent the sum of ₹2,000 crore. The MDRA was finalized on 21 December 2010. About 30 per cent of the debt was converted to equity in KFA, while the repayment schedule was extended. For the calendar year 2011, further ₹1,158 crore were 'infused' into KFA. Despite these measures, KFA could not recover from the crisis. By mid-2012, Kingfisher

Airlines had been forced to exit the low-cost carrier market. On 1 April 2012, KFA's international operations were suspended. Raghunathan sought international investment, too, by planning to raise $400 million from a 'strategic investor' who would 'understand the potential of the brand'. But all in vain. On 20 October 2012, its air operator's certificate was suspended by the Directorate General of Civil Aviation. Further hopes of rescue lay crumbled.

Endgame

In mid-2016, months before his US counterpart Donald Trump would enter the White House, Mallya's 'wannabe' political career came to an ignominious end.

In its 25 April meeting, the Ethics Panel of the Rajya Sabha, which had taken up the matter of Mallya's loan default, unanimously decided that Mallya should no longer remain an MP. Despite Janata Dal United (JDU) President Sharad Yadav's strong recommendation for Mallya's immediate expulsion, the panel decided to give Mallya a week's time to explain his conduct.

A day before the committee was set to recommend his expulsion, the liquor baron tendered his resignation. He did not have much to lose as the six-year term itself was ending and there was no chance that any political party would risk supporting him.

In his resignation letter to Rajya Sabha chairman Hamid Ansari, he said, 'I am shocked that the Department of Financial Services, Ministry of Finance, Government of India has provided factually wrong information to a Parliament Committee.

Nevertheless, since I do not want my name and reputation to be further dragged in the mud and since recent events suggest that I will not get a fair trial or justice, I am hereby resigning as a member of the Rajya Sabha with immediate effect.'

He also thanked the Rajya Sabha Chairman and his 'colleagues in the House for all the cooperation' they extended to him during his two terms. Mallya also asserted that the allegations against him were 'blatantly false and baseless'.[22]

*

Mallya lost his passport, his Rajya Sabha seat and even board memberships in most of his companies. At present, he is fighting for his personal freedom. Indian authorities have been relentless in their efforts to bring Mallya back to India and to justice.

The CBI in an affidavit before UK courts in June 2017 alleged that:

> In order to induce the consortium member banks to sanction and disburse the Term Loans/Corporate Loans aggregating to Rs. 2000 Crores, which also included the Corporate Loan of Rs. 500 Crores sanctioned by State Bank of India and Rs. 750 Crores sanctioned by IDBI bank, false representation/promises of induction of funds by way of unsecured loans, Global Depository Receipts and Equity were repeatedly made on behalf of M/s Kingfisher Airlines Ltd by fugitive Vijay Vittal Mallya. He himself addressed a letter dated 25.03.2009 to the Chairman, State Bank of India wherein, he made false representation/promise of infusing funds by way of equity/GDRs and falsely represented that the company will in any

event ensure that equity infusion takes place in Financial years 2010–11 and 2011–12 in two tranches.[23]

Evidence of unsecured loans, an 'exaggerated Brand Value' of KFA offered as 'symbolic' security, misleading forecasts, inconsistent business plans (including a Business Plan of January 2009) that contained downscaled projections of anticipated losses and inward infusion of funds by equity further strengthened the allegations against Mallya.

The CBI affidavit also accused the liquor baron of offering inadequate security for the loans in the form of negative lien twelve aircrafts despite knowing that KFA would not manage to acquire sole ownership of the aircrafts during the tenure of the loan.

It was also alleged that right from the beginning, Vijay Vittal Mallya did not have any intentions to repay his debts and that he dishonestly alienated assets with the intention to fraudulently avoid recovery of the sum after KFA's default.

Following this submission by the CBI, Mallya was briefly arrested in London twice in 2017 and released on bail.

In December 2018 after examining all the evidence and Mallya's defence, the Westminster Court's senior district judge, Emma Arbuthnot, concluded that there was a prima facie case of fraud against Mallya and allowed the extradition request.

In April 2020, a high court in the UK rejected Mallya's appeals against the order, allowing his extradition to India. The court dismissed the appeal on the grounds that the loans were conspiratorially disbursed despite KFA's weak financials, and that Mallya was 'party to false representations' about misleading data to induce the unsecured funds with a dishonest intention to repay any sums.[24]

Mallya was granted fourteen days to move the UK Supreme Court, which he did on 4 May 2020.[25] His application was consequently rejected and his extradition to India to face charges is still pending at the time of writing this book. Following this, he offered to repay £440 million to the banks on Twitter[26] and even suggested that this sum could be useful in the fight against Covid-19. But the banks are in no mood to humour him anymore.

PART II

THE DIRTY DOZEN

5

The Point of No Return?

In June 2017, the RBI chose twelve large NPAs and asked the respective lenders to move the National Company Law Tribunal (NCLT), invoking the new law of the Insolvency and Bankruptcy Code (IBC), which came into effect in 2016.

In his speech a few weeks after this move, at the inaugural session of the 'National Conference on Insolvency and Bankruptcy: Changing Paradigm' in Mumbai on 19 August 2017, the then RBI governor Urjit Patel underlined the extent and seriousness of the problem and how much depended on the success of this decision. According to him, the ratios of GNPA and stressed advances at 9.6 and 12 per cent respectively as of 31 March 2017, 'on the back of persistently high ratios in the past few years', was a matter of concern for the banking system. About 86.5 per cent of the GNPAs were connected to large borrowers with aggregate exposure of ₹5 crore and above. Such observations regarding the capital position of some banks, the PSBs in particular, had heightened the challenge of dealing with this issue.[1]

At the session, Patel also commented on addressing the challenges these large bad loans posed:

> Swift, time-bound resolution or liquidation of stressed assets will be critical for de-clogging bank balance sheets

and for efficient reallocation of capital. The Government, IBBI and the Reserve Bank have been working together to comprehensively address the challenge through a multi-pronged approach. The specific measures taken over the last few months, both by the Government and the Reserve Bank, to strengthen the legal, regulatory, supervisory and institutional framework are aimed at the ultimate objective of facilitating quick resolution of stressed assets in a time-bound manner. The sense of urgency imbued in these measures is reflective of the intent not to allow things to drag any further. The recent measures address, inter alia, two key lacunae in the earlier framework – one, the absence of a hard-coded, time-bound period for resolution; and two, the agency and coordination failures at banks and Joint Lenders Forums (JLF) in pushing through viable restructuring plans.[2]

Almost a year old, the framework under the law was still evolving when these twelve accounts were referred for resolution. A minimum outstanding amount of ₹5,000 crore was the qualifying criteria for these accounts. Close to ₹2 lakh crore was the total exposure of the banking sector to these companies. If one considered the liabilities, which included money outstanding to customers, suppliers and others, the total debt burden of these companies exceeded ₹3 lakh crore. The firms under question were not making enough operating income to meet even their interest expenses. And most of them were chronic cases, having undergone several rounds of debt restructuring already.

About 70 per cent of this exposure came from the troubled steel sector, which made up for five out of the twelve defaulter accounts. These were Bhushan Steel (₹57,505 crore), Bhushan Steel and Power (₹47,887 crore), Essar Steel (₹54,550 crore), Electrosteel (₹13,958 crore) and Monnet Ispat (₹11,478 crore).

If we were to look at the history of this sector, this stress didn't occur overnight. It had started somewhere in 2003–04. With the campaign 'India Shining' campaign gaining ground, a lot of enthusiasm and irrational exuberance had filled the air. The flashy ad was a brainchild of the NDA government, which focused on urban growth while neglecting the distress and backwardness of the rural landscape. It was supposedly implemented to improve the country's image in the international market and allure more foreign investors ashore.[3] The rising commodity prices, led by a surge of demand in China, was another plus. It was not just the price projections; everything was extremely rosy. It seemed like this upward turn in commodity prices would never end.

But business plans must always be made with a provision for shift in the price cycles. While promoters were keen to make investments, new projects were put up as debt was easily available. At times like these, enthusiasm typically overpowers rationality. The entire infrastructure was built at an inflated cost, mostly on leverage, which proved to be good while the businesses were booming, but when the cycle turned, the pain became unbearable.

Most consultants suggested that the companies should be put under CapEx – a one-time investment made in nonconsumable assets used to maintain operations and foster growth. The commodity cycle was mostly driven by China in the 2000s, given its huge capacity for industrialization, urbanization and infrastructure. Almost 50 per cent of this cycle was China. Supply always lags demand. By the time supply came online, three to four years had passed and the demand had started tapering. When the Global Financial Crisis hit, everything froze. But as far as steel was concerned, things were not completely jammed. The industry took off again in 2009. In 2013, the insiders once more realized that there was a significant overcapacity in the industry. During the intervening period between 2014 and 2019–20, there was a huge supply-demand mismatch. This drove the consolidation led by the insolvency code in this sector.

Among other sectors with large NPAs were textiles (Alok Industries, ₹30,200 crore), real estate (Jaypee Infra, ₹24,131 crore), automotive (Amtek Auto, ₹12,819 crore), infrastructure (Lanco, ₹53,158 crore; Jyoti Structure, ₹8,179 crore and Era Infra ₹15,050 crore) and shipbuilding (ABG Shipyard ₹19,316 crore).

The latest status of these accounts is as follows:

Resolution of the twelve large accounts were initiated by the banks as directed by the RBI. Together, they had an outstanding claim of ₹3.45 lakh crore as against a liquidation value of ₹73,220.23 crore.[4] Of these, the resolution plan with respect to two corporate debtors (CDs) (Electrosteel Steels Ltd and Bhushan Steel Ltd) were approved in 2018. The resolution plans of two more CDs (Monnet Ispat & Energy Ltd and Amtek Auto Ltd) were approved in the July–September 2018 quarter. As against the liquidation value of ₹2,365 crore, the claimants of Monnet Ispat & Energy Ltd realized ₹2,917.12 crore, accounting for 25.41 per cent of their admitted claims. As against the liquidation value of ₹4,129 crore, the claimants of Amtek Auto Ltd realized ₹4,385.30 crore, accounting for 34.23 per cent of their admitted claims. However, Liberty House, which was the winning bidder for Amtek, pulled out later. The resolution process for Amtek has been restarted. Jyoti Structures Ltd underwent liquidation as per the orders of the NCLT. Although, the order has since been stayed by the NCLAT. A consortium led by high net-worth individual and Netmagic CEO Sharad Sanghi has since taken charge. As for Lanco Infratech Ltd, an order for liquidation of corporate debtor has been passed. The others are at different stages of the process.

Let us now look at the people and businesses involved in these twelve large accounts and how they reached the point of no return.

Name of Corporate Debtor	Claims of Financial Creditors Dealt Under Resolution			Realization by all Claimants as a Percentage of Liquidation Value	Resolution Applicant
	Amount Admitted (in crores)	Amount Realized (in crores)	Realization Percentage of Claims		
Electrosteel Steels Ltd	13175	5320	40.38	183.45	Vedanta Ltd
Bhushan Steel Ltd	56022	35571	63.50	252.881	Bamnipal Steel Ltd
Monnet Ispat & Energy Ltd	11015	2892	26.26	1213.35	Consortium of JSW and AION Investments Pvt. Ltd
Essar Steel India Ltd	49473	41018	82.91	266.65	Arcelor Mittal India Pvt Ltd
Alok Industries Ltd	29523	5052	17.11	115.39	Reliance Industries Limited, JM Financial Asset Reconstruction Company Ltd, JMFaRC – March 2018 Trust

Jyoti Structures Ltd	7365	3691	50.12	387.44	Group of HNIs led by Sharad Sanghi
Bhushan Power & Steel Ltd	47158	19350	41.03	209.12	JSW Ltd
Amitek Auto Ltd	12641	2615	20.68	169.65	Deccan Value Investors I. P. and DVI PE (Mauritius) Ltd

Under Process

Era Infra Engineering Ltd	Under CIRP★
Jaypee Infratech Ltd⋆	Under CIRP
Lanco Infratech Ltd	Under Liquidation
ABG Shipyard Ltd	Under Liquidation

★Resolution Plan of applicant Suraksha Realty has been approved by CoC and is awaiting approval of the Adjudicating Authority.

⋆ CIRP = Corporate Insolvency Resolution Process

⋆⋆ HNI= High Net-worth Individuals

Source: IBBI newsletter; claims and realization in ₹ crores[5]

6

Lanco Infratech

Kondapalli is a village in Andhra Pradesh at the foot of the hills bearing the same name. There's nothing remarkable about it except its *bommalu*. Bommalu, a wooden toy made by local artisans, has grown popular all over the state over the last four hundred years.

Two decades ago, Kondapalli sought to break free of the toy story by writing itself a new calling card. In 1995, the Telugu Desam government that ruled Andhra Pradesh had opened the power sector to private players. Kondapalli became home to one of the first private sector power projects in India.

The state government, through its transmission companies, inked power purchase agreements (PPAs) with some of them, which was followed by fundraising and setting up the projects. The PPA and the 368-MW gas power plant in Kondapalli, which was commissioned in 2000, was a turning point in the history of a fledgling infrastructure company called Lanco.

Lanco Kondapalli Power Ltd (LKPL), a joint venture between Lanco and the Genting Group of Malaysia, marked a major milestone in the organization's growth as an independent power producer, as per its website.[1] Lanco is short for Lagadapati Amarappa Naidu and Co. In the 1960s, Amarappa Naidu and his brothers L. V. Rama Naidu and L. V. Ratnam Naidu laid the foundation of this enterprise by starting a transport business with one truck (a converted bus) that they had inherited from their father L. V. Subba Naidu. Amarappa Naidu's business expertise and the brothers' dedication led to them quickly attract orders from construction companies in need of efficient material transportation services.

By 1976, their thriving business boasted a fleet of a hundred trucks, serving the construction industry in Andhra Pradesh. Following this success, the Naidu brothers decided to enter the construction business, too. In 1980, Uma Maheshwar Rao and Company was established. The company swiftly secured a reputable presence in the construction industry by successfully delivering numerous prestigious turnkey projects in Andhra Pradesh and Karnataka. Its extensive asset portfolio included 150 trucks, eight excavators, ten bulldozers and fifteen drilling machines.

In 1985, Lagadapathi Rajagopal, a mechanical engineer and L. V. Rama Naidu's son, was inducted into the company. The venture expanded into road and other infrastructure construction activities. Over three decades later, Rajagopal would gain infamy as the 'pepper spray MP' for damaging the eyes of fellow parliamentarians in the run-up to the formation of Telangana.

In the mid-1980s though, he was still a wide-eyed engineer looking to make a mark. In 1986, Rajagopal married the daughter of a Telugu Desam politician who would go on to become a union minister – Parvathaneni Upendra – who had trained to be a journalist and was even said to have practised the trade briefly. But then he picked up a government job as a public relations officer in the Indian Railways.

As he rose through the ranks and grew close to Madhu Dandavate, the railway minister in the Janata Party government during 1977–79, politics beckoned him. When the anti-Congress wave swept his home state under the charismatic leadership of N. T. Rama Rao (NTR, the Indian actor, filmmaker and politician), Upendra joined Telugu Desam. Soon, he was nominated to the Rajya Sabha. He would go on to become the leader of Opposition in the Lok Sabha as every other party had been swept away by the sympathy wave in the 1984 elections that followed the assassination of Prime Minister Indira Gandhi.

Rajagopal's alliance with the Upendra family in 1986 came at a time when the businesses of the Lagadapathi family was going through a generational handover. As political winds changed in 1988, Upendra was picked to be the minister for information and broadcasting alongside his mentor Madhu Dandavate, the then finance minister. He also became the convenor of the National Front and held the position of general secretary in the Telugu Desam party, headed by the thespian.

When two years later, in 1991, another finance minister (Dr Manmohan Singh) under the Congress opened up the Indian economy, Lagadapathi Rajagopal, and by extension the Lanco group, were in the right place to capitalize. The shrewd P. Upendra and his sons-in-law had by now crossed over to the Congress as NTR's family members and had become more and more assertive within the party.

Upendra won two consecutive Lok Sabha elections from Vijayawada in 1996 and 1998. Unfortunately for him, both the tenures were short-lived and dissolved prematurely. In 1999, he lost by a small margin, leading to a political exile of sorts.

As he grew old and began to pull back, Upendra sought to transfer his political legacy to his son-in-law Rajagopal, who by then had finished a decent run in the construction business and had expanded his interests into the pig-iron and power sectors.

He brought in Y. Harish Chandra Prasad, a professional who had some experience in the power sector, and his own brother, L. Madhusudhan Rao. His brother-in-law Bhaskar Rao was always around.

Sometime in 2002, with the businesses up and running and seemingly in safe hands, Rajagopal took the plunge into politics. In a landmark election that saw the rout of Telugu Desam, the regional satrap of Congressman Y. S. Rajasekhara Reddy (YSR) rose to power. YSR not only managed to deliver the Andhra Pradesh Assembly to the Congress but also send forty MPs to the Lok Sabha. He also played a key role in the formation of the United Progressive Alliance (UPA) government at the Centre in 2004.

Even though Rajagopal's political journey was timely and hit the right notes early, it did not translate into a blemishless growth trajectory for Lanco. This was the time when the Lanco group was moving aggressively into the power business, winning projects and bids, having tasted success with the Kondapalli venture.

Though the company managed to win key government contracts and projects both within the state and outside, it was not very far from trouble. In March 2007, the then managing director of Lanco Infratech, G. Venkatesh Babu, was picked up by income tax officials at the Hyderabad airport.[2] Babu was carrying about ₹34 lakh in cash.

Only a few months ago in December 2006, Lanco, in partnership with Globeleq Singapore, had bagged the bid to build the 4,000 MW Sasan Ultra Mega Power Project by offering to supply power at a record low price of ₹1.196 per unit. In February 2007, it was discovered that Globeleq's promoters had changed. The promoters now included Lanco along with one of the losing bidders, Jindal Steel and Power. In April 2007, a report issued by consulting firm EY termed Lanco's bid invalid.[3] Three months later, the empowered group of ministers (EGoM), headed by Sushilkumar Shinde, the power minister, scrapped the bid. But even after this fiasco, Lanco was sitting pretty

In the same year, the Government of India had embarked on a policy to promote merchant power plants.* The Ministry of Power believed that encouraging merchant plants would enable the development of an electricity market as it would promote power trading on short-term, medium-term and spot-market basis. These plants would typically have a maximum capacity of 1,000 MW and coal linkages. They were to be set up outside the tariff-based competitive bidding process that was introduced in 1997. The scheme was formulated in response to the private sector's complaint that all new projects were being awarded through competitive bidding following the notification of the tariff policy in 1997. However, these plants would not be tied up with long-term PPAs. Merchant power plants were one option for achieving the targeted capacity addition.

Lanco had bagged several significant power projects and had inked PPAs with state electricity boards. By 2011, it had around five conventional, four mini-hydel and three non-conventional power plants. There were nine more coming up, and Lanco was targeting a total capacity of 15,000 MW by 2015.

While it had achieved a financial closure on an under-construction 6,000-MW project, another with a 6,200-MW capacity was in advanced development and required an investment of ₹35,000 crore. The group also had plans to commission a 5,000-

---

* A non-utility power plant that does not have a firm PPA in place. Under this mechanism, power producers are allowed to sell their electricity directly to retailers who then re-sell it to consumers.

MW project outside the country. Bangladesh, Indonesia and some countries in West Asia were among the nations on its radar.

Lanco had won coal blocks in Rampia in Odisha and Gare Pelma II in Chhattisgarh as well. The industry suffered a big blow when the CAG unearthed irregularities in how coal blocks were allocated in 2012. As political parties latched on to the allegations of what came to be called the 'Coalgate' scam, power sector companies went into a long and painful decline. Lanco was no exception.

This meant that the entire merchant power policy had to undergo an overhaul. By 2012, the government started actively to discourage merchant power, eliminating a key revenue stream of the power companies. A couple of years earlier, Madhusudhan Rao had told a journalist that the change of government policy around merchant power was among the key macro blows that hit power generation firms like Lanco:

> ... dip in business is related to the sale of merchant power ... Once [the] high revenues evaporated, banks, too, stopped lending to the sector. That led to a liquidity crunch which impacted both power generation companies and also state-owned distribution firms, their primary consumers.[4]

By October 2012, Lanco was in deep trouble. It had defaulted on a ₹250 crore debt. It all went downhill from there, and Rajagopal's political alienation after the formation of Telangana two years later was the last nail in Lanco's coffin. Following the default, rating agency CRISIL downgraded the firm to the default 'D' category and the ₹8,207 crore long- and short-term loans extended by banks to Lanco Power from moderate safety to moderate risk.

In 2012, CRISIL reported that:

> Lanco Infratech has total repayment obligations of ₹800 crores that it must pay in October and November 2012 and January 2013. The ratings agency believes that Lanco Infratech's liquidity will remain under pressure over the medium term because in addition to these lumpy repayments, it needs between ₹500 crores and ₹700 crores for meeting its equity investments in three power projects – Vidarbha (Maharashtra), Babandh (Odisha) and Amarkantak (Madhya Pradesh).[5]

The report further said that it had learnt from Lanco's management that the company intended to ease the liquidity pressure by selling stakes in its road, wind and hydroelectric power projects.

The rating agency also mentioned that in addition to facing liquidity challenges, Lanco Infratech's financial risk profile was expected to remain strained in the medium term. This was primarily due to the company's significant involvement in under-implementation projects through its special purpose vehicles, as well as the underperformance of Griffin Coal Mining Pty. Griffin Coal, the company that owned the second-largest coal mines (producing 4 metric tonnes per annum) in Western Australia, was bought over by Lanco in 2010 for $850 million. Debt-ridden Griffin had been kept under court-appointed administration after it had failed loan repayments. Lanco beat Chinese and Japanese buyers to buy this troubled asset, which proved to be a death sentence in retrospect. Ironically, however, when Lanco itself was put on the block for resolution in 2018 by resolution professional (RP) Savan Godiawala, there were no takers.

7

Amtek Auto

Just one ill-advised acquisition was enough to land Lanco into trouble – imagine the consequences of having some two dozen!

In a ten-year period between 2005 and 2014, Amtek Auto acquired twenty-two companies, many of them belongeing to the matured and slow-growing European market. Several of these firms were in a state of distress. Why did Amtek buy them, you might ask. Because the growth in India was not good enough. Somewhat of a contradictory logic, but everybody played along while the money flowed. Sigma Castings of UK; Rege, Scholz and Nuemayer Tekfor of Germany; and the Japanese forging firm Asahi Tec were some of these acquisitions.

'People keep telling me, "Enough is enough, now you can rest easy." But I tell them that it is in our DNA and we like to buy companies. When opportunities come, you must be able to grab them,' said Arvind Dham, the promoter of Amtek, in 2015.[1]

Dham, the son of a Haryana irrigation department official, had been a state-level cricket player, having played with the likes of Kapil Dev. Forced by his father into academics, Arvind Dham trained to be an architect in the US in the early 1980s but soon got bored of the construction business. Around this time, Maruti Suzuki had started producing cars and needed trusted component suppliers. Dham started Amtek in 1985, raising funds from banks and the Haryana government. After that, he set up a plant to make 3,00,000 connecting rod assemblies – that link a vehicle's crankshaft to its pistons – within a year, which he began supplying to the car manufacturer.

After a point, growth in the Indian market began to taper and Dham began looking for opportunities outside. Enamoured by the big auto brands, he began to scout for troubled suppliers in Europe and the US.

Bankers continued to extend liberal credit lines and justified their actions by praising Dham's abilities as a turnaround tycoon. They underwrote press articles that painted him as a savvy businessman who went after distressed assets, bought them cheap and then turned them profitable.

As per a profile on the Amtek portal in 2017 (before the company filed for bankruptcy),[2] the company was one of the world's largest integrated auto and non-auto component manufacturers. With operations spanning forging, iron casting, aluminium casting, machining and sub-assemblies, the group had a manufacturing presence in eleven countries. Together with its subsidiaries and associates, the Amtek Group generated over $3.5 billion in combined revenues.

The company produced a wide range of assembly-line components, which served various automotive sectors, such as passenger cars, two- and three-wheelers and commercial vehicles. Other products included key components for non-automotive industries, like construction, oil & gas, railways, earth-moving equipment and agriculture.

Their flagship company, Amtek Auto, transitioned from being an India-focused company with revenues of approximately $1.2 billion to a global automotive components manufacturer with annual revenues of around $2.7 billion. The share of revenues generated outside India surged from about 13 to around 70 per cent. With strategic acquisitions and expansions across Europe, the Americas and Asia, Amtek went on to become one of the world's largest forging, casting and integrated machining companies. The primary objective of their growth strategy supposedly was to support global original equipment manufacturer customers in their respective end markets.

Dham would look for companies that had suffered as a result of the senior management's lethargy rather than inherent flaws. He often sacked the top brass of his target companies but listened to what the middle- and lower-level employees had to say, reported a 2015 *Fortune* article.[3] Despite Dham's confidence, though, his debt-fuelled bravado was already bleeding his balance sheet. With interest costs alone ballooning to ₹1,500 crore, the cookie started to crumble.

For Amtek's acquisition spree, 2015 was a remarkable year. In three months, it announced three major buys. In March, it closed the deal for Scholz Edelstahl. The company, based in Germany, was a leading manufacturer of high-quality hot die forgings for the auto and non-auto component industries. The firm was also engaged in the business of trading in special steel, which, according to Amtek, would have enabled backward integration with all of its international businesses. The forging activities were carried out at a plant located in a state-of-the-art facility in Aalen, Germany. Scholz had long-standing client relationships with leading global auto OEMs and component manufacturers as well.

This was followed by the announcement of the Asahi Tec deal. In April 2015, Amtek entered into an agreement with Asahi Tec Corporation to acquire its iron casting, forging and machining business. Asahi Tec Corporation was a portfolio company of Unison Capital, a leading private equity firm based in Japan. The acquired business comprised three manufacturing facilities in Japan, two in Thailand and a strategic holding in a joint venture in China. Key products included cylinder blocks, crankshafts, front axle beams, cylinder heads, turbocharger housings and other engine- and suspension-related components. The primary end markets for the products were commercial vehicles, passenger car segments and the construction equipment sector. The business had over 1,500 employees across all locations. The acquired company had long-standing relationships with blue-chip OEM customers such as Caterpillar, Hino Motors, Mitsubishi Fuso, Mitsubishi Heavy Industries and Mitsubishi Motors.[4]

The acquisition was meant to provide a 'strategically compelling manufacturing platform' that provided access to many more high-profile OEMs in new regions. Come May 2015, before the dust settled on these two deals, Amtek announced another German acquisition – REGE, a supplier of machining and assembly solutions to auto majors such as Volkswagen and Kia Motors.

First signs of trouble

In 2015, these back-to-back acquisitions had begun to affect the stocks of Castex Technologies, formerly Amtek India Ltd, an iron casting and accessory manufacturing company. Amtek Auto had a significant stake in the company. After the announcements of the deals, the stocks of Castex, which were trading at around the ₹60 mark, started galloping. By May, it had touched the ₹180 mark and kept rising. Consequently, some bond investors smelled something fishy.

In 2012, Castex, then Amtek India, had raised funds by issuing foreign currency convertible bonds (FCCBs). The two sets of convertible bonds with coupons of 2.5 and 6 per cent for a sum of $200 million were issued by Castex between April and September 2012. These bonds were popular when Indian stock markets were booming. It led many of the promoters who had issued them to think that FCCBs would be automatically converted as stock price would soar over the conversion price in no time and investors would get their returns by selling them off in the open market without bothering them with redemptions. However, the reality was quite different. Often, for many companies, the stock price stayed well below the conversion price, leading to redemption pressures on promoters. Several FCCB holders went to court, invoking winding-up provisions as issuers failed to redeem them in time.

In the case of Castex FCCBs, rumours[5] began circulating that they were about to be defaulted. But their redemption was due only in 2017. What was actually happening was something entirely separate.

On 31 July 2015, Castex announced that it was invoking the mandatory conversion clause because the stock had stayed over 130 per cent of the conversion price for more than a month. This clause was triggered in April 2015 and could be used if the stock price remained above ₹170.

The bondholders began crying foul as the stock price had started falling even before the announcement went out, raising allegations that the company had manipulated the price to enable the conversion.[6] While the company was busy clarifying to stock exchanges, the stock came under pressure since the National Stock Exchange (NSE) removed it from the Futures and Options segment. After a 40 per cent fall in stock price in a single day on 19 August 2015, Amtek virtually hit the end of the road.

Default and the fallout

Asahi Tec, which Amtek had bought in June 2015, proved to be the proverbial last straw. When Amtek went to Asahi in April–May, funded by loans raised in Japan, the company was already sitting on a debt of ₹11,000 crore. Analysts began to question the interest servicing capabilities of the group, whose total debt was now touching ₹17,000 crore. The auto components sector simply did not deliver margins of around 9 per cent, which was necessary for servicing that kind of debt, they reasoned. While the domestic business environment was deteriorating due to pressure on the two-wheeler segment, even international operations were facing headwinds after the emissions scandal hit Volkswagen in 2014–15, involving several diesel engine VW cars being sold in America with a 'defeat device' that could alter engine performance upon detecting that the vehicle was being tested.[7]

CARE, the company that reflects the overall credit risk of the issuer, suspended ratings on the papers of Amtek, alleging that the company was not sharing critical information. In late September 2015, a few days before the fiscal year ended for Amtek, it defaulted on a bond repayment of ₹800 crore. The move sent ripples across the industry and JP Morgan Mutual Fund, which had lent money to the ancillary company, was left bearing significant losses.[8] The default also placed a large question mark over the exposure of the banking industry to Dham's costly global dream. Dham told a journalist, 'The Indian market did not keep pace as we made acquisitions. We thought the Indian market would bounce back faster in the two years, but it has not done so. So, we had to go to our bankers who have been very helpful. We did not foresee that growth in the Indian market will slow down. We will be out with our asset monetization plan soon. The reduction of debt would follow and we'll be okay.'[9]

John Flintham, the CEO of Amtek Auto, was out to convince the media and investors that the default was due to a temporary liquidity crunch and that the company was planning to de-leverage by selling non-core assets like industrial land holdings and a minority stake in the overseas business. He said a billion dollars would be raised this way and used to repay debt. This was supposed to bring down the debt to manageable levels.

Flintham, who came into Amtek with one of its earliest acquisitions, was one of the few (read *rare*) outsiders in the Amtek management. Apart from Dham, his son and nephews held top positions.

In 2002, while on his way back to India after making his first overseas deal, Arvind Dham had stopped in London and called his old friend, John Flintham, the then director of Lloyds (Brierley Hill). His company made engine ring gears, and timing and inertia rings. It was in trouble and waiting for a buyer. Dham had called Flintham to check whether the company was still on the block. It was, and Dham's stopover in Heathrow turned into a two-month stay. At the end of the two months, Dham had closed a deal to buy Lloyds for €2.2 million, almost entirely funded by Indian banks. And Flintham joined his friend's company.[10]

In hindsight, these companies were in trouble for a reason, and Indian banks no longer had the funds to keep these white elephants up and running.

The Resolution

Back in 2017, the troubled auto parts maker was among the initial group of bankrupt companies referred for insolvency resolution. During its sale, the US-based hedge fund Deccan Value Investor LP (DVI) was one of the bidders. However, DVI eventually withdrew its bid. The committee of creditors then selected Liberty House, a UK-based bidder, as the preferred buyer. Regrettably, Liberty House was found to be non-compliant with the approved norms, resulting in a fresh round of bidding. Ultimately, the US hedge fund acquired Amtek Auto with a winning bid of ₹2,700 crore. This acquisition led to lenders accepting a significant haircut of 79 per cent on the ₹12,700-crore dues owed by the auto parts maker. Only ₹500 crore of the resolution bid was transacted in cash.

The resolution process for Amtek Auto encountered numerous obstacles, including multiple rounds of bidding and litigation before tribunals and courts. However, the process was finally completed by the end of 2021, more than three years after its initiation.[11]

8

Jaypee Infratech

The irrigation departments of north Indian states must have had something to do with entrepreneurship. While Amtek was floated by the son of a Haryana state irrigation department official, its neighbour Uttar Pradesh's counterpart was not to be left behind. Only in this case, it was the official himself who quit his job midway and began his entrepreneurial journey.

Jaiprakash Gaur, an engineer with a diploma from the University of Roorkee, began his voyage as a contractor in the late 1950s. After taking up small jobs for the department he had worked in earlier, Gaur slowly ventured into bigger ventures. By 1979, he had floated Jaiprakash Associates and started eyeing larger hydel electric power projects along the tributaries of the Ganga, such as the Tehri Dam and the Narmada Valley Project.

A good relationship with successive governments stood them in good stead. Their reputation for taking care of employees and their associates preceded them. It was not until the late 1990s that Jaypee entered real estate in a big way. At that time, the government was toying with new models of infrastructure creation, where land development was offered as a barter. This model has been the source of many a failed company in the infrastructure sector.

By the early 2000s, the next generation led by Jaiprakash's son Manoj Gaur took charge. Together, they were ambitious and energetic and were keen to take the group to the next level. The Taj Expressway and the developments around it, such as golf courses and the Formula One circuit, beckoned.

While the expressway itself was commissioned despite the several environmental issues that emerged, the heavy investment in the Buddh circuit for Formula One proved bad. When the political changes came apart from this and the power sector woes caught up, the group began to sink.

The opening of the Delhi Noida Direct Flyway (DND Flyway) in 2001 brought the satellite town of Noida closer to South Delhi, triggering a flurry of development along the eastern banks of the Yamuna.[1]

What looked like a boom soon turned into a nightmare. The predicament began in the early 2000s when the Uttar Pradesh government rushed to develop vast expanses of land in Noida and Greater Noida. To attract more developers, the land authorities in Noida devised an unconventional approach of offering land at a significantly reduced price – merely 10 per cent of its actual value – for a ninety-nine-year lease. This triggered the developers' greed, leading them to acquire extensive tracts of land without foreseeing the potential challenges. Consequently, they found themselves burdened with an excessive amount of over-developed land and a struggle to find sufficient buyers for their properties. In 2003, the Jaypee Group, operating under Jaiprakash Industries, managed to secure the concession agreement for the development of the Taj Expressway, which was originally established in 2003. This agreement granted them the rights to develop a massive 2,500 hectares (25 million square feet) of land, divided into five portions of 500 hectares each.

Of these portions, three were located in the Noida and Greater Noida areas, with the remaining two in Mirzapur and Agra. Jaypee wasted no time in announcing grand real estate projects and unveiling three extravagant residential townships in the National Capital Region (NCR) – Jaypee Greens Noida, Jaypee Greens Greater Noida and Jaypee Greens Sports City.

Under the name of Jaypee Greens, the group marketed these projects with the help of Canadian architects, Arcop Associates, which designed premium properties complete with golf courses and various luxurious amenities. These three residential townships covered an area of a whopping 6,500 acres. Jaypee Greens Noida's 'Wish Town' alone spanned approximately 1,063 acres and boasted of twenty-four projects, along with residential and commercial plots, hospitals, shopping arcades, schools, golf courses, gyms and more. The group intended to construct 32,000 flats, excluding plot properties, across multiple projects within the Wish Town city, spread across five sectors in Noida along the Yamuna Expressway. Flats, penthouses, villas and plots were all part of these ambitious endeavours.

By early 2010, a staggering 88 per cent of the available space had been sold, generating over ₹900 crore in revenue for the heavily leveraged project. Although the equity amounted to around ₹1,250 crores the group's debt also surpassed ₹4,400 crore, making the real estate operations a crucial financial cushion.

While promoters raised approximately ₹600 crore through the 2010 initial public offering (IPO) by selling a portion of their shares, flat buyers continued to contribute funds. But the prevalence of corruption, regardless of the ruling party, marred the situation. Politicians and officials demanded significant cuts from builders, sometimes based on a per square foot basis. Jaypee Infratech acknowledged the political risks in Uttar Pradesh in its

IPO document from 2015, expressing concerns about potential policy revisions or hindered implementation of transportation and development policies if there was a change in power or the election of a coalition government, which could adversely affect their business.[2]

It is no secret that under Mayawati's Bahujan Samaj Party government, firms led by Jaiprakash Gaur enjoyed relative success as part of a larger conglomerate.[3] Jaypee Infratech, which was primarily a special purpose vehicle (SPV) responsible for developing the 165-kilometre Yamuna Expressway and five townships along its routes, aimed to complete most projects before the 2012 election. But because of subsequent delays, the Expressway opened in August 2012, five months after the Samajwadi Party took office. Other external factors turned less favourable, too.

'As the demand calculations were neither in sync with the job market nor with the essential infrastructure in the micro market, the projects were always going to be on a shaky wicket,' as noted by Amol Shimpi, associate dean and director of RICS School of Built Environment.[4]

In July 2012, the Noida Authority issued occupancy certificates for 1,000 flats in Jaypee's Aman Housing Project. This was out of the total proposed 5,000 flats in Sector 151 along the Noida Expressway. However, on 2 August 2012, the Yamuna Expressway Authority demanded that Jaypee refund advances received for approximately 3,000 studio apartments near the Buddh Formula 1 Circuit. These procedures were subsequently put on hold when Jaypee was referred to the insolvency court. According to its annual report for 2015–2016, Jaypee Infra had launched around 134.40 million sq ft and sold 128.20 million sq ft of it, of approximately amounting to ₹24,295 crore.[5]

Homebuyers faced their own struggles as they grappled with the implementation of the Insolvency Code. Despite efforts by the Insolvency Resolution Professional (IRP) to provide clarifications, ambiguities persisted regarding the modes of payment. The NCLT ruled that homebuyers did not fit the criteria of either 'operational creditors' or 'financial creditors', as their debts did not concern the time value of money.

In response to these challenges, real estate industry bodies called for government intervention and support to ensure the completion of the stalled projects. Their aim was to deliver the properties to homebuyers and revive the market. The road ahead remained uncertain, but efforts were underway to address the various complexities and provide a resolution to the long-standing issues faced by Jaypee Infratech and its stakeholders.

Homebuyers were angry. Chitra Sharma, a Gurgaon-based former airhostess, had used her life savings to book an apartment at Jaypee's Kensington Park Apartments. The company had floated twenty-seven such projects. When brochures had been circulated, each of these was going to be an integrated township.

'Today, there are no flats, no lawns. In many places there are just skeletons,' Sharma revealed to me. She added, 'In others even these are not there.' Many buyers had paid up to 90 per cent of their costs to the company as early as 2013. Now, they were caught in a double whammy of interests and rent payments.

Homebuyers like Sharma had marvelled at Jaypee's reputation before signing up for the projects. 'I had gone to Kedarnath and was impressed by their (Hydel) project in Vishnuprayag. They were known to take care of their employees well. I thought they would [also] treat their customers well.'

Instead, the money paid by the buyers was used to fund other business activities. 'We paid money for the building of flats. We did not give it for business. Buyers gave money for a specific purpose. He [the promoters] has used it for some other purpose. Banks are the main villain in this. Why did they do double financing?'

Sharma pointed out that the interests of the banks and the homebuyers are at loggerheads. 'They want to go to Kolkata. I want to go to Bombay. There is no meeting point.'

In September 2017, following a PIL against the NCLT, Sharma moved the Supreme Court, challenging the constitutional validity of the Insolvency and Bankruptcy Code. 'This law does not recognize the rights of the homebuyers and recent rulings have said the homebuyer is neither a financial creditor nor an operational creditor,' the petition argued.[6]

The court's initial moves raised hopes for the homebuyers, but over a year later, Sharma said it felt like they were back to square one as the court referred the matter back to the NCLT. The court managed to force the promoters to pay up a deposit of ₹750 crore.[7] But that was not enough.

Colonel S. K. Nagarath, a retired army dentist in his eighties, was a figure several homebuyers looked up to. The president of the Jaypee Aman Owners Welfare Association, he had bought two flats from the Jaypee Group. The association raised a slew of concerns, including allegations of financial irregularities and a call for a thorough forensic audit. Colonel Nagarath, a spirited advocate for the homebuyers, argued that since the buyers had parted with their hard-earned money even before the banks stepped in, they deserved to be given priority over the financial institutions.

Taking matters into their own hands, the colonel and the homebuyers wasted no time in seeking an investigation from the union Ministry of Corporate Affairs. Armed with excerpts from Jaypee Infratech's annual report and publicly available documents, they aimed to expose what they believed to be a cunning manoeuvre orchestrated in cahoots with the banks. 'Our money has been cunningly siphoned off,' exclaimed Colonel Nagarath.

He explained how the repercussions of this crisis hit countless families, particularly the middle-class and lower-income groups who had invested heavily in these properties. Many had poured in a staggering 90 per cent or more of their apartment's total cost. The amounts invested ranged from ₹25 lakh to several crores, particularly in the swanky high-end projects. In May 2017, things came to a head after a group of flat buyers lodged an FIR, accusing Jaypee Infratech's managing director, Manoj Gaur, of cheating and criminal conspiracy. Around this time, the group presented an ambitious four-phase schedule for delivering over 30,000 residential units, commencing from June 2017 and extending until 2021.

But despite the group's additional promise of refunds for some scrapped projects, many homebuyers remained unconvinced.

After five years of relentless struggle, things began to look up for the Jaypee flat buyers, when Jaypee Infratech Limited (JIL) sought a CIRP on 9 August 2017. In the case of *Anuj Jain Interim Resolution Professional for Jaypee Infratech Ltd vs Axis Bank Limited Etc.*, the Supreme Court laid down detailed principles for identifying a preferential transaction which could be voided under the Insolvency and Bankruptcy Code, 2016.[8]

The corporate debtor JIL was an SPV set up by its parent entity, Jaiprakash Associates Ltd (JAL), for certain construction, development and infrastructure projects. JAL held approximately 71 per cent of JIL's shares and had provided operational debt to JIL to the tune of ₹261 crore. The SPV had mortgaged some of its properties to secure the loans advanced by certain banks to JAL ('impugned transactions'). Among the lenders of JAL were Axis Bank, Standard Chartered Bank, ICICI Bank, State Bank of India, United Bank of India, UCO Bank, Karur Vyasa Bank, L&T Infrastructure Finance Company, Central Bank of India, Canara Bank, Karnataka Bank, IFCI, Allahabad Bank, Jammu & Kashmir Bank, South Indian Bank Limited, Bank of Maharashtra among others and some financial institutions.

IDBI Bank Ltd, a creditor of JIL, filed an application to initiate a CIRP against the debtor, alleging that JIL had committed a default in repayment of its dues approximating ₹526.11 crore.

Pursuant to this, the CIRP commenced, and a resolution professional was appointed to manage the affairs of JIL. RP Anuj Jain noticed the impugned transactions and filed an application before the NCLT under the Insolvency Code, seeking declarations that the transactions were of fraudulent, undervalued and preferential nature. The NCLT allowed the application and ordered to the 'release and discharge of the security interest created by JIL' and deem the properties mortgaged by way of the impugned transactions to be 'vested' in JIL.

However, the lenders of JAL filed separate appeals before the NCLAT. The tribunal allowed the appeals and set aside the NCLT order (the 'impugned order'). A volley of appeals against the impugned order was launched before the Supreme Court, causing delays in the CIRP that could not be completed within the designated 330-day timeframe. Further, while the SC ordered the release of the security interest, it did not provide any clarity on the status of the loan amount provided by JAL's lenders to JIL.

On 6 November 2019, the apex court resolved most of the litigations and instructed the insolvency resolution professional to finish the CIRP within ninety days. Two contenders, NBCC and Suraksha Realty, were competing to acquire Jaiprakash Infratech Ltd. The CoC favoured NBCC over Suraksha, and the former's plan was approved by the NCLT, albeit with modifications. NBCC challenged these modifications in the Supreme Court anyway. On 24 March 2021, the Supreme Court rejected NBCC's plan, ordering a restart of the CIRP process. Two months later, on 7 July 2021, the CoC approved Suraksha's resolution plan, which was then submitted to the NCLT.[9]

The case currently awaits approval from the tribunal, with only the Yamuna Expressway Industrial Development Authority (YEIDA) having presented its argument against the plan. The submissions from ICICI Bank, Bank of Baroda and JAL are still pending at the time of writing.

The judgment here is of much importance to investors and lenders, as the approach of the SC in this case highlights the risk of a transaction being set aside and the diligence required to be exercised by investors and lenders going forward. For more than 22,000 homebuyers who endured a decade-long wait for their flats, the NCLT's 491-page ruling, approving the consortium bid of Suraksha Realty and Lakshdeep Investments and Finance, on 7 March 2023, came as a relief. The announcement offered a clear path towards the fulfilment of nearly 20,000 stalled residences in Noida and Greater Noida.[10]

9

Alok Industries

In 2011, when Alok Industries celebrated its silver jubilee, SBI was a happy bank. V. S. Radhakrishnan, the then deputy general manager of SBI, wrote a congratulatory note on the occasion saying, 'We have been your bankers since inception and it is a pleasure seeing Alok growing from strength to strength, maintaining an impeccable track record through consistent growth.'[1]

Sidarth Rath, then President of Axis Bank, also complimented the group for being the largest integrated textile company in India. Both senior bankers attributed this success to the vision and strategy of the top management. Not just the bankers but global customers, such as Marks & Spencer, Carrefour and Kohl's, were also impressed with Alok's quality and timely delivery. Marquee investors such as Caledonia Investments had taken the growth ride with the company.

To add to all this, there was some glamour quotient as well. Alok was a partner in Victoria's Secret, the lingerie brand famous for their supermodel ambassadors such as Miranda Kerr and Heidi Klum. The organic free trade cotton, grown in the West African country of Burkina Faso, was one of the USPs of its global trade.

In 2007, Alok Industries brought this Burkinabe cotton to India. Here, the cotton was turned into spun yarn, which was then made into fabric and sent to its Sri Lankan partner, MAS Intimates, for producing the final garment. Alok was planning to set up a manufacturing base – a spinning unit of 68,000 spindles – in Bobo-Dioulasso, the second-largest city in the African country and a key hub of its textile and agriculture trade. The same year, the company acquired a majority stake in Mileta International in the Czech Republic, and in 2008, bought a stake in a UK retail chain, Store Twenty One. Alok Industries also set up a lifestyle retail chain in India by the name of H&A. At one point, H&A had even roped in Australian cricketer Brett Lee to be the face of its activewear range. But soon, the plans fell like Indian wickets against Lee's bowling on one of the WACA pitches.

In a matter of four years since the silver jubilee, SBI was already considering appointing a forensic auditor to find the whereabouts of ₹20,000 crore of bank funds. In May 2016, Deloitte, Alok's long-standing company auditor, resigned abruptly.[2] So, were people just glossing over the troubles of the company on the eve of its silver jubilee or did things just slide really quickly after that high?

Alok Industries had been founded by three brothers of the Jiwarajika family. Like many Marwari families of that vintage in Mumbai, the Jiwarajikas had an interest in cotton. Alok was born as a family partnership firm into trading yarn and readymade garments. Dilip Jiwarajika, the middle brother was more entrepreneurially inclined than his siblings. While he took the lead, Ashok, the elder brother who had cut his teeth working with a couple of leading textile companies, and Surendra, the youngest who was just out of college, joined hands. The trio floated the textile venture Alok Industries in 1986, named after the school-going Alok Jiwarajika, Ashok's son.

Alok Jiwarajika himself joined the company in 2002, followed by his cousins Varun and Niraj in the later years of noughties. All of them had defined roles. While Alok was already taking care of home textiles, Niraj (Dilip's son) looked after knitting and Varun (Surendra's son) oversaw the domestic retail business, H&A. Each of the brothers also handled one of the three major revenue-generating divisions independently – home textiles, polyester and apparel fabrics.

When the going was good, all six members of the Jiwarajika family – three from the first and three from the second generation – would sit together at the lunch table in the office, discussing business and other things. However, at the dinner table, business talk was avoided at all costs, unless really necessary. The Jiwarajikas would be at the plant in Silvassa and Vapi in Gujarat at least twice a week to ensure plant upkeep and discuss strategies with the plant heads to optimize efficiency. From a modest beginning in Silvassa with a ₹4.5 crore IPO in 1993, Alok clocked a turnover of ₹6,300 crore in 2011, of which ₹2,200 crore was made through exports. The next year, the turnover touched ₹8,900 crore, not to mention the mark it had made among global superstores and connections formed with supermodels.

Even though the company was putting up a brave face, there were several risks staring at it from all sides. The huge capital expenditure it had embarked upon followed by the diversification into retail and real estate had built up the leverage manifold. By 2012, the entire promoter shareholding of 33 per cent was pledged to lenders. Although there were institutional shareholders like LIC and IFCI, the stocks did not really recover from the post-financial crisis slump. The textile sector itself was caught in the global headwinds in 2011–12. But the promoters were taking solace in a September 2010 report by the consultant Technopak Advisors.

Sharing the report by the global consultants, the promoters wrote to shareholders informing them how the Indian textile industry was set to undergo significant growth in the next decade (2011–2020). Global textile trade was projected to reach $1,000 billion by 2020, while the Indian textile industry was expected to triple its size to $220 billion in that time. Key drivers of this growth would include shifting supply patterns, with a decline in the US and EU and a rise in low-cost Asian countries like India and China. The strength of India's textile manufacturing, in the form of surplus cotton and presence across the value chain, positioned it favourably to grow its market share from 4.5 to 8 per cent by 2020. In addition to this, the rising per capita income, population growth and increased organized retail were supposed to contribute towards higher domestic textile consumption.[3]

But a letter of offer filed on 20 March 2013 for a ₹551 crore rights issue underlined the risks.[4] Under point 14 of the report, the company detailed how they were competing with 'other low cost producing countries to sell our products in highly competitive markets and have limited ability to influence prices in these markets for our products'. Further stress was placed on how they must stay competitive in highly competitive markets like the US and Europe and, thereby, constantly reduce production costs, improve efficiency and enhance distribution. Failing to do this could result in losing market share to low-cost manufacturers from countries like

China, Pakistan, Indonesia and Bangladesh, which may have lower production costs, greater financial resources, economies of scale, government subsidies and broader product ranges. An inability to effectively compete with them or attract new customers could lead to negative impact on business, financial condition and profitability. Efficient cost management was crucial for maintaining profit margins.

The letter of offer also expressed concerns about the franchisee model adopted by the company to develop its retail chain H&A, highlighting how these stores were typically 'owned or rented by independent individuals or entities, and we may not be able to retain control of most of the operational factors on a daily basis'. The 'cash-and-carry' wholesale operations they had established in India through their network of independent business operators ran daily operations over which the company could not exercise absolute control. They went on to add that there could be no assurance provided for the effectiveness of their training and standards, and that the quality of the service and operations could diminish as a result of various factors beyond the company's control.

It seems that some of these risks played out, which in turn pushed the heavily leveraged structure Alok was operating on to the edge. The capital investment of previous ten years was sitting in Alok's books. The company had ₹16,000 crore of debt in its books. About half of this was long term – the company had borrowed around ₹3,505 crore under the government's Technology Upgradation Fund Scheme (TUFS) for the textile sector between 2001 and 2008, with the remaining half being short term.[5] Even then, the company knew very well that this heavy indebtedness could severely limit its ability to operate in a business that demanded a high working capital. As finance costs spiralled without a corresponding growth in revenues, the funds available for the working capital began to decrease, which in turn hit the top line.

Alok had hoped to get out of this vicious cycle by selling some of its realty assets. 'Our inability to exit the real estate business at the time or in the manner we expect would adversely affect our operations and profitability. Furthermore, we may also be unable to recover our investments and costs incurred, which may have a material adverse impact on our capital availability for our future capital expenditure requirements,' the company had warned.[6]

Alok was hoping to sell the floors it owned in Peninsula Park's B tower and Ashford Centre, both in the then emerging business hub of Lower Parel in Mumbai. It managed to sell eight floors in Peninsula, raising close to ₹425 crore.[7] But it was not enough. As early as 2013, unable to pay rentals, Alok announced that it was shutting forty-five H&A stores.[8] By 2016, the writing was on the wall. Store Twenty One, too, was floundering. It went through an insolvency-like process and witnessed the closure of eighty shops. By 2017, the remaining 122 stores were also closed down.[9] More skeletons tumbled out of the closet after the company was referred to the NCLT.

Ajay Joshi, the RP, took steps to recover over ₹11,000 crore of trade receivables from some 5,293 debtors. However, almost half of the legal notices sent by the RP returned undelivered, raising suspicions that these entities did not exist.[10] Even the notices that were delivered did not receive any response, forcing the creditors to make provisions for the missing sums.

Curiously, in August 2017, Dilip Jiwarajika was named in an FIR filed by the CBI against Indian Revenue Service officer Vivek Batra. Batra, who had served in the income tax department in Mumbai between 2008 and 2017, was alleged to have amassed assets disproportionate to his income. A lavish music programme and dinner party thrown by Batra at Gallops club in Mahalakshmi Race Course, attended by the who's who of Mumbai's business and social circles, became the talk of the income tax circles.[11]

Batra's son Arjun's admission to Boston University and the several trips the family made to the United States were also cited by the CBI. He maintained houses in posh areas in Mumbai and Delhi apart from a holiday home in Goa. Apart from Dilip Jiwarajika, the FIR also named Alok Industries among the companies and persons who had abetted Batra's crime. Alok Industries had issued an appointment order to Batra's wife Priyanka and was paying significant sums as consultancy fee.

'Shri Vivek Batra is in the process of routing ill gotten money through Alok Industries in the name of his wife Priyanka Batra by showing her as an employee,' the CBI said.[12]

Why was Alok paying Batra's wife? What was the quid pro quo? It seems the company that helped make Victoria's Secret had its own Victorian secrets buried deep in its books. Bankers have stated that Alok lost big on the forex derivatives that banks had sold to it during the 2008 Global Financial Crisis.

Since appearing in the first list of bad loans drawn up by RBI for resolution under the Insolvency and Bankruptcy Code, the textile giant was declared insolvent and eventually taken over by a consortium of JM Financial Asset Reconstruction Company (ARC) and Reliance Industries in 2018 for ₹5,050 crore. Lenders took an 83 per cent haircut on their dues worth ₹29,523 crore: a realization of 17.11 per cent. However, the NCLT rejected their claim as only 70 per cent of the creditors backed it against the minimum requirement of 75. This gave the company no option but to be liquidated.

Unhappy with the decision of the NCLT operational creditors, Reliance moved the NCLT to reconsider its decision. With the threshold reduced from 75 to 66 per cent, the Ahmedabad bench finally gave the bid to Reliance and JM in 2019. As per the plan, Reliance infused about ₹500 crore in the form of equity into the stressed unit. It acquired about a 37.7 per cent stake in the company as well. Following the epic takeover, Alok Industries, which was being dreaded by investors, soon became one among many on the must-buy list.

By early 2020, the company generated a return of 822 per cent. During the period of restructuring, the share prices were less than ₹14, which soared to ₹36 that same year.[13]

10

Era Infra Engineering

Hem Singh Bharana, a civil engineer by training, had established Era Constructions in the early 1990s, when the country stepped into a new era of business practices. As liberalization of the economy began opening opportunities, Bharana, who often managed to hold his own on business television even with his broken English, started by taking on small construction projects. His first big break into public sector projects came in 1994 when he bagged an order from the National Dairy Development Board (NDDB).

Bharana learnt the ropes of doing business with the public sector quickly. Winning government contracts meant proximity to politicians and bureaucrats, some of whom went on to serve as independent directors in Era Infra's board.

After some initial struggle, the company was able to acquire a series of projects that they successfully completed and became eligible for subsequent tenders. Bharana soon expanded into airport, highways and railways construction. Though the company had taken up airport renewal projects in the hinterland, the UP–NCR–Haryana belt became its favourite hunting ground. Power projects, institutional and industrial complexes, multiplexes and residential buildings catering to PSUs, private sector and Asian Development Bank-aided projects became

Bharana's forte. Over a fifteen-year period, beginning in the late 1990s, Era completed over fifty projects. Bharana himself was worth close to ₹200 crore at the time.

Though the Global Financial Crisis of 2008 affected a big dent in its smooth progress, the company recovered by bagging a couple of key projects in the run-up to the Commonwealth Games in 2010. It refurbished the iconic Jawaharlal Nehru Stadium as part of a ₹111 crore project. Era's troubles seem to have started just around this time. While the games themselves became controversial after several allegations of corruption against the chairman of the organizing commitee, Suresh Kalmadi, there were also question marks surrounding the way Era had conducted its operations.

Two term loans sanctioned by UCO Bank to Era in 2010 became the subject of a CBI enquiry after the forensic auditors who probed the accounts highlighted several lapses.

It turned out that in March 2010, Era had availed a ₹200 crore term loan facility from UCO Bank. As per the loan conditions, a part of the funds were supposed to be used to retire some high-cost debt availed from PNB, Central Bank of India and IFCI. PNB and Central Bank got zilch, while IFCI was paid about ₹60 lakh. And nearly ₹15 crore was diverted to sister companies Era Buildsys and Era Infra India. More on these companies later.

Further, the forensic audit revealed that out of the funds received from UCO Bank, Era had made a payment of ₹5.8 crore to Pawan Bansal. Bansal, a former IFCI employee, had turned into a middleman for bank loans and was running a firm called Altius Finserv. Altius Finserv and Bansal soon became embroiled in the Syndicate Bank loan fraud case, in which Bansal was arrested by the CBI.

A few months later, in October 2010, UCO Bank sanctioned another loan of ₹450 crore. Of this, the bank planned to hold a third, and downsell the remaining ₹300 crore. Of the ₹450 crore, about ₹239 crore was supposed to be utilized for refinancing high-cost nonconvertible debentures* (NCDs) and term loans. The remaining ₹211 crore was to be used for capital expenditure (capex).

Eventually, several irregularities were found in the end use of these funds. A sum of ₹25 crore was said to be used to repay some NCDs that had already been repaid. Of the amount earmarked for capex, more than half was diverted to meet working capital needs. There were transfers to Era Buildsys as well. Further, discrepancies were found in the documentation for the loan. Era had declared an order book of over ₹11,000 crore and, as per projections of future cash flows, justified the sanction of the loan. However, it was discovered that about ₹1,000 crore pertaining to these orders had already been received by Era several months earlier.

The account also had the direct involvement of Arun Kaul, the then chairman and managing director of UCO Bank. In its complaint to the CBI in April 2018, the bank alleged that Arun Kaul did not protect its interests and illegally altered the terms of the loan, resulting in a loss to the lender. The bank alleged a total fraud of ₹737 crore.[1]

The complaints also brought to the fore the role played by chartered accountants. According to banking rules, borrowers are required to get an end-use certificate from CAs. Often, some

---

* Long-term debt instruments issued by companies with a set interest rate for the entire investment period. Simply put, it is a type of loan that cannot be converted into company stock.

of these professionals charge a small commission to conceal the actual use of loan funds and issue these certificates, without any physical checks. The rules governing CAs are so weak that any complaints against them take years to process.

The Special Investigative Auditor (SIA) G. D. Apte and Co's report was submitted to Union Bank and circulated in Joint Lenders Meeting (JLM) on 31 January 2014. The UCO bank based its complaint on this report and is said to have raised several other red flags.[2] One of these were the figures reported under the head of 'trade receivables'. The auditor had pointed out how a majority of the ₹10,000 crore pertained to work done for one of its associate companies. Banks did not pay much heed to this at the time.

The complaints by the banks were among the lesser of the troubles that hit Bharana and his business ventures. After reporting a revenue of ₹4,701 crore and a profit after tax (PAT) of ₹168 crore, Era slipped into the red in the financial year ending March 2014, recording a net loss of ₹503 crore.[3]

As environmental clearances got held up on some road projects, heavy working capital needs amid rising interest costs began to bother the lenders. The account was referred for CDR, where about ₹8,754 crore was restructured. Promoters were asked to bring additional security and pledge all the shareholding in favour of the lenders. Bharana had to contribute ₹223 crore, a quarter of the sacrifice being made by lenders in the CDR. In its annual report of 2013–14, the following was mentioned under the business performance head:

Despite of the above said constrains, the Order Book of Company as at 31.03.2014 is maintained at ₹15,723.95 crores across sectors, to be implemented over a period of next two to three years. All ongoing projects are monitored on a regular basis by the senior management based at Noida offices ... The Company is professionally managed with well-qualified and experienced personnel in all areas including engineering, finance and administration combined with a full-fledged Enterprise Resource Planning (ERP) and MIS system. As on 31st March, 2014, the Company has on its roll approximately Two Thousand (2,000) employees.[4]

It listed some of its key ongoing projects, including the construction of a hostel complex in Mumbai's Baba Atomic Research Centre, the procurement of escalators for Mumbai Rail Vikas Corp, the civil contracts for a super thermal project by the NTPC in Bihar and works on Kochi Metro rail.

While the CDR provided some breathing space, the conglomerate at large was looking for other sources of funds. Some of the subsidiaries started collecting money from homebuyers as advances for homes, but their timing could not have been worse. With the change in the government in 2014, both at the Centre and in the key states of Haryana and Uttar Pradesh, promoters seen as close to the previous regime started facing heavy odds. Era and Bharana, who had thrived under the previous UPA regime, found themselves in a precarious spot.

The first blow came from the Securities and Exchange Board of India (SEBI) on 5 June 2014. It found that the fundraising by Adel Landmark Ltd (ALL), the new moniker of Era Landmarks since February 2014, for its three major projects in Gurgaon (Cosmocity), Faridabad (Redwood Residency) and Palwal (Era Green World), amounted to a collective investment scheme, which cannot be floated without prior SEBI permission, therefore pronouncing it illegal.

The modus operandi of Adel Landmark was described in the SEBI order as inviting applications to 'book plots of land for residential/commercial' units under schemes like 'Cosmocity at Gurgaon Sector 103', 'Era Green World at Sector 8, Palwal' and 'Redwood Residency at Sector 78, Faridabad'. Furthermore, Adel Landmark had collected ₹51,82,70,000 from 432 investors for Cosmocity, ₹80,06,11,000 from 571 investors for Green World and ₹1,19,78,92,000 from 618 investors for Redwood.[5]

The total amounted to over ₹250 crore across these three projects. However, subsequent reports quoting investor and police accounts claimed that the amount raised was well over ₹1,000 crore. The regulator ordered the directors of ALL, which included Hem Singh Bharana and his cousin Sumit Bharana, to immediately stop the money-collection activity.

It passed the following directions for the company as well:

1. To not collect any fresh money from investors under its existing scheme in Gurgaon
2. To not launch any new schemes or plans without respective licences
3. To immediately submit the full inventory of the assets owned by ALL
4. To not dispose of any of the properties or alienate the assets of the existing scheme at Gurgaon
5. To not divert any funds pertaining to the Gurgaon scheme, raised from public at large, kept in bank account(s) and/or in the custody of the company
6. To furnish all the information/details sought by SEBI within fifteen days from the date of receipt of the order, including the details of amount mobilized and refunded till date and

scheme-wise list of investors and their contact numbers, addresses and PAN.

In addition to this, in October 2015, SEBI ordered the real estate developer and its directors to refund all collected money within three months. The company was also restrained from accessing the securities market for the next four years.[6] To add to the panic, ALL ran into trouble with local authorities for building laws violations. In some cases, lenders started attaching land against which the Era group had raised loans, in turn scaring away homebuyers and investors for these schemes. As angry homebuyers started demanding flats, the company tried to pacify them by providing refunds through cheques.

Owing to insufficient funds, the cheques bounced, resulting in police cases. Several allegations started flying around. In 2015, hundreds of homebuyers from several projects, such as Cosmocity, Adel Landmark in Gurgaon, Era Greenworld in Palwal and Era Divine Court in Faridabad, were among those who filed criminal complaints.

According to the complaints filed with the Enforcement Directorate, various subsidiary companies of Bharana and his family members had siphoned off several thousand crores for investments abroad. They cited the names of some companies and mentioned Africa, UK and America as places where Bharana had parked these funds. To date, investigators are still on the job.

Bharana was arrested in July 2015 in Gurgaon for allegedly duping homebuyers. Three months later, he was admitted to a hospital in Rohtak after he complained of discomfort. Though he received bail in May 2016, things were never to be the same again.

In promoter-driven companies such as Era, where the management consists largely of family members and people close to the family, the arrest of its head means that everything comes to a standstill. As Bharana tried availing bail from prison, the affairs of Era Infra, which were already under the stress of ballooning interest payments, began to deteriorate further. Bharana and his empire could not survive the new era that dawned in 2014.

*

As for the resolution process of Era Infra, closure awaits. The insolvency proceeding is still ongoing against the company, as it owes ₹16,832 crore to financial creditors and ₹777 crore to operational creditors.[7] The case, which began on 12 April 2017 with NCLT, has been mired in one problem or another. With their petition pending in the Delhi High Court, Era thwarted NCLT's attempts at resolution by citing a conflict of jurisdiction. The tribunal then referred the case to a special bench for addressing the issue. NCLT finally admitted the insolvency application of Union Bank of India against Era Infra on 8 May 2018, almost a year after the RBI had referred it. The resolution professional Rajiv Chakraborty received two plans, but the CoC is yet to approve either because of the legal disambiguities in them. With this curious case hitting multiple walls, resolution seems far away, with no hearing having reportedly taken place since March 2020.[8]

11

Jyoti Structures

Like Era Infra, Jyoti Structures Ltd (JSL) was also an engineering, procurement and construction (EPC) firm and another victim of the various predicaments that ail the country's infrastructure sector. Jyoti, of 1970s vintage, was promoted by Bhopal-based Sanjay H. Mirchandani and Mumbai-based V. P. Valecha. In its early days, Jyoti started off by supplying the huge metal towers used in power transmission lines. It quickly expanded to global markets. By 2000, Jyoti had a revenue of ₹231 crore and a PAT of ₹15 crore. That year, it produced some 40,957 metric tonnes of towers and its export turnover stood at ₹142 crore.[1]

At this stage, the control of the company lay with Valecha and Mirchandani, who were the promoter directors. The company had three executive directors: K. R. Thakur, P. K. Thakur and S. A. Krishnan.

Though JSL began as a manufacturer of transmission line towers, it went on to become a major player in the power sector as a provider of turnkey solutions for high-voltage transmission lines, substations and distribution lines. It executed large projects across the globe, partnering with companies such as National Grid in the UK, Hydel Quebec in Canada and several Australian utilities.

K. R. Thakur, then the face of the company, was a former public sector executive associated with Engineers India Ltd and Nuclear Power Corporation of India Ltd. A transmission industry veteran with experience dating back to the early 1980s, Thakur had been in the thick of things at Jyoti since 1989.

Three main lines of operation, namely, transmission lines, substations and rural electrification, lay at the core of JSL's business. In each of these, it undertook turnkey projects on a global scale. Turnkey projects refer to work assignments where the service provider offers a completed product, taking care of a complete range of services. In JSL's case, it included design, engineering, tower testing, manufacturing, construction and project management.

The company had manufacturing plants in Nashik and Raipur, with a combined manufacturing capacity of 110,000 MT of transmission line towers. It also had an in-house tower testing facility at Ghoti, Igatpuri. Close to 2,000 people worked in these factories.

The Vajpayee-led NDA government had made a name for itself by planning and executing the world-class Golden Quadrilateral and North–South and East–West corridors of the National Highway. The subsequent UPA government in turn took up rural electrification in a big way.

This was an opportunity for JSL. Rural electrification under the Rajiv Gandhi Grameen Vidyutikaran Yojana, introduced in April 2005, aimed to provide electricity to all villages and habitations. In order to supply power to the entire country, an expansion of the regional transmission network and inter-regional capacity to transmit power was essential. The total number of inhabited villages in India as per the 2001 census was approximately 593,732, of which 489,532 were electrified as on

31 March 2009, with the remaining number of un-electrified villages at 104,200.[2]

As the push for electrification gathered pace, the contribution of rural electrification to JSL's revenues increased from 12 per cent of the total revenue to 14 per cent in 2009. Rural electrification was a strong growing sector at a compound annual growth rate (CAGR) of 28.81 per cent. Jyoti bet big on this segment. On revenues of ₹1,724 crore, it reported a net profits of ₹79.74 crore in the financial year 2008–09.[3]

International expansion

Over the next few years, the company became aggressive with international projects and even set up manufacturing facilities in Dubai and Houston, Texas.

Providing an update on international operations in a letter of offer filed in 2014, the company highlighted that their subsidiaries and joint ventures had previously collaborated with customers from over thirty countries around the world. Their international revenues witnessed substantial growth, rising from ₹61,033 lakh in FY 2013 to ₹103,485 lakh in FY 2014, reflecting a y-o-y growth of 69.56 per cent. And while in 2009 only one of their joint ventures served in the Middle East, as of 30 June 2014, JSL had undertaken EPC turnkey contracts across the Middle East, the US and Africa.

Africa held particular importance in the company's international operations, taking on power transmission contracts in many African countries. Through actively pursuing business development opportunities and establishing subsidiaries, they aimed to play a significant role in the power transmission and distribution sector in the continent. In all of this, expanding their global presence remained a priority.[4]

However, it appears that these global bets did not produce the desired results and proved to be a drag on the company's finances. JSL did not even have in place some basic systems, such as data management softwares, that would be considered a given in a company of its size. The auditors had started making qualifications to the accounts of the company, indicating certain issues, uncertainties or discrepancies in the financial statements, from 2014 itself.[5]

Emphasis on international subsidiaries

In the company's FY 2015–16 annual report, which also contained R. M. Ajgaonkar & Associates' independent and qualified auditor's report, red flags were raised about JSL's international arms, which seemed to be bankrupt.[6] Jyoti International (JII), JSL's wholly owned subsidiary company had seen investments of ₹6,000 lakh in its equity shares. As per the report, 'As on 31st March, 2016, the Company has also advanced loan of ₹7,647.53 Lacs to JII.' The losses incurred resulted in total erosion of the company's net worth with no provision whatsoever made for outstanding amounts because the management was 'optimistic of turning around the business of that company'.

Another subsidiary, Jyoti Americas LLC, had received an advanced loan of about ₹800 lakh with an outstanding sum of ₹4,739 lakh.

The company had made an investment of ₹419 in the equity shares of its subsidiary Jyoti Structures Africa (Pty) limited

(JSAPL), with an advanced loan of about ₹2,819 lakh. The outstanding credit here was reportedly ₹3,026 lakh. But in both these cases, too, the company remained 'optimistic' despite the worth of these ventures having fully eroded as of 31 March 2016.

Another major red flag pointed out by the auditors was the company's current financial crunch because of inadequate liquidity. This had resulted in delays in implementing contracted projects, which could cause future liability. As per the report, 'The Company has made a provision of ₹1,300 lakhs for any such liability which in the view of the Company would be adequate.' The auditors refrained from commenting further on the matter, citing it was technical in nature.

Several joint ventures (JVs) also looked dubious. As of 31 March 2016, the company had trade receivables of ₹7,045 lakh from a joint venture called Lauren Jyoti Private Ltd (LJPL). The company also paid ₹5,507 lakh for a bank guarantee encashed by one of LJPL's customers, which was considered receivable from the joint venture. The remaining outstanding amount from LJPL, including interest for the FY was ₹2,534 lakh. The auditors noted: '[Given] the financial statements of the JV are not available and it is not regular in repayment of the above outstanding, we are not able to comment on the recovery of the debt and impact of the same on the financial statements of the Company for the year.'

The company had invested ₹5,000 lakh in 5 million equity shares of LJPL. However, with the financial statements of LJPL unavailable, and based on the last audited financial statements from 31 March 2013, it was found that the entity's net worth was 'completely eroded'. JSL had, again, not made any provision for this loss. As a result, the company's loss for the year was understated, and its reserves overstated, by ₹5,000 lakh.

Another suspicious area was that of bank guarantees (BGs). Auditors noted how during the year, a customer encashed bank guarantees worth ₹1,823 lakh. JSL did not include this amount in its P&L statement, as it had done in previous years. They had also not recognized a portion of the interest on outstanding loans claimed by certain banks, as they believed the interest charges were excessive and expected them to be waived. As a result, the auditors reported that they were 'unable to comment on the impact of the same on the financial statements'.

The auditors were also upset that JSL did not even have a proper enterprise resource planning (ERP) system. R. M. Ajgaonkar & Associates mentioned in their audit report that the company faced limitations in its control system and processes, requiring manual intervention and reconciliations. They suggested that the SAP postings and physical documents needed to undergo harmonization to ensure accurate accounting.

An independent report by KPMG (engaged by Jyoti Structures on 21 October 2014) highlighted the poor state of the company's ERP system and reviewed its debts. Confirmation letters were received from 229 projects, but key information such as client personnel names and designations were missing in many cases. Bank guarantees were issued for 142 projects, and a sample review showed that some guarantees were invoked but later debited back to the customer's account as on 30 June 2015.

What was more surprising was the lack of client acknowledgements and provision for guarantees. It was also uncertain whether the amount debited due to invoked guarantees could be recovered. There were 307 projects and sub-projects with a total outstanding amount of ₹3,781.85 crore as of June 2015. After analyzing collections from December 2014 to June 2015, KPMG found that twenty-two debtors had outstanding amounts of ₹792.49 crore, including ₹142 crore as retention money. Of these, ₹511.60 crore had been outstanding for over a year. Additionally, ten terminated projects had an outstanding balance of ₹394.80 crore, which couldn't be determined. On 31 March 2015, the company had total outstanding debts of ₹3,620 crore, and by June 2015, only ₹278 crore (8 per cent) had been realized.[7] The findings of the KPMG report raised several uncomfortable questions about the systems in place at Jyoti Structures. The worst-case scenario was that the management had been in the know about the state of affairs and ignored it deliberately. This then raised questions of whether there was any collusion.[8]

Initially, JSL was ordered to be liquidated by the NCLT in 2018. However, after a legal battle, in March 2019 it was awarded to a group of high-net-worth investors, led by Netmagic CEO Sharad Sanghi. He had submitted a revised bid as per the order of NCLAT. Sanghi had offered to pay almost ₹4,000 crore in twelve years against the original fifteen years.[9]

This amounted to more than the liquidation value of about ₹1112.5 crore. The deal involved an upfront payment of ₹50 crore, followed by ₹75 crore distributed over the next twelve months. The remaining amount was to be paid in staggered payments over the next twelve years.

Even this proposal was contested in the Supreme Court by one of the lenders, DBS Bank, the sole first charge holder over certain assets of the firm. The bank argued that the company owed ₹53.77 crore to it and that the liquidation value of the assets charged to DBS was thrice this amount. DBS also said that the tribunal had ignored the principles of the law of mortgages, which provide sanctity of property rights, more so the right of a creditor holding the first and sole charge.

An SC Bench, led by Justice R. F. Nariman, dismissed the DBS appeal against the NCLT order which accepted the amended resolution plan for Jyoti Structures.[10] Following the acquisition, JSL formally became a 100 per cent public listed company in June 2021.[11]

12

ABG Shipyard

Between 2003 and 2007, the Indian stock market saw an unprecedented bull run, with stocks trending upwards.[1] The index grew seven times in the period, while some stock prices multiplied ten times. This surplus of capital made promoters consider new ventures. Analysts lost track of price-earnings ratios as the market's blistering rise made them look absurd. They had to come up with something new; the answer was SOTP. Although the concept was not invented then, it quickly gained currency. SOTP, which stands for 'sum of the parts', is a valuation methodology where a certain valuation is attached to each part of the business and the total valuation is the 'sum' of these parts.

This theory helped justify the large premiums being commanded by some large business houses to a certain extent. Other promoters also wanted a piece of this cake. This drove a spree of diversifications. As a result, some real estate players wanted to get into mutual funds, another realtor wanted a share of the telecom story, a telecom player wanted a play in financial services, a drug maker wanted to open a bank and so on. Nobody cared about synergy, experience, risks or competition.

Amid this madness, a young Rishi Agarwal's logical and pragmatic idea of getting into the business of building offshore rigs came off as conservative. Oil rigs are huge apparatuses built for drilling – to explore, extract and process petroleum or natural gas that lies in the rock formations beneath the seabed. Agarwal's ABG Shipyard, established in 1985, originally had a presence in ship repairs, with its facility located in Magdalla, near Surat. It was in the process of setting up a shipbuilding yard in Dahej, about 130 kilometres north along the Gulf of Khambhat. Rig-building seemed like natural progression, even though there were very few players in this business globally. Offshore rigs can take two to three years to build and can eat up a lot of capital, but global banks were flush with cash at the time and keen to extend funds. A management graduate from Purdue University, in the US, the twenty-three-year-old had embarked on an acquisition spree in 1989 by buying the Magdalla Shipyard. It was the first Indian shipyard to export a ship when it delivered a newsprint carrier to Lys-Line, Oslo, Norway in 1998. He also led ABG Shipyard to become the first company to use a diesel electric propulsion plant in its vessel *CCC Pioneer*.

In early 2007, Agarwal's ABG Shipyard announced its plans to build a plant to manufacture rigs at a projected outlay of ₹550 crore. American major Friede & Goldman was to help with the designs. As if by providence, even before the plant was in place, ABG managed to get orders for two rigs, then worth close to ₹2,000 crore, from Essar Oil. Incidentally, Essar's rig, which was deployed for the exploration in the Krishna-Godavari (KG) basin for Gujarat State Petroleum Corporation (GSPC), went kaput and had to be sent back to the UK for repair. Around the same time, a few hundred miles south at Dabhol in Maharashtra, ABG's rival in the shipyard business, Bharati Shipyard, was building India's first rig for a company called Great Offshore.

Established by the Mumbai-based Sheth family in 1983 as a division of Great Eastern Shipping (GE Shipping),

Great Offshore was the leading player in this niche segment and at that time contracted by ONGC, the state-owned explorer. The Sheths, a set of five cousins and their families, were third-generation businessmen. Maneklal Ujamshi Mulji and his younger brother Jagjivan Ujamshi Mulji set up GE Shipping in the 1940s. Maneklal's two sons, Kanaiyalal and Sevantilal, and Jagjivan's three sons, Jayantilal, Kantilal and Vasanth, formed the second generation. In 2005, things boiled down to the Kanaiyalal and Kantilal branches of the family on the stakes in GE shipping. It was decided that the offshore business would be spun off into a separate entity called Great Offshore under Vijay Kantilal Sheth while Kanaiyalal Sheth's sons Bharath and Ravi Sheth would receive control of the demerged GE Shipping.

Though Vijay took control of Great Offshore, he had to borrow a few hundred crores to shore up his stake and take control of the company. He raised this amount from institutions such as Infrastructure Leasing and Financial Services (IL&FS). As the shares kept growing in value, things seemed under control for a while. The rising crude oil prices meant that exploration work continued briskly, encouraging Sheth to invest in building rigs. Sheth entrusted this task to his old friend P. C. Kapoor, who was running Bharati Shipyard Ltd (BSL) along with Vijaykumar.

Then the US investment bank Lehman Brothers collapsed in September 2008, taking down the entire market with it and triggering a set of events now known as the Global Financial Crisis. As credit froze, global trade crashed and stock markets plunged to historic lows. The shares of Great Offshore were no exception. By December 2008, lenders were breathing down Vijay Sheth's neck, demanding that he top up the margin money for the loans against shares. Already leveraged heavily, Sheth parked his stake with his vendor and friend at BSL. Over the next six months, things did not improve dramatically. In hindsight, they would not have improved even if he had waited another ten years.

By entrusting those shares to Bharati, however, Sheth had inadvertently passed on his misfortune to multiple entities. Following a bidding war between ABG and Bharati, which stretched to the second half of 2009, the control over Great Offshore went to the latter, while Sheth was allowed to continue at the helm. Eventually, all three companies would file for bankruptcy.

Why was ABG attracted to Great Offshore Ltd (GOL)? According to Nishith Desai Associates' report from 16 December 2019 titled 'Great Offshore Takeover Saga – Bharati Shipyard v/s ABG Shipyard', GOL was a prized possession for the shipping giants.[2] It was a valued player in the industry, having made a net profit of ₹211 crore on a turnover of ₹950 crore in the previous fiscal year. Bidders BSL and ABG looked beyond GOL's economic position and recognized the potential in the offshore sector. With a fleet of over forty floating assets, including offshore support vessels, GOL had a significant opportunity for replacement and captive business in the following years. Additionally, GOL's vessels offered potential for dry-docking and repair services, making it an attractive prospect for potential acquirers.

In addition, buying GOL would have deprived the competitor Bharati Shipyard of a captive asset. ABG, with better financial back-up, naturally felt uneasy at the prospect of BSL acquiring a large captive business.

It was also a golden opportunity for ABG to eliminate competition from BSL in the sector once and for all by grabbing its major client. Moreover, this could be a positive step for ABG in order to prepare itself for a superior performance in the recovering market. The services provided by ABG would have perfectly matched GOL's business, lending to a perfect case of forward integration. Alternatively, there was a possibility that ABG intended to wield a double-edged sword by participating in the race against BSL to make the acquisition a costly affair for the latter while simultaneously amassing profits for itself.

However, had ABG won the race for GOL, things would have perhaps played out differently. Despite pulling out at the last minute, ABG had to shell out close to ₹300 crore for buying shares tendered in the open offer. A captive client like Great Offshore could have propped up ABG's finances in a market where prospects for shipping had dried up in the Global Financial Crisis years.

With a ₹16,000 crore debt in the books already, ABG had been struggling to service the loan. In 2014, lenders led by ICICI Bank sanctioned a corporate debt restructuring proposal for ₹11,000 crore to the company, among the biggest at that time. It involved a two-year interest moratorium. But the business seemed beyond recovery. A year later, lenders took control of the company through the strategic debt restructuring mechanism.

Was it just a business failure or was there something more to it? Where did all the money go? At least one of the lenders, Standard Chartered Bank, seemed to think that a portion of the entire sum had been siphoned off by Agarwal.

In October 2017, the Metropolitan Magistrate's Court in Bandra ordered an investigation against ABG Shipyard by Mumbai's Bandra Kurla Police Station was prompted by a complaint of criminal conspiracy filed by the Standard Chartered as the company had failed to repay ₹200 crore to the lender.[3]

'The complaint discloses cognizable offenses. This complaint is necessary to be investigated by the police,' Vishwas Mane, the metropolitan magistrate, wrote in the court order. 'Therefore, the original complaint along with documents [needs to] be sent to police inspector of BKC police station, for investigation.'

Standard Chartered Bank had filed a complaint in 2006 with the Economic Offences Wing, Mumbai Police, through its legal counsel MZM Legal. It claimed that ABG Shipyard had siphoned off about ₹794 crore to its other group companies, including Western India Shipyard, PFS Shipping India and ABG Resources. Standard Chartered had been the company's banker since 2005, extending different credit facilities. It had in fact been a part of the thirteen-bank consortium led by ICICI Bank.

Another transaction that ran into trouble was ABG's dealing with Religare Finvest Ltd. In November 2016, Religare Finvest wrote off a sum of ₹793.67 crore. Its holding company, Religare Enterprises Ltd, in a Bombay Stock Exchange (BSE) filing, reported:

> The board of directors of Religare Finvest Ltd, a material subsidiary company ... has considered and approved one-time write-off of entire amount of ₹519.92 crores in the profit and loss account pursuant to non-receipt of dues towards assignment of certain loan accounts by RFL. In addition to the above, the board of directors of RFL have further approved write-off of an entire amount of ₹273.75 crores standing overdue in other accounts related to the same transaction.[4]

In a separate statement to *VCCircle*, the company spokesperson confirmed that the write-off was associated with exposure to

ABG Shipyard. 'In the loans against shares book of Religare Finvest, the company had entered into an assignment transaction for various client accounts, wherein the underlying scrip was ABG Shipyard.'[5]

Curiously, the sum in Standard Chartered's complaint alleging siphoning-off by the promoters and the one written-off by Religare is almost the same. Religare had assigned these loans to a company called Strategic Credit Capital Pvt Ltd. Several premises in Delhi and Mumbai of this company and its sister concerns that were controlled by a man called Mohnish Mukkar were subjected to search-and-survey operations of the income tax department in January 2017.

In the *Strategic Credit Capital Pvt ... vs Ratnakar Bank Ltd &Anr* case at the Delhi high court on 29 May 2017, these companies argued that there were SPVs (special purpose vehicles) involved in 'transactions for the purposes of restructuring; that over the past ten years they have, at times material to their operations, managed, for their own debt recoveries and third party actions, a substantial number of entities, which term includes companies incorporated under the Companies Act and Trusts'.[6]

In a separate response, the companies also submitted that the funds in their accounts 'are the proceeds of a transaction with Religare Finvest Limited', which were made available by it to enable a 'large ticket restructuring'.

An alternative prayer was made for 'at least the funds of EFER L' (Exsto Foundation Enterprises and Reserves), the proceeds of the joint venture for debt restructuring with Religare Finvest, to be released. Interestingly, the lawyer representing the companies in this case was none other than a certain P. Chidambaram. But the court did not find enough grounds to provide any relief.

Everything in Agarwal's life turned rapidly. The slide after the failed bid to acquire Great Offshore was also quick. Before his fiftieth birthday, he had all but lost everything. In September 2022, following a complaint lodged by SBI in 2019 – one of the banks involved in the ICICI consortium – the CBI arrested Rishi Kamlesh Agarwal, in connection with the alleged bank frauds.

Sanjeev Gupta of Liberty House, the UK metals house and bidder for ABG, summed up the state of ABG facilities on 27 August 2018:

> ABG is a junkyard. It has been vandalized and now you will only find stray dogs there. The shipbuilding business is not something we're planning on. The yard is well-located; it's got a good shiplift. It can be used for breaking ships for scrap and that serves our green steel (recycled steel) objective.

Gupta's business model for ABG was, in the long term, to transform it into a steel plant.[7]

Soon, Gupta himself got into trouble, struggling to shore up funds for his other acquisitions, such as Amtek Auto and Adhunik Metaliks. The jinx seemed to continue. ABG, which allegedly caused India's biggest scam by defrauding twenty-eight banks of over ₹22,000 crore between 2005 and 2012, was one of the companies staring at the prospect of entering liquidation as per RBI guidelines. But with the suspension of its insolvency regulation professional, Sundaresh Bhat, on 28 September 2022, the story of ABG Shipyards has become even murkier, and a resolution remains pending.[8]

13

Essar Steel

Remember how Rishi Agarwal's rig-building venture had received a fillip due to an order from Essar Group's oil firm in 2007? Now, we turn to its own story. Essar makes up the initials of Shashi and Ravi Ruia, Agarwal's maternal uncles.

In February 2014, about an acre of dry land had been cleared off the road to Sakkanthi village near Sivaganga. A stage had been set along with a pandal, where a few dozen locals had gathered. The then union Finance Minister P. Chidambaram and his son Karti smiled from flex banners that had come up around the venue.

A backward district in southern Tamil Nadu, Sivaganga was the home constituency of the finance minister. Aegis, the BPO business of the Essar Group, was starting a delivery-experience centre. 'Aegis will give jobs to the youth of the area. First non-agri entry to youth of many families. It will bring about 500 jobs directly and another 1500 indirectly,' Chidambaram said after laying the foundation stone.[1]

Shashi Ruia, who had flown down for the event, was amazed at the number of educational institutions that had sprung up on the road from the Madurai airport. He also highlighted the five hundred jobs they would create, expressing excitement about the potential improvement in the 'quality of life' among the people living in the area. Anshuman, Shashi Ruia's son, said that the centre would open in about four to five months.

Though the Ruias spent their early years in Chennai, their choice of location seemed to be largely influenced by their eagerness to humour the minister. With over ₹1.5 lakh crore in debt across various companies, the Ruias were among the largest borrowers in the country and the minister controlled some eighteen public sector banks. Chidambaram had allegedly even said that once the centre was a success and the group liked the friendly nature of the people there, he would ask the Ruias to make a bigger investment. It made sense for a politician to take these initiatives, especially in an election year. And if the people also benefited, there was no problem. It seemed like a win-win situation for all.

Five years later, the Aegis call centre wore a sorry look. A skeleton of a building stood with a lone security guard dozing away at the entrance. That was probably the only job that was created, with no proof that it was given to a local youth. The other 499 jobs never materialized.

By 2017, lenders had begun squeezing the group as debt pressure kept piling. The group started to sell assets in response. Essar Oil was sold to the Russian major Rosneft. Aegis itself was bought by Capital Square Partners for ₹2,000 crore. But this could not prevent the group flagship, Essar Steel, from being referred to bankruptcy courts.

The largest and most significant of its operations, the 10 MTPA facility in Hazira, Gujarat, lies at the core of Essar Steel and dates back to the 1970s. Essar Steel was classified as an NPA during the April 2015 results shared by HDFC Bank and was sold to asset reconstruction companies after lenders agreed to a 40 per cent loss.[2] The lender's unwillingness to continue being part of the consortium that had offered loans to the tune of ₹500 crore to Essar was echoed in May of the same year by Bank of India, which also labelled the account as an NPA.[3] Other banks of the consortium followed suit over the next few quarters.

The company's troubles were also not new and followed a very similar template every time – when times were bad, the group bargained for a restructure, sold non-core assets and once the environment improved, they borrowed aggressively and diversified again.

A case study on the group carried out in 2001, available on the ICMR website, said, 'Moreover, many of these diversification moves failed to deliver the desired results and the group's image took a beating. The simultaneous launch of various projects during the mid-1990s pushed the group towards a liquidity crunch. As a result of these diversification efforts, Essar Steel got entangled in a complex mesh of cross holdings in other Essar companies, which created serious problems.'[4]

At that time, the Essar Group, the parent company of Essar Steel, was involved in various sectors such as power, telecom, shipping, oil and iron-and-steel. Essar Steel was the second-largest private steel manufacturer in India, trailing only after TISCO. The origins of the Essar Group goes back to 1956 when Nand Kishore Ruia (also known as NKR), the founder, started undertaking independent contract works in construction and shipping under the name Essar Construction and Carriers Ltd. After NKR's passing in 1969, his sons Shashi and Ravi Ruia took over the business.

During the seventies and eighties, the company expanded into power, steel and oil. The Essar Group continued to grow in related industries such as offshore construction, pipeline laying, contract drilling and marine transport. The liberalization of the Indian economy in the early nineties presented new opportunities for the Essar Group. This led to further diversification and solidified its status as a conglomerate of companies.

The Beginning

Essar Steel Ltd was established in 1976, with the Ruia family playing a significant role in the Indian steel industry's development. As the first private sector company permitted to set up a 2-million-metric-tonne steel plant, Essar faced challenges when acquiring long-term funds for capital-intensive projects in India by the late 1980s. The group's profits declined in the late 1990s due to unrelated diversification, ineffective project planning, delays, dumping, poor financial choices and reduced returns on investments. In 1998, the group incurred a loss of ₹4.13 billion, a considerable decline from the ₹1 billion profit earned in 1997.

The FRN debacle

In July 1999, the leading company of the Essar Group encountered a severe financial crisis, becoming the first Indian firm to default on its international debt repayment obligations. It failed to repay its $250 million of floating rate notes* (FRNs) issued to foreign investors, which had matured on 20 July 1999. This default raised concerns about the credibility

---

* A type of bond for which the interest rate changes periodically based on market rates.

of Indian companies and debts in international markets. Essar acknowledged its inability to make the repayment and pledged to present a concrete solution by the end of October 1999. Notices were sent to FRN holders, offering options for rollover or refinancing, with the company's future course depending on their responses. If immediate payment was demanded, the issue could escalate to international courts and result in asset liquidation. Refinancing was deemed challenging due to the default's damaging effect on Essar's borrowing credibility and potentially triggering loan recalls by other creditors. The default had been anticipated by industry observers who attributed the problems to poor asset-liability management practices at the company.

Is the worst behind?

By late 1999, the global steel industry saw a recovery with steel prices peaking at $450 per tonne in 2000. Analysts predicted that Essar would benefit from this upturn, improving its cash flows and enabling it to gradually repay its debts. To address liquidity challenges and enhance financial stability, Essar underwent a significant financial restructuring in 2000. As part of this process, it requested an extension from FRN holders, which was granted, along with an eight-year maturity period extension. Partly secured creditors also extended their maturity periods by five to six years to align with other creditors.[5]

Restructuring requests

In 2002, Essar Steel found itself grappling with financial strains, prompting the company to seek restructuring from banks.

Shashikant Ruia, in an effort to address the situation, proposed settling with lending institutions at the actual cost they had incurred, which was approximately 16 per cent at that time. The financial strain arose from high-interest rates that the economy struggled to sustain.

One significant factor contributing to Essar's plight, Ruia pointed out, was the overcapacity in the domestic market, particularly around 25 per cent excess capacity in the flat product segment. This affected Essar Steel's performance, even though the company was earning operating profits. The proposed restructuring aimed not only to fortify operations but also to generate sustainable cash flows, meeting obligations and benefitting stakeholders.

Over the next three years, Essar Steel, buoyed by the new bull run in the stock markets, strategically positioned itself for another phase. The company took steps to exit corporate debt restructuring by prepaying ₹2,500 crore, enabling it to secure fresh loans. This move aligned with the bullish market conditions, which triggered fervent capacity expansion across the entire steel sector to meet the growing demand from the Chinese economy.

In February 2008, the high-profile marriage of Smiti Ruia, Ravi's daughter, to Nishant Kanodia of the Matix Group marked a significant social event. The star-studded reception, attended by prominent figures like L. K. Advani, Uddhav Thackeray, Venugopal Dhoot, Narendra Modi, Kumarmangalam Birla, and Nita and Mukesh Ambani, hinted at the convergence of business and social circles.

As Essar expanded, by 2011 the company had invested close to ₹50,000 crore in various manufacturing facilities across the country. These included a 10 MTPA integrated steel manufacturing facility in Hazira, a 12 MTPA iron-ore beneficiation and pelletization facility in Paradeep, Odisha, and an 8 MTPA facility in Vizag, Andhra Pradesh. Essar also owned and operated iron-ore slurry pipelines in Odisha and Andhra Pradesh.

Yet, challenges began to mount again. The Hazira plant, which operated on gas, faced uncertainties when the central government, contrary to earlier assurances, changed its gas-supply policy in March 2011. The government reclassified the steel sector from a 'priority sector to a non-core sector' and directed KG-D6 field contractors to cut off gas supply disproportionately in case of shortages, dealing a severe blow to Essar.

This policy shift, amid the business climate post the Global Financial Crisis, resulted in a substantial ₹26,000-crore loss for Essar Steel over the next five years. Additionally, external disruptions, such as a Naxalite attack on the pipeline between Kirandul and Vizag, further impeded operations in 2010 and between 2012 and 2014.

Essar Steel's journey, marked by attempts at restructuring, market dynamics and external challenges, reflects the complex interplay of economic, policy and operational factors influencing a company's trajectory.

In 2015, CARE downgraded the company's ratings and filed a report that is no longer available in the public domain. According to it, the company was facing cashflow issues because earlier challenges had affected the steel plant's optimal functioning. Delays in getting regulatory approvals for the Odisha Slurry Pipeline and ongoing damage to the Kirandul-Vizag Slurry Pipeline impacted pellet production until FY 2014. Operations were also hindered by the lack of natural gas for the sponge iron plant and captive power plants at Hazira. The delay in stabilizing projects and the upcoming repayment of project debt caused a cashflow mismatch.

Lower natural-gas prices and merchant power tariffs were anticipated to help the steel-making operations recover. The company attempted to improve its financial situation through various initiatives, including selling identified assets, financial support from promoters, increasing working capital limits with banks, converting a part of long-term debt from rupees to dollars and refinancing the remaining rupee-denominated debt with longer maturity under the RBI's 5/25 structure. Several exposés have been published over the last couple of years on how the group used different methods to win friends and influence people.

To do this, Essar employed two methods, one introduced earlier. The second method came to light when an Essar insider allegedly leaked a CD containing details of gifts, including iPads, given to influential figures in politics, bureaucracy and the media.[6] Leaked correspondence involved emails and memos detailing meetings with government officials and alleged favours to ministers, bureaucrats and journalists. This triggered a public interest litigation seeking a court-monitored investigation into Essar's alleged nexus with politicians, bureaucrats and journalists for business gain.

In 2015, the Centre for Public Interest Litigation (CPIL), led by senior advocate Prashant Bhushan, filed the PIL. In a subsequent affidavit, the CPIL alleged that then President Pranab Mukherjee had sought a favour from Essar for the appointment of his granddaughter at the company's London office. In 2018, another whistleblower highlighted transactions more directly linked to the group's debt issues.

The whistleblower alleged that the group had tried to influence the decisions of ICICI Bank chief Chanda Kochhar by funnelling investments into a company run by her husband, Deepak Kochhar.[7] The investments were routed through a Mauritius-based company that also held investments in a Kanodia family venture.

The letter from whistleblower Arvind Gupta also disclosed, using information obtained from NuPower Renewables' Registrar of Companies (RoC) filings, that Nishant Kanodia (who is Ravi Ruia's son-in-law) invested in NuPower through Firstland Holdings in Mauritius. This company is the holding entity of the Matix Group, which is co-promoted by Kanodia.

Firstland Holdings of Mauritius, subscribed to a total of 3,243,752 shares of ₹1,000 each of NuPower Renewable Ltd during 31 December 2010 to 21 March 2012 in four different tranches, amounting to a total of ₹324.37 crore.

According to the letter widely reported by the Press Trust of India (PTI) and other news outlets, these transactions took place when Essar Group received favourable deals from ICICI Bank's overseas branches in Singapore, the UK and New York for acquiring Essar Steel, Minnesota, in the US, and Algoma Steel in Canada. In 2010, ICICI Bank, the lead banker in a consortium, lent $530 million to Essar Steel and $350 million to Essar Oil for the acquisition of the Stanlow refinery in the UK. However, all these investments by the Essar Group encountered financial difficulties, leading to liquidation and bankruptcy proceedings for investment recovery.

The whistleblower further claimed that Essar Capital Holdings, Mauritius, compensated Matix for funding NuPower Renewable Group by subscribing to the equity offering by Matix

Fertilisers and Chemicals from December 2010 to August 2011, purchasing 163,540,343 shares of ₹10 each for ₹163.53 crore.

Despite the allegations, Essar Group insisted that its dealings with ICICI dated back to 1980 were transparent, and the Kanodias asserted that their investment in NuPower was a means to participate in the renewables sector, from which they later exited. Firstland, they emphasized, had no connection to Essar.

ICICI Bank maintained that the loans to Essar's overseas arms were part of consortium lending and adhered to norms. However, this second letter, following an earlier one linking NuPower to Videocon, proved crucial, marking the turning point in Chanda Kochhar's career.

On 4 October 2018, Kochhar was eventually forced to step down as MD and CEO of the bank in disgrace.

★

In April 2021, ArcelorMittal's resolution plan was approved, which provided for an upfront payment of ₹42,000 crore and an equity infusion of ₹8,000 crore. Unsecured financial creditors were to be paid about 4 per cent of their admitted claims. The approval was challenged by various parties, including Standard Chartered Bank, several operational creditors, the suspended board of directors and even former promoters of Essar Steel, but nothing much came of it. In March 2022, market watchdog SEBI penalized erstwhile Essar Steel India Ltd for its disclosure lapses and imposed on it a ₹2 lakh fine.[8]

14

The Bhushan Twins
Bhushan Steel and Bhushan Power & Steel

As we have observed, the Essar Group had sophisticated ways of dealing with people in influential positions, yet everything eventually came out in the open. On the other hand, the Bhushan scam was more overt. In August 2014, the then vice chairman of Bhushan Steel Ltd (BSL) Neeraj Singal, was arrested for allegedly bribing the chairman of Syndicate Bank, S. K. Jain, with ₹50 lakh for extending credit facilities.[1]

The events leading up to the arrest were quite dramatic. It was the early days of the Modi government and there was little focus on bank frauds and arrest of top officials, let alone a serving chairman of a bank. The CBI, through a call intercept, came to know about cash being carried to Jain through some middlemen for concessions towards two companies, Prakash Industries and Bhushan Steel. Jain was arrested on 2 August along with the middlemen, including Pawan Bansal, the managing director of Altius Finserv Pvt Ltd, who was earlier also involved in the Era Infra Engineering case.

The CBI chief Ranjit Sinha was furious that Neeraj Singal was not picked up the same day. It would later be revealed that the CBI officials who searched Singal's residence on 1 August had instructions to pick him up that night, but Singal managed to get a reprieve by promising to present himself at the CBI office for questioning the next day. Of course, he did not turn up.

After a little cat-and-mouse chase across Delhi's posh hotels, he was picked up within a week. The arrest was a shock for the markets, and it dawned on investors that all was not well with Bhushan Steel, which at the time had over ₹35,000 crore of debt on its books. Warning bells had tolled as early as March that year. In a ratings revision report, CARE Ratings downgraded the company's long-term debt, which at the time was about ₹30,000 crore, to CARE BB from CARE A+. It also slashed the ratings of other instruments of the company, such as short-term loans (about ₹5,100 crore), debentures and preference shares, by a few notches.[2]

CARE had seen several red flags in the financial performance of the company in the preceding nine months. Profits were shrinking and cash flows were becoming errant. In turn this was beginning to affect liquidity since the company had large interest-payment commitments to the lender. Between 2012 and 2014, Bhushan's debt had doubled from around ₹19,000 to ₹30,000 crore. A lot of the funds had been tied up in the third-phase expansion plans in Dhenkanal, Odisha, which was completed in March 2013. There were cost overruns in this project, which was eventually completed for some ₹7,500 crore against an estimated ₹6,500 crore.

Despite this, if the expanded capacity of 4.4 MTPA had become online immediately, Bhushan would have breathed easy. However, that was not the case. An explosion that killed three and injured dozens of workers in November 2013 proved to be a blow Bhushan never recovered from. Though the facility was reportedly up and running by January 2014, before the benefits could kick in and reflect in numbers, things went awry.

An analysis by Deepak Shenoy of *Capitalmind* showed that the interest costs kept increasing as the revenues kept falling. Shenoy wrote about the revelations in a column on his portal:

> It's not easy to run this company – they paid over 1800 cr. in interest in the last 12 months, which is a 50% increase from the 1,200 cr. in FY13. (Some of the loans are denominated in dollars, which lets them be cheaper) In fact, in the last quarter, they earned an EBIDTA of ₹700 cr. of which ₹500 cr. was paid out as interest alone! Banks should have been worried ages ago, but they apparently aren't paid to be worried as long as there is no default. There wasn't one – and Bhushan Steel was getting even more loans (their debt increased substantially, from 19,000 cr. in 2012 to nearly 40,000 cr. in 2014).
>
> Now, as the Syndicate Bank story comes out, it's obvious that they are not creditworthy and are trying all they can to just stay afloat. With the bribe case, no bank will want to lend more to them.[3]

One of the problems was the extreme reaction from the stock market. The Bhushan Steel stock had hovered around the ₹400 mark despite all the rating downgrades and lender concerns. But the arrest of the promoter broke the investors' trust in the company. As the stock fell to ₹140, and what with valuing the entire company at ₹3,300 crore, the Singals knew it was going to be a long winter.

A few days before Neeraj was picked up by the CBI, the agency had also arrested Arun Agarwal, the chief financial officer of a company called Bhushan Power & Steel Ltd (BPSL).

Though it was it was initially thought to be a case of mistaken identity, the connections between the two entities were too close to ignore.

BPSL was controlled by Singal's estranged older brother, Sanjay Singal. Although Sanjay's company, being unlisted, did not enjoy the same mindspace in Mumbai as its listed cousin, the older brother's family shot into prominence in the commercial capital, especially in the Marwari circles after a glitzy wedding in 2010. Sanjay's daughter had married Saurabh Dhoot, the son of Videocon President Pradeep Kumar Dhoot, in February that year. The families hosted the who's who of business, Bollywood and politics at glittering ceremonies that took place in Mumbai and Delhi. The guests included Shahrukh Khan, Katrina Kaif, Mukesh Ambani, Subrata Roy Sahara, Vilasrao Deshmukh and Sushil Kumar Shinde.

Though Sanjay maintained a low profile, his name got embroiled in the controversies surrounding Robert Vadra, the influential son-in-law of the Gandhi family. In early 2013, I had written about how Vadra's companies Skylight Hospitality, Skylight Realty, Real Earth Estate, North India IT Parks and Blue Breeze Trading had sold over 190 hectares of land in Rajasthan's Bikaner district to a Faridabad-based company called Poly Medicure Ltd.[4] This company, which had diversified shareholding but not much strength in the balance sheet, was funded by BPSL in the form of unsecured loans. I learnt that BPSL had extended these interest-bearing loans in the form of inter-corporate deposits (ICDs). Another company called BS Trade, which had bought land from Vadra, was also the recipient of loans from BPSL.

People familiar with the sector claim that this perceived closeness to the previous regime also became a liability. Though some players jumped across the fence swiftly and bought peace with the new dispensation, the Bhushan twins were clearly not among them as the events that unfolded over the next four years would show.

Early days

Among the two, though BSL had problems, its asset quality was good. It produced flats – a form of steel used in producing sheets, plates, etc. – which had good demand in the local market. BPSL, however, had a fundamental problem – it relied on coal-based production.

According to a steel-sector analyst I spoke with, BPSL had many coal-based units. The Supreme Court's deallocation of coal blocks had resulted in the loss of affordable coal. They were not accustomed to making it viable if coal wasn't available at zero cost. They tried to put up non-coal-based units for which they needed another ₹7,000 crore, which no one was ready to give them.

The two Bhushan companies derived their name from the brothers' father – Brij Bhushan Singal. The senior Singal had started off in Ambala, Haryana, with his father Kishori Lal in the cement transport business. In the late 1970s, Brij Bhushan set up a facility to produce door hinges and track fasteners for the Indian Railways. It was Brij Bhushan's vision that made the regional railway contractor into one of the largest steel mills in India.

The first opportunity came in 1987 in the form of Sahibabad-based Jawahar Metal Industries. The four-year-old company had fallen into bad times and Brij Bhushan saw the potential in steel.

Jawahar was bought over and renamed Bhushan Steel and Strips. Sanjay was already helping out in the business. Neeraj, seven years younger, joined subsequently.

With the opening up of the economy in 1991, new opportunities also sprung up. By 1993, Bhushan Steel was listed in the bourses. Using the fresh capital, the company invested in Japanese machinery from Hitachi. The high-quality steel that was subsequently produced placed Bhushan Steel among the few who could cater to the rising demand for automobiles. The company was able to attract top clients in the auto sector, including Maruti Suzuki. Proximity became an added advantage. A partnership with Sumitomo of Japan further strengthened the company's operations.

However, differences began to crop up between Brij Bhushan and his older son. In 2002, this became a full-blown war. Yet, it remained contained within the family for a while, with the father and the younger son looking after the affairs of the listed flagship Bhushan Steel and Sanjay taking control of the Faridabad-based Bhushan Power & Steel, which specialized in galvanized steel and other value-added products.

According to an oral agreement in 2003, Sanjay was made the managing director of Bhushan Power & Steel Ltd (BPSL) and Neeraj the managing director of Bhushan Steel and Strips Ltd (BSSL). Brij Bhushan Singal got one-third of the paid-up capital shares in both the companies. He was also to remain the chairman of BSSL and BPSL for his lifetime, being the founder, promoter director and patriarch of the Bhushan family.

An attempt by Sanjay to remove his father and brother from BPSL culminated into a legal dispute with the angry father moving to the Company Law Board (CLB) in 2005–06. Acting on the complaint, CLB Chairman N. Balasubramanian directed Brij Bhushan Singhal and son Sanjay to not intervene in each other's business and ordered a status quo in the group companies.[5]

In his petition filed before CLB under Section 396 (suppression of facts) and 397 (mismanagement) of the Companies Act, Brij Bhushan had alleged that his son Sanjay removed him from the post of chairman and director of BPSL in the annual general meeting of the company on 17 June 2005. Brij Bhushan's lawyers argued that Sanjay had removed his father from BPSL in a fraudulent manner, violating the provisions of company law. He also removed Neeraj, his younger brother, from the post of director from BPSL, 'illegally and unlawfully' violating the family agreement, they submitted to the CLB.

They further alleged that Sanjay had seized documents of nineteen investment companies belonging to the Bhushan group. As per the family agreement of June 2003, these companies were to come under the father's control.

Brij Bhushan also asserted that BPSL and Sanjay had continued to unlawfully retain essential statutory records and documents. Moreover, they controlled the companies and wouldn't give them to the petitioners, despite many requests. Some shares, too, were transferred to new dummy companies owned by BPSL.

The dispute had also made both companies prisoners of debt as, during the intervening years, equity capital could not be raised from the market and they borrowed extensively to keep their ambitious capex plans going. Although these disputes between father, son and brother were eventually settled by agreeing to divide the $6-billion empire equally among family members and cross-holdings disentangled by 2011,[6] the multiple investment companies and their dealings landed both families in trouble. But before that, a big blow came in the form of coal-block deallocation.

The UPA government had opened up underexplored coal mines across the country for the private sector and had allocated them to different industry groups. Both the Bhushan companies had won coal blocks in Odisha and had mounted ambitious expansion plans to set up integrated steel plants there. In a draft letter of offer in 2012, Bhushan Steel proposed to raise about ₹425 crore through a rights issue. It made the following declaration about large related party transactions:[7]

> We have entered into certain transactions with related parties, including our Promoters and associates and may continue to do so in future. These transactions or any future transactions with our related parties could potentially involve conflicts of interest. For instance, in fiscal 2011, we entered into related party transaction with Bhushan Energy Limited aggregating ₹40,752.46 lacs towards purchase of goods and services and ₹2,166.57 lacs towards sale of goods and services, respectively. Similarly, we also entered into related party transactions aggregating ₹5,217.80 lacs and ₹1,853.04 lacs with Arshiya International Limited and Bhushan Aviation Limited, respectively, in fiscal 2011.

> We cannot assure you that we could not have achieved more favourable terms had such transactions been entered into with unrelated parties. There can be no assurance that such transactions, individually or in the aggregate, will not have an adverse effect on our business, prospects, financial condition and results of operations, including because of potential conflicts of interest or otherwise. In addition, our business and growth prospects may decline if we cannot

benefit from our relationships with our Promoters and associates in the future.

Related party transactions are usually red flags, as these could be abusive for minority shareholders considering promoters tend to enrich themselves at the expense of the other shareholders.

A large uncertainty was encountered when a draft report by the CAG in March 2012 accused the government of inefficient allocation of coal blocks between 2004 and 2009, leading to windfall gains of ₹10.7 lakh crore to the allottees.[8] In September 2012, an inter-ministerial group recommended cancellation of the allocation of New Patrapara block given to Bhushan Steel in 2006 on the grounds that it had not commenced production from it.[9]

Bhushan Steel petitioned the Delhi high court, challenging the move by saying that its end-use project was almost ready and a confirmation to this effect had been offered by the steel ministry. Even as the judicial process dragged on, in September 2014, a month after Neeraj was arrested by the CBI in the Syndicate Bank bribery case,[10] the Supreme Court cancelled all the 194 coal-block allocations, plunging numerous allottees and their projects into crisis. Later, more issues hit the Singal family during 2014 and 2016.

In 2014, during a routine assessment, an assessing officer of the income tax department observed that the BSL Group was suppressing taxable profits on a large scale. The unaccounted income thus generated was being introduced into the books of family members and promoters of the BSL Group. The tax-exempt, bogus long-term capital gains of hundreds of crores by pre-arranged trading in shares of some nondescript listed companies was evidenced. Such fraudulent capital gains were an accommodation entry obtained with the help of some entry operator.

In a coordinated search-and-seizure operation conducted on 13 June 2014, the income tax department gathered several incriminating documents from the premises of the BSL Group and Raj Kumar Kedia, a known accommodation entry operator.[11] Such an entry represents a financial transaction between two parties, wherein one party records the transaction in its books to accommodate another. These transactions occur mostly in lieu of cash of equal amount and commission charged over and above at a certain fixed percentage for providing the entry.

Apart from statements from the staff of Bhushan Group, the income tax department also seized a pen drive containing details of the long-term capital gains (LTCG) book of Singal family members – Brij Bhushan, Neeraj Singal and their respective spouses Uma and Ritu. These pertained to several penny stock* companies, such as Rander Corporation, Ankuran Commercial and so on.

The assessing officer submitted that of the eighteen companies that SEBI was probing for misallotment of shares to launder money and avoid taxes, the Singal family members and entities had conducted transactions with nine – Radford Global, Mishka Finance and Trading, Parag Shilpa Investments, Dhenu Buildcon Infra, First Financial Services, Pine Animation, Rander Corporation, Action Financial and Prraneta Industries.[12]

Separately, a SEBI investigation found that First Financial Services Ltd (FFSL), a Kolkata-based listed firm, had made

---

* Penny stocks are shares of small publicly traded companies that are listed on stock exchanges for less than ten cents. They are not widely traded securities, and their potential gains are usually determined by sharp spikes in market volatility. Penny stocks can be risky to invest in due to their lack of liquidity.

preferential allotments of shares to several entities in the Singal family and investment companies connected to them. In what was came to be known as the LTCG scam, SEBI took up investigation after receiving information from the income tax department, showing that the share prices had been manipulated artificially to generate long-term capital gains for the preferential allottees.

Show Cause Notices (SCNs) were issued to the Singals and their respective spouses, and companies such as Marsh Steel Trading and Vision Steel. In an interim order, some of these entities were barred from participating in markets until further orders.

In the final order in April 2018,[13] SEBI said that there was not enough evidence to proceed against these entities in the first financial matter. As per the Income Tax Appellate Tribunal, Brij Bhushan Singal, Neeraj Singal and Uma Singal were given preference in allotment. On 19 September 2011, FFSL transferred ₹1 crore and ₹50 lakh to Marsh Steel Trading Ltd and Vision Steel Ltd respectively. Aarti Singal, a relative of the Singal group, was a director in both companies. As per the show cause notice, she was also a promoter in Bhushan Steel Ltd until 30 September 2011. The transfer of ₹1.50 crore from the allotment proceeds to Marsh Steel Trading Ltd and Vision Steel Ltd indirectly benefitted the Singal group of allottees.

Further, the two companies stated that the ₹100 lakh received from FFSL on 16 September 2011 and 14 December 2011 were capital contributions. They allotted 40,000 equity shares to FFSL on 31 December 2011 and filed the necessary documents with the Registrar of Companies. Similarly, Vision Steel Ltd received ₹50 lakh from FFSL on 16 September 2011 which was also a capital contribution. They allotted 20,000 equity shares to FFSL on 13 December 2011 and made the required filings. It was claimed that the funds received were invested in BPSL.

Brij Bhushan, Neeraj and Uma Singal also brought to light the decade-long family dispute, settled in November 2011, because of which the funds received from FFSL were not transferred to the BPSL Group. Since the settlement terms were fully implemented only by February 2012, the three clarified that they had no role in the affairs of Marsh Steel Trading and Vision Steel, where Aarti Singal (wife of Sanjay Singal) served as Director. In the case of the transaction between Neeraj Singal and Pine Animation Ltd, ₹80 lakh were paid for preference shares on 12 December 2012, and ₹40 lakh on 15 March 2013. Furthermore, the shares of FFSL were purchased based on information and feedback received from professionals and individuals with knowledge of the securities market. Based on their explanations and all circumstantial evidence, it was determined that no further action should be taken against Brij Bhushan Singal, Uma Singal, Neeraj Singal, Marsh Steel and Vision Steel Ltd.

However, some analysts were not convinced by the order and felt that the group was let go easily. These concerns were not without reason, given the detailed accounts put out by the income tax department. But SFIO took over from where SEBI and the income tax department left off. Neeraj Singal was arrested for a second time four years later in August 2018.

As per the release in the Press Information Bureau (PIB), Neeraj Singhal, former Promoter and Managing Director of Bhushan Steel Ltd, was arrested by the SFIO after being found 'guilty of indulging in serious corporate fraud punishable under Section 447 of the Companies Act, 2013'.[14] The arrest was made during the investigation into the company's affairs, prompted by complaints received from various sources. It was found that the erstwhile promoters engaged in complex fraudulent activities to divert and siphon off funds, causing significant losses to banks and investors. Throughout the investigation, the former promoters failed to cooperate and concealed crucial information and 'material facts'.

Separately, the SFIO also grilled the elder brother Sanjay Singal.

Brushes with law and investigators were not new for the Singals. In 2016, the CBI court awarded a three-year prison sentence to Brij Bhushan Singal and six former officials of the UT Electricity Department in Chandigarh and Bhakra Beas Management Board (BBMB).[15] A fine of ₹15,000 each was ordered in the twenty-three-year-old power-theft case that caused a loss of ₹3.06 crore to the union territory. Six others were sentenced to imprisonment by the court. They included the UT Electricity Department employees – XEN V. K. Mahendru, Commercial Engineer Deepak Chopra, Junior Engineer Tarsem Lal Aggarwal and Assistant Executive Engineer Harjinder Singh Brar. Two BBMB officials also made the list – Junior Engineer Mangat Pal and Substation Engineer Jagir Singh.

The case dated back to 1993, the year Bhushan Steel made its IPO. The CBI had registered a case against six officers and the managing director of Bhushan Industries on 14 December 1993. The charges were filed under the Indian Electricity Act, 1910, as well as the Prevention of Corruption Act. However, it took another eight years for the CBI to submit the charge sheet in February 2001. By February 2006, the court formally framed charges related to the case, which pertained to power theft from

April 1985 to July 1988. As the timeline clearly shows, cases in India typically drag on for generations. Even those filed by the CBI. The only difference now is that the Singals no longer own their company.

In 2019, the NCLT approved the Sajjan Jindal-controlled JSW Steel's resolution plan for BPSL and Tata Steel's resolution plan for BSL. In 2021, Tata Steel turned around Bhushan Steel's bankrupt fate by strengthening its financial performance and doubling its share price in a single month. In more recent news, Neeraj Singal was once again put behind bars by the ED in June 2023, following a search operation at his residence in connection to a bank fraud case of ₹56,000 crore.[16] The businessman had allegedly formed an array of shell companies.

15

Monnet Ispat & Energy

The promoter of Monnet Ispat & Energy Ltd, Sandeep Jajodia, shared an equal enthusiasm for big-ticket acquisitions as his brother-in-law Sajjan Jindal. A few years ago, on Monnet's website, Jajodia wrote the following ode to himself:

> The self-motivated, young and dynamic visionary, Mr Sandeep Jajodia is a man of strong judgement and deep insight, who has concertedly led Monnet Group's emergence into a formidable corporate entity shining bright on the Indian economic horizon. With his committed focus and dedicated passion, Mr Jajodia has steered the Group's evolution as the second largest coal-based sponge iron producer and also the first private sector company to operate the single largest underground coal mine in India.[1]

Up to a point, these praises did not seem misplaced. At one point, Jajodia had built a $2 billion empire by setting up a 1.5 MTPA integrated steel-manufacturing facility in Raigarh, Chattisgarh, and had closed several challenging approvals and power purchase agreements for a 1050 MW thermal power plant in Angul, Odisha. But like the great king Ashoka, though his expeditions into Odisha were successful, they were in some sense pyrrhic.

In 2009, Monnet was locked in a three-way fight for the acquisition of Orissa Sponge Iron and Steel company. In an uncanny resemblance to the doomed acquisition of Great Offshore, all the suitors and the target ended up in dire straits and eventually became bankrupt. The other suitors of Orissa Sponge in that summer of 2009 were the Bhushan twins BSL and BPSL. Unitech's Sanjay Chandra had also picked up a stake even as promoters P. K. Mohanty and family were accused of illegally shoring up their stake.[2]

Multiple suitors and murky deals notwithstanding, Orissa Sponge seemed attractive because it was sitting on iron-ore reserves of around 120 million metric tonnes and coal reserves of a similar level. It was also running sponge iron and steel billet plants in Palaspanga, Odisha, with an installed capacity of 250,000 tonnes.

Though Neeraj Singal, who controlled Bhushan Steel, had first entered the fray by buying some 9 per cent shares from Unitech and warrants which could take their stake to 21 per cent by June 2009 on conversion, it was his brother Sanjay who first threw a spanner in the works. In early February 2009, Sanjay made an open offer, forcing Neeraj to make a competitive bid.

Jajodia joined the bid quite late but surprised the brothers by acquiring 27 per cent shares and some warrants from the Mohantys. The open price had already risen to ₹320 per share. Jajodia and Monnet were playing the proverbial white knight, similar to the role played by Bharati Shipyard in the Great Offshore case. While Monnet eventually managed to raise its stake to 35 per cent, control eluded the company as Bhushan dragged it to court. Some investor groups also got involved, alleging siphoning of funds by the Mohantys. After three years of going through different forums, the petition by Bhushan Energy, the Bhushan Steel subsidiary, failed to convince the Supreme Court. Things were back to square one.

A fresh round of open offers by Bhushan Steel began at ₹360. However, since about 60 per cent shares were locked in the hands of the promoters and Monnet, the offers did not yield success. Elsewhere, other steps Monnet had taken to secure coal linkages were causing them trouble.

In 2011, Jajodia had led an ambitious acquisition by Monnet of a coal mine in Sumatra, Indonesia. In an interview with the *Economic Times* in March 2011, he had said that the company was targeting 3,000 MW of power generation capacity by 2017, riding on coal assets in Indonesia and India.[3] He mentioned that the Indonesian coal mine was set to begin production from June 2013. The plan was to trade excess coal after consumption into 1,200–1,300 MW power plants. Due to its location in Sumatra, the logistical costs for transporting the coal to India would have minimized. It was expected that the reserves, then established at 65 million metric tonnes, would substantially increase upon complete exploration.

Jajodia added that Monnet was looking for coastal sites in Andhra Pradesh and Gujarat to set up projects that could be fuelled by their Indonesian coal mine. At the time, he was implementing a 1,050-MW thermal power plant at Angul in Odisha at an investment of ₹9,000 crore. The project would be one of the most low-cost generating stations in the world. Funds and contracts were in place and another 660-MW expansion project, expected to be commissioned by December 2014, was being planned at the same site. Jajodia was confident that as far as funds were concerned, they would not face any problem as banks were keen to lend, given the strong credentials of the company and the project.

But soon, cracks began to appear in these well-laid plans. Following the draft report by the CAG that slammed the processes followed by the government in coal allocation because of which, per the report, the allottees were enjoying windfall gains of ₹10.7 lakh crore (which was later revised to ₹1.86 lakh crore in the final report), the CBI registered two preliminary enquiries between June and September 2012.[4] The first one, registered in June, was to look into the allocation of coal blocks from 2006 to 2009. The Rajgamar Dipside block in the Korba district of Chattisgarh allotted to Monnet fell into this category. The other PE registered three months later went into the allocations between 1993 and 2005. Monnet's other coal block in Gare Palma, about 100 kilometres away, had been awarded to Monnet in 1996 for captive use in the proposed expansion of 0.5 MTPA in its sponge iron plant in Raipur, the capital city of Chattisgarh, some 300 kilometres away. The company started mining the block eight years later in 2004. By this time, Monnet had set up another plant in Raigarh, about 50 kilometres from the Gare Palma block. It was alleged that Monnet was illegally utilizing the coal allotted for the Raipur plant in Raigarh and using more coal in the latter location than the former.

Further, there were accusations of other end-use irregularities, including the misuse of coal for the captive power plant though the allocation was for sponge iron only. A second block at Rajgamar, which Monnet had proposed for its Raigarh plant, faced allegations of allocation based on misrepresentation. It was claimed that there was no coal linkage to this plant and, in reality, the second block was using coal from the first one.

Even as the CBI took its time to complete these inquiries, the reports of its investigations and proceedings initiated in the Supreme Court created an overhang for the company. This in turn affected the bankers' confidence in Jajodia. As funding sources dried up, the new ventures began to face difficulties. By the time the SC cancelled the allocation of some 214 coal blocks in 2014, the crisis had reached its doorstep.[5] Monnet, which had five blocks in all, was among the worst affected.

A report in the *Telegraph* said that the proposed 1,050-MW merchant power plant in Angul was one of the first to be hit by the decision:

> Monnet was looking to source coal from the Mandakini block in Odisha. Jindal Photo and Tata Power have also been allocated the block for captive use.[6]

Amitabh Mudgal, the president of the marketing and corporate affairs for Monnet Ispat & Energy, was quoted as saying, 'This plant is built based on the coal block and it is too late for such a decision to be coming.' He was referring to the Angul plant, which was supposed to significantly add to the company's revenue through major power purchase agreements. The subsidiary Monnet Power Company Ltd started work on the plant in 2009. However, delays in obtaining environment clearance and credit disbursement pushed back the commissioning of the project. Mudgal expressed the company's optimism about a favourable outcome in the allocation of the coal block, considering the substantial investment of approximately ₹5,000 crore made in the plant. The cancellation began to impact the finances and reflect in the accounts of the company, leading to questions from the auditors. They pointed out that the company had invested directly or through joint ventures an aggregate amount of ₹109.04 crore in the five coal blocks that had been cancelled pursuant to the court order. 'No adjustment has been made against impairment of assets since the final compensation amount is not yet ascertained/under litigation,' the auditor said.[7] The management in turn attributed the impact on the financial wealth of the company to the loss of advantage of concessional coal from the block. The company was now exposed to coal's market rates.

Meanwhile, in Indonesia, the company's wholly owned subsidiary Monnet Global's acquisition of the local company PT Sarwa Sembada Karya Bumi's mine in Sumatra had run into political trouble. Changes in the mining policy created new challenges in areas with regards to taxation and human resources. The Southeast Asian nation had brought up domestic value addition, some increase in royalty and cess and domestic employment.

Facing troubles everywhere, Monnet began to accumulate losses, resulting in erosion of net worth. It incurred net cash losses in FY 2016 and FY 2017.[8] The current liabilities of the company exceeded its current assets in the balance sheet date in 2017. Up until March 2017, the company had a total debt of about ₹8,900 crore, including interest and all the penalties paid for the coal mines.

As per the annual report in 2017, the accounts received a qualification from the auditors. According to their qualified opinion, the borrowings in one subsidiary, Monnet Power Company Ltd, were classified as non-performing by most lenders. The company had not provided interest and other dues on these borrowings owing to uncertainty, resulting in a potential increase in losses and liability. Had the interest been accounted for, the losses for the current and previous year would have been higher, with a corresponding decrease in equity. The management's response to this was that the subsidiary had a stalled project, and lenders were planning to auction the power plant. Cash flow issues had also affected debt serviceability. The bidding process, which was expected to conclude in the first half of the current financial year, was pending agreement on terms and conditions. Interest payments were not being made, and the management would account for all of this once the project was revived and the lenders determined the debt and interest treatment.

The auditors pointed out that the financial statements of one joint venture, Mandakini Coal Company Ltd, had not been received for the year ending 31 March 2017.

The management said that the company was pursuing the matter with both the entities for the FY 2017 balance sheets but both firms were unable to provide them.

As key financial indicators had started turning red, the lenders implemented SDR, whereby they took 51 per cent stake through part conversion of the existing debt. According to the terms of the scheme, the lenders decided to identify a new investor to take over management control of the company. Two rounds of bidding followed. In the first, six parties expressed interest, but Monnet received only one official bid from Synergy Capital, a London-based company.

The bankers re-invited an expression of interest (EoI) after nearly nine months. Four companies submitted them, but finally, it was the family that had to come to the rescue. JSW Steel, run by Sajjan Jindal, whose sister Seema was married to Jajodia, had made the single largest bid in the second round held in February 2017. But the lenders seemed to have developed cold feet again.

As the fate of that deal remained in limbo, the 2017 annual report of Monnet Ispat & Energy Ltd said, 'Other steps are also, being taken to augment the financial resources to ramp up the operations.'[9] However, none of these steps saw the light of day. By this time, Monnet was already on the verge of being referred to the National Company Law Tribunal under the IBC. In 2017, the CBI had just finished its preliminary enquiry and filed an FIR over irregularities in allocation of the Rajgamar and Gare Palma mines to Monnet.

A half-hearted effort was put up by a Blackstone-led consortium. But eventually, it was blood that proved thicker than steel, as a resolution plan offered by AION Investments and JSW Steel amounting to ₹2,875 crore was approved by the NCLT in 2018.

16

Electrosteel Steels

Many players in the steel industry have landed in trouble because of expanding capacities or diversifying into other sectors such as power. But this is the story of a ductile iron pipes company, also famous for supplying covers for manholes in New York, which it did by trying to venture into steel.

Electrosteel's origins can be traced back to the business empire established by the Dalmia brothers – Ramkrishna and Jaidayal – in the pre-independence era. The Dalmia Bharat Group (DGB) owned several cement plants and other industries set up across British India. Post Independence, the brothers split and Jaidayal set up Dalmia Iron and Steel in 1955. The company was soon listed on the Calcutta Stock Exchange.

Ghanshyam Kejriwal, who was married to Uma Devi, Jaidayal Dalmia's daughter, joined the company in the 1960s. At the time, the Dalmias were facing the wrath of the Nehru government, which did not have a great opinion of Ramkrishna, the then chairman of *Times of India*. He had once been described by Nehru as 'an ugly man with an ugly face and an ugly mind and an ugly heart'. The Dalmia Group encountered issues with tax authorities, and Ramkrishna Dalmia was jailed in 1962 for tax evasion, perjury and criminal misappropriation of funds. This brush with politicians and law would be a recurring feature. More on that later.

A few years on, the iron and steel plant was incurring heavy losses. At one point, Jaidayal Dalmia decided to sell it, but as a last effort, he popped the question, 'Ghanshyam, can you run it?'

For a moment, the man from Kanpur was perplexed. But egged on by his uncle and Jaidayal's friend M. L. Goenka, Ghanshyam picked up the gauntlet. He had only one condition – that Dalmia would not enter the plant without him. The son-in-law was apprehensive that if the elderly man was around, he would not be able to get the employees on his side. Once the condition was accepted, there was no looking back.

Old timers now reminisce about how Ghanshyam would reach the plant as early as six in the morning. He would give engineers on the shop floor a free hand. 'I felt like a racehorse. If I run, I will win. That is the kind of confidence that it gave me,' he would say.

Towards the end of the 1970s, he brought over his sons Umang and Mayank into the business. Second-generation businessmen, the brothers worked under the shadow of their father through much of the 1970s and 1980s. From 1972 to 1975, Umang oversaw the sale of Electrosteel Castings Ltd (ECL) products in his role as the executive director of the company's then sole selling agents, Electrocast Sales India Ltd. He was appointed as an executive director of ECL in 1975 and subsequently promoted to Deputy Managing Director in 1979. In 1981, he was promoted to Managing Director of ECL, a role in which he continues to date. His brother Mayank is the joint managing director.

The venture into steel

In 1994, Electrosteel decided to expand into the manufacturing of ductile iron pipes. The project, built almost completely in-house with homegrown engineers, had become a big success and the first mover advantage gave the company near monopoly.

Ductile pipes are omnipresent nowadays in most urban water management systems, as they are used in every stage of the process, from lifting of water from source and distribution to sewage disposal. Apart from a dominant presence in the local market, Electrosteel had also built a significant export business, taking on global giants such as Saint-Gobain.

About a dozen years after this successful venture, Umang Kejriwal, ably supported by his younger brother and some trusted lieutenants, sought a new challenge. The construction activity in China in the lead-up to the Beijing Olympics, among other things, had driven a tremendous bull run in steel. India's stock markets saw an unprecedented rise in share prices, which spilled over to real estate and construction sectors. This in turn triggered local demand for steel, though nowhere near China's.

During the period 2001 to 2007, the consumption of finished steel worldwide increased from 777 tonnes to 1,209 million metric tonnes, registering a CAGR of 7.6 per cent. Though developed economies such as the US and Japan saw demand tapering, growth in crude steel production was mainly driven by emerging countries like China and India, which registered a CAGR of 18.7 and 10.6 per cent from 2001 to 2008.

Then Electrosteel had the audacious idea of taking a giant leap. A slightly built, bearded man often seen in whites, Umang Kejriwal might like to forget this entire episode as a bad dream today. In his own words, 'As far as we were concerned, this was the only way to move forward and that's what we did.'

Twelve years back, they had the vision and the will. But putting up a large steel plant is like conducting a giant orchestra – a million small things have to fall in place along with some big things. Among the big things are coal and raw material linkages.

The Kejriwals managed the allocation of Parbatpur coal mines, near Bokaro in Jharkhand, famous for one of the four integrated public sector steel plants built in the 1960s with Soviet help. The coal block allocation came through during the first UPA regime in 2005, and scouts were assigned to find suitable land for the plant in closeby areas. A special purpose vehicle called Electrosteel Integrated was incorporated in 2006. Separately, as part of the memorandum of understanding with the Jharkhand government in 2004 to set up the steel plant, ECL requested allocation of land for mining iron ore.

Somewhere in mid-2007, when the markets were still going strong, Kejriwal announced the group's plans to put up an integrated steel plant. The initial plan was a plant of 1.3 million metric tonnes per annum capacity and Umang Kejriwal himself was quoted estimating the outlay at around ₹4,900 crore. Electrosteel Castings, as the promoter, would infuse around ₹500 crore, while the rest would be funded by a consortium of banks.

Soon renamed Electrosteel Steels, the entity launched its IPO. The plant's biggest advantage was that it was promoted by Electrosteel Castings, which owned the Parbatpur coal mine with 231 million metric tonnes of reserves, an iron ore mine and a non-coking coal mine in Jharkhand. The new plant was to source iron ore and coking coal from Electrosteel Castings for a period of twenty years.

The group obtained some coal and iron ore blocks in Jharia Coalfields near Bokaro, an iron ore mine in Kodolibad near Barajamda and a mine block for non-coking coal in North Dhadu. According to the company leaflets from the time, it was in discussion with the Odisha government for acquiring more coal mines in the state.

The plant's location also had some advantages. It was near the village Siyaljori in the Bokaro district, around 22 kilometres from Bokaro Steel City, giving it access to all modern amenities and offering a significant competitive edge.

This belt had a low-cost manpower pool as well as key raw materials, such as dolomite, quartzite, ferro alloys and additives, thereby reducing transportation and procurement costs. Electrosteel made plans to build a private railway siding located at the plant, which would further reduce the logistical costs. The plant was also well connected with railways and highways. The state highway was about 18 kilometres away and the nearest railway station was in Talgheria at a distance of about 6 kilometres. The company said at the time:

> The unit's power requirements, other than our captive power plant, will be fulfilled by Damodar Valley Corporation (DVC) from their substation near Dhanbad, which is located at a distance of about 52 km from the plant. The plant's water requirement is sourced through a dedicated pipeline from the Damodar River located about 8 km from our plant.[1]

In another first, the group commissioned Chinese steelmaker Laiwu Steel for setting up the plant, going against the tradition of collaborating with Russians and Germans. The experience would be similar but a lot lighter on the purse – Electrosteel was not averse to applying the Indian consumer's street logic. Laiwu had built an annual capacity of 15 million metric tonnes and was known for quickly ramping up production to peak capacity. This was the first time that a manufacturing process from China was being used in India. The Chinese were also to train the Electrosteel staff in the best manufacturing practices followed in China. Chinese consulting and construction firms were hired to execute design and engineering. Even the construction, construction management and training contracts were outsourced to them. But first-time efforts like this one often run into unexpected difficulties. Over 1,500 Chinese workers had to be brought on site.

In its draft Red Herring Prospectus (dRHP), Electrosteel described the visa-related issues it faced:

> In light of the fact that the equipments are being procured by us from China, the Chinese contractors are appointed so that there are no problems in integration of the equipments used in the Project. We require approximately 1,500 Chinese personnel, all of whom were working at site on August 31, 2010.[2]

The dHRP further stated that all the Chinese contractors employed at the project site possessed valid work permits and their visas were regularly renewed. However, the project's progress had experienced a slowdown since the Chinese contractors left, following visa guidelines set by the central government. Although some employees had been approved to return to the project, the fact that future approvals might face uncertainty or delays, potentially impacting the project's implementation, development and commercial production.

Another dampener in the run-up to the IPO was an insider trading case in which both Umang and Mayank along with Electrosteel Castings were fined. In December 2009, SEBI imposed fines totalling ₹1.6 lakh for not conforming to the insider trading regulations related to model code of conduct:

> With regard to Mr Mayank Kejriwal and Mr Umang Kejriwal, the Investigating Authority, in the investigation report had observed that on March 04, 2002, 14 cross deals were executed by Dalmia Securities Private Limited on behalf of Mr Mayank Kejriwal and Mr Umang Kejriwal but had not made the necessary disclosures to ECL in terms of Regulation 13 (4) of the Insider Trading Regulations in respect of acquisition of shares made on March 04, 2002, thereby violating Regulation 13 (4) of the Insider Trading Regulations.[3]

ECL, Umang Kejriwal and Mayank Kejriwal paid the penalty imposed by SEBI, but challenged the order in the Securities Appellate Tribunal (SAT). In February 2010, SAT threw out the appeal without even considering any reduction in sentence.

Despite these hiccups, the fact that Electrosteel had raw material supply in place attracted blue-chip investors such as Franklin Templeton to take a bunch of shares in pre-IPO placement. The company also performed well in its IPO, listing at a 12 per cent premium on the BSE in October 2010. But things would change dramatically over the next couple of years as the CAG report and subsequent cancellation of coal blocks triggered setbacks.

By 2012–13, when the project was commissioned, global steel prices had crashed amid slowing Chinese demand. The Indian scenario also began to look downbeat as the construction industry, which would pick up products such as TMT bars, took a hit. Before long, the company approached the lenders with a CDR proposal, unable to meet the interest costs of over ₹7,000 crore. Lenders were supportive of the proposal because the problems seemed cyclical in nature and things would improve once steel demand increased, resulting in higher prices.

Under the CDR package, the banks reworked Electrosteel's loan terms by extending the repayment period, slashing interest rates and sometimes offering 'interest free periods' of a couple of years to tide over the cyclicality. However, perhaps even the banks were not prepared for the death blow dealt by the Supreme Court.

As Electrosteel's Parbatpur mines had to be handed over back to Coal India and the company was in no position to afford expensive raw material from the market, the plant had to be shut down, leading to labour unrest. The company filed for a refund of ₹1,300 crore that was sunk in the development of the mines. But of course government dues take forever to arrive.

In January 2014 at an election rally, Gujarat chief minister and the BJP's prime ministerial candidate Narendra Modi launched a broadside on UPA-II's controversial environment minister Jayanthi Natarajan:

> Environment *ministry mein ek toofan macha hua tha. Saari file rok di jaati thin. Humne toh income tax suna tha, sales tax suna tha, excise ka naam ka tax suna tha. Pehli baar humare kaan mein aaya, Dilli mein ek Jayanthi Tax chalta hai. Jab tak yeh Jayanthi tax poora nahi hota, Parayavaran mein file idhar udhar nahi hoti, aisa log kehte hain.*[4] [There was a storm over at the environment ministry and all files were blocked. No file was moving without money. We had heard of income, sales and excise taxes but for

the first time, we heard about a Jayanthi tax in Delhi without which nothing was moving. Till the time that was not paid, files could not be moved in the environment ministry.]

Electrosteel Steels had said in its prospectus from 2013–14 that the construction and operation of their project had encountered opposition from various parties, including local communities and special interest groups. The critics had expressed concerns about the potential negative impacts on the communities and the environment in the project's location.[5] There was no guarantee that objections or disputes would not arise around the project, possibly leading to litigation and significant expenses for resettlement, which would adversely affect the company's financial standing and operational outcomes.

Between Modi's rhetoric and this innocuous disclaimer lay another major issue that continued to haunt Kejriwal and Electrosteel. Jharkhand, a tribal-dominated state, had been sensitive to land issues. The Kejriwals had, in quick succession, taken up over 1,800 acres. Of this, about 200 acres were sold to the steel plant. 'We have acquired approximately 210.82 acres of land at our plant site from our promoter out of total 1,804.70 acres, for a total consideration of ₹44.05 million. While we believe that the past arrangement has been conducted on an arm's length basis, we cannot assure you that we could not have achieved more favourable terms had such arrangement been entered into with unrelated parties,' the company had said.[6]

In early 2009, the state forest department had filed several cases against the company and promoters for allegedly encroaching forest land. Elsewhere, the land allocation for iron ore mines cleared by Natarajan also ran into trouble. Soon after Modi stormed into power in 2014, the CBI initiated a preliminary enquiry into cases cleared by the former environment minister.

Electrosteel's proposal for iron ore mines had been doing rounds in the environment ministry since 2009. It was initially rejected by the Forest Advisory Committee (FAC) because the proposed region fell in the core area of Singhbhum Elephant Reserve, which was critical to forest conservation. Jairam Ramesh, then the junior minister for environment, had observed that not only should Electrosteel proposal be rejected but even the four existing mines in the area should be shut down. In 2010, the company made a representation to the prime minister, yet the FAC continued to reject its moves.

In 2011, once Natarajan took over, the chief minister of Jharkhand wrote to her again, asking her to reconsider the proposal considering the benefits that the steel plant would bring to the underdeveloped region. After this, Umang Kejriwal had a meeting with Natarajan. Some back-and-forth between the state government and the environment ministry ensued. The ministry sought an update on the existing mines in the region. On receipt of this report in February 2012, Natarajan cleared the proposal for diversion of 55.79 hectares of forest land for mining purposes. She did not refer the matter to FAC again.

The CBI eventually filed an FIR, naming Natarajan, Umang Kejriwal and Electrosteel Castings in the alleged criminal conspiracy. The premises of Electrosteel were subsequently searched. By this time, the steel plant was incurring losses continuously and its current liabilities exceeded the worth of its assets. Its net worth had eroded by more than 50 per cent. Even the relaxed terms under the CDR package were too much for Electrosteel to comply with.

Electrosteel earned the dubious distinction of being the first company for which the lenders invoked SDR, and where the debt was converted into equity and lenders became the owners of the company. Though attempts were made to find a buyer, ultimately nothing worked out. From there, the company landed at the door of the NCLT. It was among the first of the dirty dozen to be sold off. Vedanta, which had lost out to Electrosteel in the race to put up the plant, was able to buy it at half the price of what it cost the Kejriwals and banks. For just ₹1,800 crore, it now controlled 90 per cent of Electrosteel Steels' equity, while the 90 per cent stake the banks originally owned had now reduced to a paltry 9 per cent. It would take a further ₹3,550 crore as debt to revive the company, bringing the total amount of the resolution plan to approximately ₹5,320 crore.[7] The dream lives on, but for the Kejriwals it was a nightmare they would rather forget.

PART III

THE AFTERMATH

17

Conquerors, Survivors and Hindustan Leavers

By now, it is sufficiently clear that even among the select group of twelve large companies put through the corporate insolvency resolution process, there were different shades of grey. In fact, in nine of these companies, resolution professionals have filed reports under Section 66 of the Insolvency Code, which deals with corporate frauds. It reads:

> If during the corporate insolvency resolution process or a liquidation process, it is found that any business of the corporate debtor has been carried on with intent to defraud creditors of the corporate debtor or for any fraudulent purpose, the Adjudicating Authority may on the application of the resolution professional pass an order that any persons who were knowingly parties to the carrying on of the business in such manner shall be liable to make such contributions to the assets of the corporate debtor as it may deem fit.

The RBI had set up a fraud-monitoring cell to coordinate early reporting of fraud cases to the investigating agencies. However, as we have seen, there can be significant lag between banks identifying frauds or wilful defaults and agencies getting on the chase. Sometimes, banks resort to reporting fraud as the last option because they fear the entry of sleuths to mean having to shelve any hopes of immediate recovery, as judicial proceedings can take forever in India, even if the agencies wrap up a case quickly. Often, high-value debtors move to foreign locations, thumbing their noses at the entire system. This was evident in the case of Vijay Mallya, but there are more like him – Nirav Modi, who ran the eponymous diamond jewellery house, Mehul Choksi of Gitanjali Gems, Nitin Sandesara of Sterling and Jatin Mehta of Winsome.

The Hindustan Leavers

1. *Nirav Modi and Mehul Choksi*

In February 2018, PPNB told the stock exchanges that it had unearthed certain fraudulent transactions in Mumbai. Analysts were wondering and double-checking the figures because the number was too large to fathom. Could it really be $1,771 million (over ₹11,000 crore) or was it a decimal placement error?

Soon, the sensational scam brewing at the Brady House branch and the names of the main perpetrators – the nephew–uncle duo of Nirav Modi and Mehul Choksi – were revealed. Modi ran a diamond business and was planning to take his company Firestar Diamonds to an IPO and raise funds, while his uncle already managed a listed company called Gitanjali Gems. Though they rubbed shoulders with the bold and beautiful in society circles, there was a whiff of incredulity surrounding them, particularly Choksi.

Avneesh Nepalia was a senior executive of the bank in Delhi, looking after the communications department, which interacts with journalists and the media. A little over a month before the scam broke out, in January 2018, he was posted to the zonal office in Mumbai as the deputy general manager. The task of reporting the scam to the CBI fell to him.

Describing the events in the complaint, Nepalia wrote that on 16 January 2018, a group of partnership firms belonging to Modi and Choksi had approached the bank's mid-corporate branch at Brady House. They presented a set of import documents and requested the branch to provide buyers' credit for making payments to overseas suppliers. Since there was no sanctioned credit limit for these companies, the bank officials asked them to furnish at least 100 per cent cash margins for issuing Letters of Undertakings (LoUs).

There is a widely accepted provision of guarantees, known as an LoU, under which a bank can allow its customer to raise money from another Indian bank's foreign branch in the form of a short-term credit. The LoU serves the purpose of a bank guarantee for the customer who has to make payment to its offshore suppliers in the foreign currency.

The firms had said they regularly availed this facility in the past. Surprisingly, when the bank checked the records, they found the firms had indeed availed these facilities earlier. Gokulnath Shetty, a junior official of the bank, who had recently retired after spending over seven years at the branch, and Manoj Kharat became the fall guys.

Nepalia's complaint stated that the LoUs were fraudulently issued by these two PNB officials and kept concealed from the system for several years. By the time Shetty was arrested, both Modi and Choksi had already fled the country. Over the next few months, several lapses and ignored red flags surfaced. The bank's former MD and CEO, Usha Ananthasubramanian, was named one of the accused in the chargesheet and dismissed from her position as the MD and CEO of Allahabad Bank.

Modi has since taken asylum in London. His uncle is cooling his heels in the Caribbean. It emerged that just two months before the scam broke out, Choksi managed to buy the citizenship of Antigua for himself. Official efforts to bring these two fraudsters back are currently on. But the bank has already booked these losses. In the latest development, the High Court of Antigua and Barbuda has ruled that 'the government cannot forcefully remove the alleged absconding diamantaire' from the Caribbean.[1] On the other hand, Nirav Modi continues to remain imprisoned, left with no more legal options in the UK.

2. *Nitin and Chetan Sandesara*

Nitin Sandesara was a chartered accountant with big dreams. His brother Chetan, too, was a connoisseur of good things, who lived large. Together, they were out to build a diversified conglomerate with interests in oil, ports and special economic zones.

But they made their money in gelatin. Sandesara was the CA for Sterling Biotech, a listed firm that produced gelatin, which is a key ingredient in several pharmaceutical products including capsules. At one point, Sterling Biotech had grown to a ₹1,000 crore company. It developed interests in oil by winning a 29-square-kilometre field for exploration. Though the firm claimed to have struck oil, the claim did not seem to be substantial.

As early as 2012, trouble had started with holders of foreign currency convertible bonds (FCCBs) issued by Sterling Biotech moving UK courts for recovery of $184 million (around ₹1,000 crore). The five-year bonds were due for payment in May 2012.

In 2007, Sterling Biotech issued convertible bonds worth $250 million. However, only $115 million (46 per cent) of the initial issue was redeemed and converted, as the company was mired in debt problems and its share price dropped significantly. As a result, the company defaulted on a repayment of $184 million due on 17 May 2012. The gelatin maker's plants were operating below capacity due to a lack of working capital loans, leading to lawsuits from lenders the State Bank of Mysore and IDBI Bank. Bondholders raised concerns about transactions involving Sterling's oil venture in Nigeria, questioning the discrepancy between the company's valuation of the reserves ($10 billion) and the sale of a 17 per cent stake for only $20 million. Despite the company's efforts to restructure with the help of advisers, bondholders refused to accept the proposed terms because of the discrepancies they uncovered in the company's financial records.[2]

A CBI FIR filed in 2017 said that the Sandesaras had hatched a criminal conspiracy to cheat Andhra Bank and other public sector banks. As of 2010, Sterling Biotech had outstanding liabilities to the banks totalling ₹2,890 crore. Group companies Sterling Oil Resources (₹1,392 crore), Sterling SEZ and Infrastructure (₹992 crore) and PMT Machines (₹446 crore) had also run up significant debt under different credit facilities. As of 2016, the total liabilities of the group stood at ₹5,383 crore, making it an NPA.

Several investigation agencies, including the income tax department, the ED and SEBI, had been probing the group for years. It turned out that the promoter being a chartered accountant, the Sandesaras' core competency seemed to be cooking their books. Investigators found that almost all figures related to sales, production and investments had been fudged and inflated. False documents were created on the basis of which manipulated balance sheets were prepared in order to induce the banks to sanction larger amounts of loans that were then diverted for personal purposes.

Chetan and his wife Dipti lived the high life in their farmhouse on the outskirts of Vadodara, often throwing parties to which Bollywood celebrities were invited. They also had a health mall in Vadodara frequented by socialites. At one point, the Sandesaras bought a Gulfstream private jet in which they flew to oversee their Nigerian operations. This jet was also used by Dipti to ferry her showbiz friends to a holiday in Turkey.

Investigators found that the brothers had also rigged their stock by holding shares under *benami* (fictitious) names, both in India and abroad. For example, in the financial year ending March 2008, while the actual investment in capital goods was ₹50 crore, the books of accounts mentioned ₹405 crore. Thus, ₹355 crore were siphoned out of the company. There were differences between income tax returns and the company's balance sheet, too. The brothers also used *angariyas* (local couriers) to launder their money and keep some bank officials in good humour.

After the attachment of assets worth over ₹4,500 crore by the enforcement directorate, the brothers were declared fugitives. They seemed to have joined the club of Hindustan Leavers by flying off sometime in 2017. They are said to have taken the Nigerian route, where they're reportedly flourishing and drilling oil wells.[3]

3. Jatin Mehta

Before Nirav Modi and Mehul Choksi, there was Jatin Mehta. A native of Palanpur like Modi and Choksi, Mehta's whereabouts are unknown, but he is said to be now cooling his heels in Saint Kitts, not very far from Choksi, who is in Antigua. Mehta was among the top diamond jewellers in Mumbai, running a listed firm called Winsome Diamonds. It is alleged that Mehta was acting in tandem with a Jordanian national named Haytham Salman Ali Abu Obaidah. Winsome bought gold from bullion banks abroad, such as Bank of Nova Scotia, Standard Chartered and HSBC, against the standby letters of credit (SBLCs) issued by the Indian banks.

Winsome had adopted a business model in which it imported gold and gems from foreign banks and private parties against SBLC/LC/cash credit for value addition. These were then used to produce jewellery for export to its customers foreign customers. The company availed credit facilities from the banks under a consortium arrangement.

Their modus operandi went something like this.

The companies inflated the valuation of diamonds and jewellery with the mala fide intention of securing higher credit facilities from the lenders. This also served to misrepresent the security coverage available with the lenders. Export bills that remained unpaid by the due date were purchased by the consortium banks. Simultaneously, the disruption in the cash flow led to the devolvement of SBLCs, leaving the outstanding cash credit unpaid.

The thirteen companies controlled by Ali Obaidah explained that they couldn't fulfil their SBLC commitment on time because their receivables were delayed due to financial problems faced by foreign buyers. The companies provided manipulated and false details of their receivables and debtors to the bank to obtain credit facilities. All of them cleverly used innovative funding ideas, convincing the consortium to grant the entire pre-shipment as SBLCs instead of packing credit loans. They also secured post-shipment finance by discounting export bills from one bank and pre-shipment finance from another using SBLC, resulting in double financing. The Central Vigilance Commission (CVC) spotted several loopholes and lapses in the banking system in such cases of fraud in the jewellery sector, highlighting them in their 'Analysis of Top 100 Bank Frauds' in 2018. As per the CVC, due diligence reports on borrowers 'were not obtained before submitting the sanction/renewal proposal'. The banks primarily focused on enhancing the export limits without insisting on payment guarantees for exports. While the imports were on the basis of SBLC, comforts like letters of credit or SBLC were not insisted upon to ensure timely payments for exports.

The existing buyers' companies were controlled by a single individual and no credit assessment was conducted for these customers. Moreover, there was no evidence to show proof of goods delivery to customers, particularly in sales of gold and diamond jewellery to foreign companies, which led the investigating agency to raise concerns.

The CVC also noticed that in the absence of effective monitoring of discounted export bill proceeds for SBLC liquidation, the companies diverted funds to related/shell companies. The consortium mechanism failed to adequately oversee transactions.

Information exchange was merely ceremonial, lacking thorough scrutiny. The lead bank failed to address concerns and warnings from business rating reports and did not alert other member banks early on. Bullion trade and merchant trading were not genuine transactions, rather deliberate actions to siphon off funds from the consortium. The high-value transactions were made without the consortium's approval, which resulted in default on payment or repayment.

Between them, the leading trio of Hindustan Leavers – Modi, Sandesaras and Mehta – scooted with a whopping ₹25,000 crore.

The House of Debt

Let us now take a look at some large business groups for whom the borrowing begins at such a number. A few of them owe the banks several times more. Not all of them have been able to do justice to the faith their lenders had placed in them.

As early as 2012, Ashish Gupta and his fellow analysts at the investment bank Credit Suisse (CS) coined the term 'House of Debt' to refer to highly indebted corporate houses. Gupta had identified ten large business groups whose exposure accounted for a major chunk of the credits provided by the banking system. In its House of Debt Report from August 2012, Credit Suisse noted:

> Over last five years, Indian banks have witnessed strong (20 percent CAGR) loan growth. However, this has increasingly been driven by select few corporate groups; aggregate debt of these ten groups has jumped 5 times in the

past five years and now equates to 13 percent of bank loans and 98 percent of the banking system's networth.[4]

In the October 2015 report of these companies, Credit Suisse analysts said eight of the ten groups had already faced defaults and the sums at default were estimated at a whopping $53 billion (at ₹65/$, this would be in excess of ₹3.4 lakh crore).

> Going through the annual reports available for 'House of Debt' companies, we find instances where auditors have highlighted that the company has been in default for a period of up to 360 days. According to their auditor's report, eight of the ten 'House of Debt' groups were in default last year. Total debt with these companies in default was at US$53 bn (~48% of total debt with the groups) of which US$37 bn were reported to be in default for 0–90 days by the auditors.[5]

While some of these accounts were restructured by the banks, most of them continue to be classified as 'standard'. Such deliberate blindness of the banks to stressed assests led the RBI to take certain steps forcing the banks to recognize bad loans. They have been described in the next chapter. But first, let's look at the ten members of the House of Debt.

Conquerors, Survivors and the Not-So-Lucky

The ten large borrower groups listed by Credit Suisse could be broadly classified into three categories, depending on how they have fared in recent years.

Conquerors: The Sajjan Jindal-promoted JSW Group, Anil Agarwal's Vedanta and Gautam Adani's Adani Group are better off than others, not just because of close ties with the ruling dispensation but also because they have been buying stressed assets in the market.

Survivors: The GMR Group, GVK Industries and Anil Ambani's Reliance ADAG fall under this category. GMR and GVK, the two infrastructure groups that made their names by building the modern airports in Delhi and Mumbai, respectively, have been largely keeping to themselves, trying to deleverage by selling assets and bringing debt under control.

Not-So-Lucky: Venugopal Dhoot's Videocon Group, which has already been referred to insolvency resolution, headlines this bunch consisting of Essar Steel, Jaypee Infratech and Lanco Infratech. They have faced a similar fate with their key companies as the dirty dozen.

The Conquerors

JSW Group

Gross Debt as of 31 March 2023: $9.4 billion or ₹81,000 crore

Sajjan Jindal, the chief of JSW group, is an influential man today. In April 2017, the Pakistani media went into a tizzy when he had a secret meeting with their then prime minister Nawaz Sharif. As speculations regarding Jindal facilitating some back-channel diplomacy on behalf of Prime Minister Modi grew rife, Sharif's daughter Maryam tweeted, clarifying that 'Mr Jindal is an old friend of the prime minister. Nothing secret about the meeting and should not be blown out of proportion.'[6]

A few months later, Jindal's own tweets created ripples in policy circles and triggered amendments in the insolvency and bankruptcy framework. Right after Essar Steel's promoters, the Ruia family, floated Numetal Mauritius to launch a bid to buy their own company back through the insolvency resolution process, Jindal tweeted several times about the need to keep 'dubious promoters' out of the system. Soon, the government, by way of an ordinance, barred promoters and their associates with outstanding dues to the lenders from taking part in the resolution process unless they paid up.

JSW was a key player in the sale of many distressed companies through the IBC framework. It has already successfully snapped up Monnet Ispat & Energy and Bhushan Power & Steel Ltd. With these buys, JSW Steel has emerged as India's leading integrated steel company with a capacity of 28.5 MTPA as of May 2023.[7] By 2025, Jindal wants to produce 40 MTPA domestically and another 8 to 10 MTPA overseas.[8] A possible consolidation and listing of JSW in New York or London are also on the cards.

Things weren't always this rosy. In the early 2000s, Jindal Vijaynagar Steel, as the company was called back then, had to go through a painful restructuring process after it struggled to service the ₹5,000-crore debt taken out for building a plant near Hospet in Karnataka. As a part of the process, the investments of the company were hived off into Jindal South West Holdings, and it was merged with Jindal Iron and Steel Company (JISCO) in 2005 to form the company JSW Steel that exists today.

Even as this process was ongoing, Sajjan Jindal lost his father, Om Prakash Jindal, who was also the Haryana education minister at the time, in a helicopter crash. A family succession saga ensued wherein Sajjan and his brothers Prithviraj, Rattan and Navin took up the management of specific companies. JSW Steel and JSW Energy went to Sajjan Jindal, Prithviraj took control of Jindal Saw, Ratan Jindal got Jindal Stainless while Navin took over Jindal Steel and Power.

Though the managements had been separated, ownership continued to be entangled in cross-holdings through three listed holding companies, namely Nalwasons, JSW Holdings and Hexa Trading. Sajjan, being the strongest, had to enter into a couple of related party transactions – first to buy out some US assets under his elder brother Prithviraj Jindal in 2008 and then the Chhattisgarh power plant run by Navin Jindal that got into trouble following the coal block cancellation. Investors had not been too happy about these deals.

In FY 2015, Credit Suisse analysts expressed concerns about the company's worsening debt servicing ability.[9] As per the report from October 2015, around 84 per cent of JSW Group's debt was from the account of JSW Steel, which had seen 'muted operating performance'. Revenue had increased 3 per cent y-o-y and EBIT remained flat y-o-y as interest costs rose by 15 per cent. Debt increased by 8 per cent year-on-year, resulting in 'worsening of debt servicing ratios'. The company also reported a loss in the first quarter of 2016. 'The weakening in commodity prices is likely to keep profitability under pressure,' JSW stated in the same report. Nearly 40 per cent of JSW Steel's borrowings were in foreign currencies.

JSW Energy, on the other hand, was relatively better placed as it accounted for 16 per cent of the group's debt. The subsidiary saw improvement in its operating performance, with EBITDA growing at 11 per cent y-o-y in FY 2015. However, JSW Energy sold 41 per cent of its power through the merchant route. The company cited 'weakness in power demand' as the reason behind the drop in profitability during the first quarter of FY 2016.

'The group has had no trouble meeting its debt obligations so far,' JSW commented in the report against debt servicing.

But the outlook for the steel sector has improved since, with the prices recovering, and JSW Steel seems confident about servicing debt through internal accruals. At present, JSW has debt levels of 3.75 times its EBITDA and 1.75 times the equity, which is among the best for the steel industry. In the company's corporate presentation in May 2023, the credit ratings were quoted as being stable.[10] As per a senior company executive that the *Economic Times* spoke to, the company plans to use the entirety of the freshly raised funds amounting to ₹18,000 crore to refinance its upcoming debt maturities of around ₹14,000 crore in FY 2024.[11]

Adani Group

Gross Debt as of 31 March 2023: ₹2.27 trillion

Gautam Adani's rise over the last decade or so has surprised many. His political connections are no secret. But the college drop-out turned commodity tycoon sees himself as a self-made entrepreneur who benefited from opportunities thrown up by the 1991 liberalization.

The son of a textile merchant, Adani began as a diamond sorter in Mumbai's Zaveri Bazaar in the late 1970s. He eventually became a diamond broker himself.

Then a call from his brother took him to a different kind of trading in Ahmedabad. Here, Adani dealt in the import of polyvinyl chloride (PVC), starting in the 1980s. The international trading experience put him in the right place to benefit from the post-liberalization opportunities. He did so well that he was kidnapped by the underworld in 1998. Though the exact circumstances of the kidnap and release are unclear, most reports talk of a hefty ransom being paid, with figures varying from ₹3 crore to ₹15 crore.

When businesses in Gujarat tried to distance themselves from Narendra Modi, the then chief minister in 2002, Adani, along with other like-minded businessmen such as Karsanbhai Patel of Nirma and Anil Bakeri of Bakeri Engineers, started a group called the Resurgent Group of Gujarat (RGG).

This group was the brain behind the first Vibrant Gujarat Summit in 2003. Adani's stock has been on the rise since, largely in line with Modi's political ascension, or so has been alleged. The Adani Group now has interests in mining, ports and the power sector. Adani Enterprises owns coal mines in India, Australia and Indonesia, with reserves in excess of 10 billion tonnes.

Its power company has a 12,450 MW operating capacity (including acquisitions), probably the largest in the country.[12] The group's seven operating ports handle 339 MMT of cargo.[13]

In 2015–16, when most other groups were looking to deleverage, the Adani Group acquired port assets (in FY 2015) and two power plants (in FY 2016), taking its debt levels to ₹84,000 crore.

'Within the group, Adani Ports was well placed operationally and had healthy debt servicing ratios,' wrote Gupta and co in their report from 2015. But this accounted for only 20 per cent of the group's debt. Even prior to the recent acquisition, Adani Power accounted for more than 50 per cent of the group's debt, having been incurring losses for the past eight years.

Adani Enterprises had also faced issues at its $4.2 billion Carmichael Mine, as the environmental clearance had been delayed. As a result of the delay in obtaining clearances, the company saw project costs rise by 20 per cent. According to earlier estimates, Adani Enterprises was required to spend $7.7 billion at Carmichael Mine – $4.2 billion to get the mine operational and another $3.5 billion to set up the rail link to Abbott Point and build a terminal to transport 60 MTPA of coal once the mine was operating at full capacity.

In November 2018, Adani announced that a scaled-down version of its project with a capacity of about 27.5 MTPA and a narrow-gauge railway line would come up. These would be self-financed after local protests derailed the efforts to get support from the government.

Unlike others, the company has not sought to reduce debt through asset sales but has boldly acquired capacities in the power sector. It bought Reliance ADAG's power distribution utility in Mumbai and Ambuja Cement more recently.

Adani Power had also entered into an agreement with the government of Rajasthan to set up a 10 GW solar power park in 2015. An MoU signed with the Chhattisgarh government had brought them an investment of ₹25,000 crore for two projects.

The group has since set up a 40 MW solar power project in Gujarat. Adani Ports has also recorded 9 per cent y-o-y growth in FY 2023 and reported to have handled the largest port cargo volumes ever.

But a big blow was waiting for the group in 2023. According to an investigation carried out by Hindenburg Research, Gautam Adani, the founder and chairman of the group, has significantly increased his net worth by more than $100 billion in the past three years. This growth is primarily attributed to the rise in stock prices of the group's seven main publicly traded companies, which have experienced a remarkable surge of approximately 819 per cent during the same period.[14]

According to the Hindenburg Research report, the Adani Group has encountered challenges and losses in various industries. It highlights the following areas of business:

1. *Ports*: Adani's port business is facing tough competition, resulting in declining profits.
2. *Power*: The Hindenburg report argues that Adani's power business is struggling due to high debt levels and low returns.
3. *Real Estate*: Adani's real estate projects have been slow to gain momentum, leading to financial losses.
4. *Agribusiness*: The report suggests that Adani's agribusiness ventures have faced difficulties due to mismanagement and underperformance.
5. *Trading and Distribution*: Adani's trading and distribution businesses have experienced significant losses due to their lack of competitiveness.

This report has sparked controversy in the financial and business communities, with Adani Group refuting the claims made in it. Nonetheless, the report raises important concerns regarding the financial performance and business practices of the group.[15]

Despite this, in a presentation shared with the RBI, the group said that it had raised fresh funds amounting to ₹19,235 crore in the two months following the Hindenburg report. Adani Group's net debt is 17 per cent more than the previous year's. They are supposedly going to use the fresh debt for the Navi Mumbai airport and the Mundra Petrochem project that fall under Adani Enterprises. The group also added that owing to their access to credit facilities, they are currently working on domestic and international debt capital market programmes.[16]

Vedanta Group

Gross debt as of May 2023: ₹52,760 crore or $6.4 billion

When James Cameron's blockbuster film *Avatar* was released in 2009, people were quick to point out the parallels between its storyline and the struggles of the Dongria Kondh tribals. The indigenous people who lived on the Niyamgiri hills in Odisha fought the efforts of Sterlite Industries and Orissa Mining Corporation to mine bauxite. Armed with a Supreme Court order that made their consent a pre-condition for the project, the tribals pushed out the miners. For London-based billionaire Anil Agarwal, who built the multibillion-dollar Vedanta Group starting from a scrap business in Mumbai, such setbacks were a part-and-parcel in extractive industries.

Agarwal, who grew up in Bihar, assumed control of his father's aluminium conductors business in the 1970s and later diversified into the scrap metal trade. He expanded Vedanta Ltd through a series of ambitious acquisitions, starting with the purchase of a controlling stake in the government-owned Bharat Aluminium Co in 2001. This was followed by the acquisition of another state-run entity, Hindustan Zinc. In 2007, he successfully bid for the iron ore producer Sesa Goa Ltd and Cairn India. Vedanta Resources also holds copper and zinc operations in Africa.

The company achieved a milestone as the first Indian firm to list in London in 2003. Agarwal later privatized the firm after fifteen years when his company, now recognized as Vedanta Inc, acquired minority investors to streamline the group's structure. Agarwal subsequently renamed Volcan Investments Ltd to Vedanta Inc. However, this spree of acquisitions led to a significant increase in the conglomerate's debt, with Vedanta Resources' total debt reaching $6.4 billion by the end of June 2023.

Founded in Bombay in 1976 by Anil Agarwal as a scrap-metal dealership, the company expanded its portfolio over the years. In 1979, it acquired Shamsher Sterling Corporation (later renamed Sterlite Industries), specializing in power and control cables. Significant milestones include acquiring a majority stake in Balco, the Indian state aluminium business, in 2001.

Vedanta went public in 2003, raising $876 million through an IPO on the London Stock Exchange. Over the years, it made strategic acquisitions, including Sterlite Gold in 2006 and a 51 per cent stake in Sesa Goa, the country's leading iron ore producer, in 2007. In 2008, Vedanta purchased the assets of Asarco, a copper mining business, and in 2010, it acquired Zinc assets in South Africa, Namibia and Ireland.

In July 2010, Sterlite Industries had received a tax notice of about ₹3.24 billion and was charged with violating several rules by the excise department. Excise officials accused Sterlite Industries of misdeclaration, asserting that the company attempted to export copper waste with the intention of extracting gold and silver. But, the waste was found to contain additional precious metals, such as platinum and palladium.

Key acquisitions continued, like the 2011 purchase of a 58.5 per cent controlling stake in Cairn India, the largest private sector oil and gas company in the country. In 2013, Sterlite Industries and Sesa Goa merged to form Sesa Sterlite Ltd, now known as Vedanta Ltd. In January 2014, the income tax department revelead that Vedanta owed ₹10,247 crore in retrospective tax.

In September 2018, Anil Agarwal announced plans to take Vedanta Resources private, effective from 1 October 2018.

But only a few months prior, in May 2018, in Tamil Nadu's Thoothukudi city, Sterlite's two-decade-old copper smelter ran into trouble after locals protested an expansion plan, citing health hazards. The protests led to shooting that saw the deaths of thirteen people. But that did not stop the group from paying ₹5,320 crore to buy Jharkhand-based Electrosteel Steels through the insolvency process in 2018. Vedanta Resources had interests across oil, zinc, copper, aluminium, iron ore and power already. When it wrapped up Electrosteel's sale, it would also have a play in steel. A losing bidder, Renaissance Steel moved the court demanding disqualification of Vedanta's offers, which did not find favour in the appellate tribunal.

The Supreme Court issued a notice to Sterlite on the Renaissance appeal. Meanwhile, the National Green Tribunal gave a nod to Sterlite for reopening its Thoothukudi factory. The Supreme Court began hearing an appeal lodged by Vedanta against the Madras high court's decision to not reopen the Sterlite Copper smelting plant. This plant had been ordered to halt operations back in 2013, following an order from the TNPCB after the leakage of noxious gases from the plant in March of that year. Around the same time in the previous year, the company was being sued by Zambian villagers over alleged pollution of their village resources. In 2019 again, the company was faced with legal and human rights charges in the Supreme Court of the United Kingdom.

More importantly, the *Wire* reported in 2021 how an investigation by the Rajasthan government uncovered substantial irregularities in the operations of Hindustan Zinc Ltd (HZL), a Vedanta Group subsidiary, suggesting potential royalty losses of ₹3,613 crore to the government between 2013–14 and 2018–19.[17] The State Directorate of

Revenue Intelligence (SDRI) detected discrepancies in the declared mineral produce of silver, lead and zinc, with HZL allegedly evading royalties worth ₹2,537 crore on silver and ₹1,113.67 crore on lead and zinc. HZL, India's largest zinc mining corporation and the world's second-largest, denied the allegations and awaits further investigation.

The SDRI's analysis revealed significant underreporting of silver and lead-zinc quantities by HZL to the state government compared to the company's declarations to the Indian Bureau of Mines and its annual reports. While the directorate recommended recovering the evaded royalties, HZL argued that it also extracted silver from imported minerals. The Rajasthan government has served notices to HZL and initiated additional investigations since, with the authorities being instructed to complete their assessments and submit a report by 2023.

The conglomerate is presently seeking liquidity, aiming to restructure approximately $3 billion in bonds maturing in 2024 and 2025.[18] Simultaneously, the group is considering dividing its extensive portfolio to enhance the individual value of its businesses. Despite these efforts, skepticism among debt investors persists, leading to a decline in the group's dollar bonds.

The Survivors

GMR Group

Gross Debt as of 31 December 2022: ₹299 billion

Grandhi Mallikarjuna Rao started his life as a junior engineer in the public works department. Hailing from the village of Rajam in Srikakulam district in erstwhile Andhra Pradesh, Rao brushed off early failures to become the first graduate in his family. Though he managed to land a government job as a junior engineer in the public works department, his mother was keen that he become a businessman, true to the entrepreneurial heritage of the Vysya community to which the family belonged.

Following her wish, Rao soon quit his job and joined the agricultural commodities trading business with his brothers. This took him to major markets in Chennai, Nagpur and Kolkata. On one such trip, he learnt that a Chennai-based jute mill was bring out up for sale.

In those days of strict government controls on the industry, the licence was often more valuable than the plant itself. As the mill fitted into the brothers' plans of getting into the 'industry' from trading, Rao led this buyout. It took several months to get all the required permissions. This theme of striking promising, yet challenging deals would repeat in Rao's journey.

Rao's movement from the hinterland to the mainstream began in the mid-1980s, when Ramesh Gelli, the chairman of Vysya Bank, was looking for members from the community to become directors. The RBI had, at the time, capped the tenure of bank directors at eight years. Vysya Bank, a small private entity with operations in Andhra Pradesh, Karnataka and Tamil Nadu, saw most of its board stepping down. New directors were to be hired. 'At that time, they requested me to join the board. I accepted the directorship. It was a profitable bank, had 200 branches, paid a good dividend and was a listed entity,' Rao told the *Moneylife* magazine in 2010.[19]

By 1994, when Gelli left to found Global Trust Bank, Rao was already the largest shareholder of Vysya Bank, having got the lion's share in a couple of its rights issues. He went on to take over the reins of Vysya, shifting base to Bengaluru. Being an outsider, he struggled in the initial years to learn how to deal with a tough regulator. But he came into his own soon, bringing in foreign shareholders.

By this time, he had also developed significant interests in the power sector, owing plants in Chennai and Mangaluru with his American partners. He incorporated a public limited company called Varalakshmi Vasavi Power Projects Ltd in 1996 and changed its name to GMR Vasavi Infrastructure Finance Ltd in 1999. Following the Enron scandal in the US in the early 2000s, when his American partners wanted to exit, Rao bought them out. The funds for this buyout largely came from the sale of stake in Vysya bank. Thereafter, on 24 July 2000, the name of the company was changed to GMR Infrastructure Ltd. On 4 October 2004 the registered office of the company was shifted from Andhra Pradesh to Karnataka.

By now, GMR had started taking on road projects as the Vajpayee government set about building the Golden Quadrilateral connecting the metros and the North–South and East–West corridors, with the foundation stone laid in 1999.

Despite all these successes, Rao had one unfulfilled wish. Though he owned sugar mills, he did not have a large project in his home state. This dream came true when GMR isgned a pact with the Andhra Government and Malaysian Airport Authority in 2005 to develop a greenfield airport in Hyderabad. This and the later projects, such as the Delhi airport in 2006, catapulted the company to the big leagues and turned it into a household name.

The airport business also brought some infamy when, in 2012, the group's venture in the Maldives was in choppy waters. GMR had to exit the project to modernize the Hulhulé airport after nationalist sentiments and allegations of corruption created massive resistance to the project among the local community.

Locals alleged that GMR was trying to convert the airport into a large shopping mall when it actually needed an additional runway that would help in quick check-ins and check-outs for tourists.

The airports arm, GMR Airports, too, ran into disputes with private equity investors such as the Macquarie Group and Standard Chartered. These investments, made in 2011–12, included some milestones, such as providing exits through an IPO within a specified time period. However, during FY 2015, the airport segment turned a loss, with revenue for the segment down 16 per cent on y-o-y basis. In February 2015, the airport regulator issued a draft order to reduce the airport charges by nearly 78 per cent. From 2014 to 2019 for the Delhi airport, as against an increase of 43 per cent requested by GMR. This, among other factors, threw a spanner in the IPO plans. Then, the private equity (PE) investors wanted their pound of flesh, demanding they be given an exit through the buyback route. The matter moved into arbitration.

With the revised charges set to kick in from 2019–24, the outlook for the airports business looks bright again. This has raised hopes of the IPO coming back, even as there have been reports of settlement with PE investors. In 2020, GMR signed another contract with the Andhra government to develop a greenfield airport near Vizag in Bhogapuram.[20] The group also signed an MoU with Airbus SE to collaborate on aircraft maintenance and airport services, changing its name to GMR Airports Infrastructure Ltd in 2022.[21]

The company's power projects, both in coal and gas, have faced raw material issues. A hydel project in Alkananda, Uttarakhand, suffered severe delays due to the massive floods in 2013.

In 2013–14, GMR sold several key assets. It sold twenty-three assets to raise over ₹11,000 crore by 2015 in an effort to deleverage. But the debt levels have remained high.

In an interview with the *Economic Times* in April 2023, Executive Director of GMR Saurabh Chawla said that their main focus is to 'strengthen our balance sheet' and cited their net debt as ₹250 billion. The group sounds hopeful of upstreaming cash flows and driving value for shareholders despite the huge debt.[22]

GVK Group

Gross debt as of 1 December 2023: ₹58.1 billion

The life and times of G. Venkata Krishna Reddy have run almost parallel with his country cousin G. M. Rao. Their infrastructure groups have grown, competing for many projects over the past two decades. For example, while GMR was constructing a hydel project on the Alaknanda river near Badrinath, GVK was building one downstream near Srinagar. If GMR built the Delhi and Hyderabad airports, GVK won the projects in Mumbai and Bengaluru. Both cut their teeth as contractors on the irrigation and power projects in Andhra in the early 1990s. Today, both are struggling with debt problems.

A photograph of GVK Reddy's son Sanjay Reddy from the 1980s features the then chief minister N. T. Rama Rao (NTR) blessing him and his new bride, Aparna aka Pinky Reddy, the vivacious daughter of Congress politician T. Subbarami Reddy. Reddy, known for his lavish parties in Hyderabad and Delhi, had interests in movies and the entertainment industry besides politics.

Given that Congress and Telugu Desam, founded by NTR, were at opposing ends of the political spectrum in the state, the Reddys had mastered the art of political tightrope walking even in those early days. Such tactfulness was put to good use when the group set about developing the new T2 terminal of the Mumbai airport. The land for the terminal was home to numerous government offices, private buildings, temples and a police station. While the group dealt with each of these stakeholders and managed to move them, a statue of Shivaji became the centre of much controversy. Shiv Sena, the political outfit espousing the cause of the Marathi community, jumped in, giving sleepless nights to the Reddys.

Even private property holders were not easy to handle. Sanjay Reddy recalled an incident where a sixty-year-old woman who had come to his office pulled out a gun. Though the group managed to navigate such difficult situations and completed the project, it took nearly eight years and ₹12,500 crore.

The group also faced cost overruns in hydel, coal and gas-powered plants due to varying reasons. The 330 MW hydro project in Uttarkhand saw a 75 per cent cost overruns, largely owing to a two-year delay on account of the 2013 floods in Uttarakhand. Coal block cancellations by the Supreme Court led to heavy escalation in raw material costs. The gas-based plants, which relied on natural gas from Reliance's Krishna–Godavari basin fields, virtually shut down as Reliance stopped production. In its annual report from FY 2017–18, GVK commented: '40% of India's gas requirements are being met from a single field i.e. KG-D6 Basin has proved to be hot air.' As per the group, India witnessed a surge of gas-based power plants between 2009 and 2014 because of the hype. However, the drop in production from the KG-D6 field was the main reason why the industry was upset. 'It's a do-or-die situation gas-based power plants are facing, notwithstanding the government's target of increasing the share of natural gas in India's primary energy mix to 15% from 7% at present,' the report further stated.[23] In the 2021–22 annual report, GVK Energy Ltd, a subsidiary of the GVK Group confidently claimed that 'Government of India will take necessary steps/initiatives to improve the situation of natural gas'.[24] Their energy assests, like the Gautami Power power project, the Alaknanda hydroelectric project and the Goindwal Sahib power plant were reportedly making good progress.

In 2011, the company had acquired coal mines in Australia with a capacity of 80 MTPA for $1.26 billion. The project was estimated to require an additional $10 billion. There were delays in GVK Hancock receiving the mining permit. GVK Power had a 10 per cent stake in GVK Coal Developers, which is the group's holding company for its Australian projects. Loans for this acquisition had been downgraded to NPA recently by one of the state-owned banks. At one point in 2015, the debt-equity ratio of the company stood at over a prohibitive twenty-eight times. It had also defaulted on several interest payments.

The Reddys went on a selling spree to cut debt. They offloaded their entire 43 per cent stake in the Bengaluru International Airport in two tranches to Fairfax Holdings, raising close to ₹3,500 crore in the process.

In the 2017–18 annual report, GVK had said that all infrastructure companies across India were facing challenging times due to their financial exposure to banks and lending institutions and that the company was no exception to this. In the 2021–22 report, the group went on to say:

The challenges faced by the renewable energy industry are many. Political pressures, government policies, corporate influence, age-old infrastructure, lack of proper battery storage system, and present market scenario stand in its way for a wider adoption worldwide.

As part of recent developments, in October 2022, GVK Power (Goindwal Sahib) has been admitted for corporate resolution and insolvency based on the petition filed by Axis Bank.[25] Previously, in September 2020, the group had agreed to cede control of its airport business to the Adani Group, following a reported debt of ₹3,739 crore at the end of FY 2019. The Mumbai International Airport Ltd (MIAL) reportedly had a gross debt of ₹8,109 crore and was also taken over by the Adani Group in December 2022.[26] The lender consortium included Goldman Sachs, HDFC Bank and SBI, among others.[27]

The Not-So-Lucky

Reliance ADA Group

Gross Debt as in September 2021: ₹40,000 crore*

In 2019, Anil Ambani was busy suing journalists and media organizations for publishing defamatory reports on the alleged corruption in the Rafale fighter jets deal. Ambani's firm Reliance Defence was the chosen offset partner for Dassault Aviation, triggering allegations of kickbacks and crony capitalism in the multibillion-dollar contract. The Congress party, led by Rahul Gandhi, alleged corruption in the transaction and implicated

---

* ADAG is now insolvent.

the name of Prime Minister Narendra Modi as well. One of the key charges was the poor financial condition of the group.

The telecom business, Reliance Communications or RCOM had run aground and the bankers were desperate to recover some money by selling its tower, optical fibre and other assets to Reliance Jio, the new company floated by Mukesh Ambani that has disrupted the entire sector. However, Ericsson, one of its vendors, had already dragged RCOM to the NCLT, seeking resolution of insolvency. Though RCOM managed to pull itself out after agreeing to settle with Ericsson, delays in execution of the deal with the older brother caused jitters in the market.

Before the death of his father Dhirubhai Ambani, Anil Ambani used to be the finance whiz-kid of the group. His interest in project implementation were minimal, as older brother Mukesh was responsible for helping their father put up large projects, such as the grassroots refinery in Jamnagar.

Mukesh had also chalked the group's telecom foray in the early 2000s through Reliance Infocomm, but the business fell into Anil's lap after an equal partition of assets in 2005. While Mukesh got the reins of Reliance Industries and IPCL, Anil was handed over Reliance Communications, Reliance Capital and Reliance Energy.

Though Anil ventured into power, infrastructure and defence, he could not make much of a mark except in his core area – finance. Reliance Capital was the island of good performance amid a sea of red within it. Since 2018, the group has been taking steps to reduce its debt. While ADAG's debt in March 2018 was around ₹1.7 lakh crore, it came down to ₹93,900 crore in July 2019. Then, in September 2019, Reliance Capital – the last bastion in Anil Ambani's business empire – decided to shut its two lending arms, Reliance Commercial Finance and Reliance Home Finance to settle its debt of ₹15,000 crore with its creditors.[28] Tata and Adani were amongst the groups that queued up to take over the debt-laden company, which is currently under corporate insolvency resolution.

From $42 billion in 2008, Anil Ambani's net worth reduced to almost nothing in 2020.[29] The completion of the NCLT-ordered resolution process will see the group's debt reduce by 50 per cent or ₹20,000 crore. In December 2022, after a close race with the Hinduja Group, Ahmedabad-based Torrent Group, specializing in pharmaceuticals and power, acquired Reliance Capital with a bid of ₹8,640 crore and entered the financial services sector.[30]

The lesson to learn here, apparently, is that though good, too much diversification can backfire and debt loops can lead to complete downfall.

Videocon Group

Gross Debt FY 2019: ₹45,405 crore*

Videocon Industries, an Indian electronic appliances maker, reported a ₹1,367.94 crore loss in 2016, an amount 24.5 times its loss in 2015. The whopping increase was mainly because of two reasons: falling revenues and high debt.

The Videocon Group, led by Venugopal Dhoot, had interests in oil and gas exploration, consumer electronic, telecom and power. Venugopal wanted to convert the company from a

---

*The group since went into insolvency.

consumer durable firm to a global oil and gas exploration and production companies, setting his sights on Brazil, Indonesia, Australia and East Timor for the same.

Videocon spent ₹9,000 crore in capex in the segment, while its EBIT continued to remain in the red. One of the smaller telecom operators in India, Videocon operated in six circles serving around 7.6 million customers. It acquired the 5 MHz spectrum in the November 2012 auction in six bands for around ₹2,200 crore. Since then, the company has not incurred significant capex in the telecom segment and has continued to turn losses at the EBIT level.

The journey of the Videocon Group began in 1955, when Nandlal Dhoot established a sugar mill, importing machinery from Europe. In 1986, his three sons, Venugopal, Rajkumar and Pradipkumar, ventured into Adhigam Trading, initially selling paper tubes before expanding into the production of television sets and washing machines.

During the 1990s, the company experienced significant growth as it introduced additional products like air conditioners, refrigerators and home entertainment systems. This period of expansion coincided with India's economic liberalization. On 14 February 1991, Adhigam Trading changed its name to Videocon Leasing and Industrial Finance.

In subsequent years, Videocon expanded rapidly by diversifying into sectors such as oil and gas in the late nineties, followed by telecom, DTH entertainment and retail. Throughout the 2000s, the company underwent substantial growth, but this was accompanied by a significant increase in debt.

Post 2007, Videocon's debt multiplied seven times. Moreover, the group's capacity to pay interest deteriorated.[31] With not much to write home about, the company has already been admitted to the insolvency resolution process after SBI moved the NCLT Mumbai bench in June 2018. It is part of the second lot of twenty-eight companies that have been referred by the RBI for resolution. Venugopal Dhoot offered to settle the ₹31,289 crore debt by raising money from monetization of assets, affordable housing and its consumer electronics and home appliance businesses, but creditors saw no good in his decade-long plans.[32]

Meanwhile, the business links between Dhoot and Deepak Kochhar became the subject of a CBI inquiry. A whistleblower alleged that the Dhoots had favoured Kochhar's renewables company NuPower as a quid pro quo for extending credit facilities to the Videocon Group.

ICICI Bank and the Kochhars had initially denied any wrongdoing. The ICICI board had stood by Kochhar and given her a clean chit. However, after a second whistleblower complaint surfaced with further details, Chanda went on leave. In 2018, investigations by SEBI and a panel headed by former Supreme Court judge B. N. Srikrishna commenced. Kochhar stepped down from her position in October the same year, perhaps the biggest scalp in the war on distressed assets.

In mid-2021, Vedanta Group company Twin Star Technologies had offered ₹2,962 crore for Videocon Industries. In 2022, three big players – Adani, Jindal and Mukesh Ambani-owned Reliance Industries – joined the race to buy the stressed company's assets. The NCLT also observed that the creditors were taking a haircut of nearly 96 per cent on their loans, with the bidder paying 'almost nothing' for the company.[33]

In June 2023, the government-owned Bharat Petroleum Corporation (BPCL) exercised its right of first refusal in a bid to take control of the bankrupt Videocon Oil Ventures' (VOVL) Brazilian assets. The Supreme Court is still hearing a petition by Twin Star, and has appealed against the NCLAT's order to seek rebids for the company.

The Videocon case is a classic example of companies aggressively borrowing to expand but failing to repay.

18

The Central Bank's Response

On 2 July 1997, Bank of Thailand, running out of dollars to defend the *baht*, its national currency, delinked it from the US dollar. This triggered a contagion that spread across the region and came to be known as the 'Asian Financial Crisis'. The crisis saw a multi-year growth, fuelled by dollar loans, collapse in Thailand, Indonesia and South Korea. Malaysia and the Philippines, were also not spared.

As companies struggled for survival, banks stared at a mountain of NPAs. One of the several measures that came out of a multibillion package from an international financial institution was an out-of-court corporate debt restructuring mechanism.

As the first step, Bank of Thailand set up the Corporate Debt Restructuring Advisory Committee (CDRAC) in August 1998 and established the framework for corporate debt restructuring – the so-called Bangkok Approach – which involved the reorganization of a distressed company's outstanding obligations to its creditors that we've discussed before. It laid down the broad framework for inter-creditor and debtor–creditor engagements. In a little over a year, the CDR framework was handling nearly 1,700 cases with total outstanding loans of over 2.1 trillion baht, according to a paper presented by the Bank of Thailand official Tumnong

Dasri at the International Conference on Systemic Resolution of Corporate and Bank Distress in Crisis-Affected East Asian Countries held in Tokyo. By the end of 1999, the Thai CDRA had already approved plans worth 500 billion baht.

India was largely insulated from the Asian crisis because of tight capital controls, some of which are in place even today. But other troubles came its way. The Vajpayee government decided to conduct nuclear tests in Pokhran in May 1998, taking on international opposition. It was the beginning of an avalanche of major local and international events that hit the economy in a span of about three years. The halo of the Pokhran tests dimmed a bit as Pakistan soon followed suit, but it also brought with it global sanctions. The sanctions imposed by the United States included a 'no exports' list featuring some two hundred Indian entities. American corporations were barred from exporting 'anything' to the companies on this list. L&T, Godrej & Boyce, Kirloskar Brothers, Walchandnagar Industries, BHEL and HAL were among the firms included in it. This was followed by more tumultuous times, with the Kargil War, Kandahar hijack and the dotcom bust which began in 2000.

Hit by multiple blows, the Indian economy was faltering and the corporate sector was no exception. Even as the government tried to do its bit by kickstarting infrastructure spending in the form of development of national highways, Delhi metro and other large projects, the RBI had to step in.

The Thailand experiment seemed worth learning from. The RBI, then under Bimal Jalan, studied mechanisms in other countries such as Korea and the UK before coming up with detailed guidelines for India's own CDR. The framework came into effect in August 2001. Within a couple of weeks of this announcement, the deadly 9/11 attacks in New York plunged the global economy into distress with multiple sectors, including aviation, tourism and finance, getting hit.

As early as 1993, India had put in a system of Debt Recovery Tribunals. But bankers had little incentive to move these bodies, where cases could drag on for years. Even in the rare instance of a favourable verdict from the DRT and the appeals process, the lengthy time lapse meant most of the value of the asset would already have been eroded.

Such an environment where numerous external factors affect genuine businesses is precisely what the CDR mechanism sought to address by providing a meeting ground for lenders and borrowers. Two rounds of revisions were done to the initial guidelines, first based on recommendations by a working group headed by deputy governor Vepa Kamesam in 2003 and then, after proposals, by another group headed by S. Gopinath, another deputy governor of the central bank. As per an annex on CDR by the RBI:

> The Corporate Debt Restructuring (CDR) Mechanism is a voluntary, non-statutory system based on Debtor-Creditor Agreement (DCA) and Inter-Creditor Agreement (ICA) and the principle of approvals by super-majority of 75% creditors (by value) which makes it binding on the remaining 25% to fall in line with the majority decision. The CDR Mechanism covers only multiple banking accounts (MBA), syndication/consortium accounts, where all banks and institutions together have an outstanding aggregate exposure of ₹100 million and above.[1]

According to the RBI, even cases filed in DRTs or the BIFR as well as other suit-filed cases were eligible for restructuring under CDR.

The mechanism could be triggered by a reference from creditors who account for a fifth of either the term finance or working capital. The borrowing company could also prompt CDR if it was backed by lenders who held 20 per cent of the debt. The RBI put up a three-tier structure for CDR that included:

1. CDR Standing Forum and its Core Group
2. CDR Empowered Group
3. CDR Cell

The CDR Standing Forum was a general body that included all banks and financial institutions that were participating in the system. The RBI itself would stay out of this group, its role limited to setting the rules of the game. The standing forum had the chairpersons of key institutions such as SBI, IDBI, ICICI Bank, the Indian Banks Association and all other member banks. A core group was carved out of this broader forum. This group in turn drafted policies and guidelines for functioning of the Empowered Group and the CDR Cell.

The CDR Empowered Group consisted of executive director-level officers of various banks. The group was mandated to investigate each case of debt restructuring, examine the viability and rehabilitation potential of the company and approve the restructuring package within a specified time frame of ninety days or at most within 180 days of reference.

It looked at some of following key parameters and applied these based on the merits of each case:

1. Return on capital employed (ROCE)
2. Debt service coverage ratio (DSCR)

3. Gap between the internal rate of return (IRR) and the cost of fund (CoF)
4. Extent of sacrifice

The system also envisaged a dedicated CDR Cell that would assist the Empowered Group and the Standing Forum in their activities. The cell would perform the initial scrutiny of the proposals received from borrowers or creditors, call for the proposed rehabilitation plan and other information before putting up the matter before the CDR Empowered Group within one month to decide whether rehabilitation was prima facie feasible.

If the group agreed, the CDR Cell would prepare a detailed rehabilitation plan with the help of creditors and, if necessary, engage experts from outside. If not found prima facie feasible, the creditors could initiate action for recovery of their dues.

The CDR was a win-win situation and worked well at the time. The stock markets and economy had started looking up from 2003 to 2008. In fact, as this period drew to a close, things had moved to the other end of the spectrum. An abundance of liquidity was sloshing around the globe, credit was cheap and too many bankers were chasing very few promoters.

Two key areas where financing peaked were realty-driven infrastructure projects and power projects based on coal. Buoyant realty prices boosted the infrastructure development model, where companies would get compensated in terms of development rights for the land alongside the projects. The UPA government under Manmohan Singh allocated coal blocks which were previously lying undeveloped to the private sector.

A senior banker at Corporation Bank recounts how each member of the consortium would throw his hat in for the account:

Imagine a hundred bankers chasing a single promoter. Often bankers were under pressure to be part of large projects. They were keen to grow their balance sheets. When the projects were underwritten by consultants such as SBI Capital Markets and anchored by SBI or other large banks as lead lenders, smaller banks did not have much option but to grab their share. If one missed out, calls flew from head office asking if SBI could lend ₹1,000 crore, could you not do even ₹15 crore. This led to a situation where promoters borrowed more than what they required. Forget due diligence or difficult questions, most bankers who were desperate to lend were in no position to ask any questions at all. Because if you did, the borrower would simply go to someone else.

In his 2016 speech in Bengaluru, the RBI governor Raghuram Rajan described the situation:

> Why have bad loans been made? A number of these loans were made in 2007–2008. Economic growth was strong and the possibilities limitless. Deposit growth in public sector banks was rapid and a number of infrastructure projects such as power plants had been completed on time and within budgets. It is at times as these bankers make mistakes.[2]

He went on to explain how bankers tend to extrapolate past growth and performance into the future. So they are willing to 'accept higher leverage in projects and lesser promoter equity'.

A former Syndicate Bank executive recounted instances of how some institutions, such as IL&FS, tried to prop up individuals without much track record as promoters. There were cases when funds for the subscription of shares in the project were financed against the pledge of those same shares.

Such boom time excesses would come back to haunt the bankers. If they were helpless while lending, they were even more so when it came to recovery:

> The borrower would come in his BMW, dressed in a three-piece suit. But, he would say the company did not have money and he can't repay. You would be able to do nothing. Money loses its colour once it leaves the books. Even though you might know that some diversion has happened, it is very difficult to prove. It is with this same money that was lent that this personal asset was purchased.

The collapse of Lehman Brothers and the Global Financial Crisis wrecked the stock markets and the corporate sector. The Supreme Court order cancelling allocations of over 200 coal blocks came as a death blow for many projects which had invested significantly in power projects, largely based on borrowed funds. In many cases, the structures were such that there was little or no promoter equity in these companies.

Deprived of their captive mines and unable to meet the costs of sourcing raw materials from outside, most of these plants and projects ground to a halt. Cyclical factors such as the collapse of Chinese demand after Beijing Olympics hit the steel sector. Fear of investigation slowed down project approvals further causing delays.

Soon, all of these problems started to surface as stressed assets at the doorstep of the CDR Cell.

Bankers, too, were caught in a fear psychosis. A chief financial officer of a large corporate group revealed to me how many of the restructurings that took place in the 2012–14 period were evergreening exercises.

> The promoter had built this whole ecosystem around his company. He did not want to let go any of these by way of selling. There were emotions involved. Companies wanted to continue without deep restructuring, that would have helped them survive and recover. Even the bankers were scared of taking big haircuts and providing for these in their books. So, they postponed the problem to their successor. This is what led to evergreening.

Before the government changed in 2014, there was a change of guard in the RBI on 1 September 2013. The IIT-educated Rajan's claim to fame was his 2005 Jackson Hole speech warning policymakers about the risks of housing-driven growth supported by loose financial regulation.[3]

In a couple of months after taking charge, Rajan floated a discussion paper on a framework for revitalizing distressed assets in the economy.

A month later, in January 2014, the RBI released a new framework titled 'Early Recognition of Financial Distress, Prompt Steps for Resolution and Fair Recovery for Lenders: Framework for Revitalising Distressed Assets in the Economy' that laid out a framework for dealing with wilful defaulters.[4]

The main proposals of the framework were:

1. Centralized reporting and dissemination of information on large credit
2. Early formation of a lenders' committee with timelines to agree to a plan for resolution

3. Incentives for lenders to agree collectively and quickly to a plan – better regulatory treatment of stressed assets if a resolution plan is under way, or accelerated provisioning if no agreement can be reached
4. Improvement in current restructuring process: Independent evaluation of large-value restructurings mandated, with a focus on viable plans and a fair sharing of losses (and future possible upside) between promoters and creditors
5. More expensive future borrowing for borrowers who do not cooperate with lenders in resolution
6. More liberal regulatory treatment of asset sales:
    a. Lenders can spread loss on sale of loan assets over two years provided the loss is fully disclosed
    b. Takeout financing or refinancing will be possible over a longer period and not be construed as restructuring
    c. Leveraged buyouts will be allowed for specialized entities to allow acquisition of 'stressed companies'
    d. Steps to enable better functioning of Asset Reconstruction Companies mooted
    e. Sector-specific Companies/Private Equity (PE) firms encouraged to play active role in stressed assets market.[5]

The report required banks to be more proactive and focus on large credit of ₹5 crore or more. It came up with a few acronyms that gained currency during Rajan's tenure.

CRILC (Central Repository of Information on Large Credit): The RBI wanted all banks to have information on who had lent to a borrower. Often borrowers used the same underlying asset to raise loans several times with different borrowers. This large-loan database included loans of ₹5 crore or more and was shared with all lenders. It would help all lenders be on the same page.

SMA-0, 1 and 2 (Sub-categories in Special Mention Accounts): Though the concept of SMA was in vogue since 2002, the central bank introduced sub-categories within these so as to enable early detection of stress. SMA-0 would cover cases, where the interest or principal payments were not due for more than thirty days, but there were signs of stress. SMA-1 referred to accounts in which payments were due for thirty-one to sixty days. SMA-2 referred to payment overdue for sixty-one to 180 days.

JLF (Joint Lenders Forum): Once an account becomes SMA-2, the RBI wanted a JLF to be convened. In consortium lending, the lender would convene the forum. In case of multiple banking arrangements or multiple consortiums, the lender with highest exposure would be the leader. JLF formation became mandatory when the total exposure crossed ₹100 crore. However, lenders were free to convene JLFs for smaller accounts, too.

CAP (Corrective Action Plan): Once a JLF was convened, it was required to work on a CAP to resolve the stress in the account through a suitable process, either recovery or restructuring. For cases to be restructured by JLF, a techno-economic viability (TEV) study was prescribed. For accounts, where the aggregate exposure was above ₹500 crore, the TEV study was put up before an independent evaluation council.

As lenders grappled with these changes and new frameworks became popular, the CDR mechanism began losing its primacy. Fewer cases were referred to the CDR Cell, though the new framework provided for JLF to refer some of the restructuring cases to CDR.

While it allowed additional funding by banks for restructuring or rectification, the RBI made it clear that these options could not be done for evergreening of loans. 'JLF may also consider providing need based additional finance to the borrower, if considered necessary, as part of the rectification process. However, it should be strictly ensured that additional financing is not provided with a view to evergreen the account,' the report on the new framework said.

Non-cooperative Borrowers and Wilful Defaulters

A huge amount of data was generated because of these initiatives, enabling the RBI to have a closer monitoring of the system. It asked banks to report non-cooperative borrowers who were not supporting their legitimate efforts to restructure or rectify stressed accounts.

The central bank created a database of directors on the boards of companies classified as non-cooperative borrowers for dissemination to lenders. Further, the list of suit-filed accounts of wilful defaulters (₹25 lakh and above) was already being submitted by banks to the credit information companies (CICs). These names were displayed on their respective websites as and when received.

As per the RBI report, 'The list of non-suit filed accounts of Wilful Defaulters (₹2.5 million and above) is confidential and is disseminated by RBI among banks and FIs only for their own use.'[6]

The system of banks/FIs reporting names of suit filed accounts and non-suit filed accounts of wilful defaulters and its availability to the banks by CICs/RBI was also said to be enhanced to make it as current as possible, as against the current 3–4 months' time lag from the date of reporting by a bank.

This confidentiality became a subject of public scrutiny. Several RTI applications and PILs were filed trying to force the central bank to reveal the list of wilful defaulters. But it steadfastly resisted all such attempts, citing client confidentiality.

While the RBI had its own fraud monitoring cell, it also turned up the heat on the prominent cases, such as Winsome Diamonds and Zoom Developers*, by sending a list of such cases to the Prime Minister's Office.

New Schemes for Stressed Credits

The concerns around evergreening lingered as banks continued to restructure unviable accounts to avoid recognition or provisioning of losses. Eventually, in April 2015, the RBI ended the ability of banks to restructure accounts without marking them as NPAs. In the meantime, it continued to provide new avenues for genuine borrowers to resolve stress.

5/25 Scheme: Banks usually lent for a maximum period of ten to twelve years. Several large infrastructure projects had cash flows spanning several decades, whereas repayments were front-loaded. This scheme allowed banks to lend up to twenty-five years with periodic refinancing at regular intervals.

Strategic Debt Restructuring (SDR): This initiative was announced in collaboration with SEBI. Under this, banks could replace promoters unable to bring in fresh equity by

---

*The Mumbai-based company had been allegedly charged in six bank fraud cases amounting to Rs 558.16 crores by the CBI in 2019.

converting their loans into equity or convertible preference shares. The banks were then required to find a new promoter within a specified period.

Scheme for Sustainable Structuring of Stressed Assets (S4A): This framework was meant for the not-so-weak promoters, who might be overleveraged in some of their projects. A sustainable debt level was to be determined and the remaining debt was to be converted into equity or quasi-equity instruments. This was supposed to provide an upside in case the project turned around successfully. Only large accounts with aggregate exposure of over ₹500 crore were eligible for this scheme.

In Rajan's own words, these initiatives created an informal out-of-court bankruptcy mechanism. These multiple schemes and frequent modifications were made necessary because of the diverse nature of businesses and sources of borrower distress. But the success of these initiatives was, at best, mixed. Some critics say that these did not work at all, as bankers continued to fear recognizing losses. They wanted a stamp of approval for their commercial decisions, which no one could give – neither the RBI nor the government.

Religare Capital analysts pointed out several negatives in these schemes. There were concerns that many of the old CDR cases got through to SDR. Banks tended to misused it to delay NPA recognition, as asset classification remained at a standstill for eighteen months. Some banks also ended up with equity ownership of bad companies. But they were unable to find new buyers for these assets. In the midst of all this, there were attempts by the government to force PSUs to acquire stakes. Another drawback was that the portion of debt converted to acquire 51 per cent equity was often minor as a percentage of the total debt, leaving unsustainably high debt levels. Being significantly higher than market capitalization, the share of debt to be converted was also smaller.[7]

Similarly, criticism of the 5/25 scheme was that it only delayed the recognition of the problem, even for projects that were clearly stressed. This scheme was used in a large number of cases where the asset was stressed and despite pushing back principal repayments, the firms were unable to meet interest obligations. Analysts also said that the initiative resulted in additional loans being given to stressed companies and the required haircut was refused by the lenders.

However, a reply in the Parliament by the government to a question on 15 December 2017 was kinder to them. The minister of state for finance Shiv Pratap Shukla suggested that the popularity of these schemes had killed CDR. 'Public Sector Banks have apprised that with introduction of other restructuring schemes like Strategic Debt Restructuring, Scheme for Sustainable Structuring of Stressed Assets, etc., CDR mechanism has lost significance and is no longer preferred,' he said.[8]

Asset Quality Review (AQR)

Before the effectiveness of these schemes could be verified, the RBI embarked upon another ambitious exercise. Banks were not following uniform procedures – a loan that was 'non-performing' in one bank could be labelled as 'performing' in others. They were not making adequate provisions for loans that had stayed NPA for a long time. The lenders were doing little to get the projects back on track and had also slowed credit growth.

The central bank wanted to get the banks to recognize NPAs on a timely basis and make provisions for them. So, a crack team of supervisors armed with data went about evaluating asset quality. It completed an Asset Quality Review in October 2015 and shared it with the banks.

The AQR covered thirty-six banks, including all PSBs, which accounted for 93 per cent of the SCBs' gross advances. The sample reviewed under AQR constituted more than 80 per cent of the total credit outstanding and 5 per cent of the number of accounts of the banking system reported through CRILC. The exercise sought to validate objective compliance of banks with applicable income recognition, asset classification and provisioning (IRACP) norms, and exceptions were reported by the supervisors as divergences in asset classification or provisioning.

The major objectives of the AQR exercise were to:

1. Examine the assessment of asset quality at the bank level and at the system level as a whole
2. Uniformly deal with cases of divergence in identifying NPAs and additional provisioning across banks
3. Ensure early finalization and communication of divergences in provisioning, giving banks sufficient time to plan the additional provisioning requirements so that they could present clean and fully provisioned balance sheets by March 2017.

The findings of the review were conveyed to the banks to affirm there was effective compliance with regulatory prescriptions. Following this, most banks recognizing NPAs and started making provisions for them. Every passing quarter, the amount of NPAs ballooned and crossed ₹10 lakh crore in 2018.

This led to some critics of the RBI accusing it of derailing the economy with AQRs. There was also speculation that this was one of the reasons Rajan did not get a two-year extension that some thought he richly deserved.

Two years after he demitted office, Rajan was called upon by a parliamentary committee to depose on the stressed assets issue. Before the Estimates Committee of the Parliament, Rajan answered two questions.[9] First, did NPA recognition slow credit and hence economic growth? Rajan said:

> Simply eye-balling the evidence suggests the claim is ludicrous, and made by people who have not done their homework.
>
> In sum, the Indian evidence, supported by the experiences from other parts of the world such as Europe and Japan, suggests that what we were seeing was classic behaviour by a banking system with balance sheet problems. We were able to identify the effects because parts of our banking system – the private banks – did not suffer as much from such problems. The obvious remedy to anyone with an open mind would be to tackle the source of the problem – to clean the balance sheets of public sector banks, a remedy that has worked well in other countries where it has been implemented. This is not a 'foreign' solution, it is an economically sensible solution. It is something that has been repeatedly flagged by the government's own Economic Survey, under the guidance of the respected Dr Arvind Subramanian. Clean up was part of the solution, not the problem.

He went on to explain the second question: Why did the NPAs continued to mount after the AQR was over?

> The AQR was meant to stop the evergreening and concealment of bad loans, and force banks to revive stalled projects. The hope was that once the mass of bad loans were disclosed, the

banks, with the aid of the government, would undertake the surgery that was necessary to put the projects back on track. Unfortunately, this process has not played out as well. As NPAs age, they require more provisioning, so projects that have not been revived simply add to the stock. A fair amount of the increase in NPAs may be due to ageing rather than as a result of a fresh lot of NPAs.

Weeks after Rajan left office in September 2016, the Insolvency and Bankruptcy Framework, which he had sought to replicate with many of his schemes, came into being.

The central bank, under its new governor Urjit Patel, got busy with the government's demonetization initiative. It returned to the NPA problem after the amendment of the Banking Regulation Act of 1949, first by an ordinance in May 2017 and then an Act in August 2017, which gave powers to direct lenders to refer stressed companies to the bankruptcy courts. Speaking at a conference 'Insolvency and Bankruptcy: Changing Paradigm', Patel said:[10]

> The size and nature of the NPA problem necessitated concomitant measures to signal intent and commitment of the Government and the Reserve Bank to meet the challenge squarely. The IBC was in place but the required action in respect of the large stressed accounts was not forthcoming on the part of banks and JLFs. Part of the inertia may have to do with the initial days of the IBC; but part of it was also the typical (and severe) agency and moral hazard problems of not resolving NPAs when the banking sector is majorly government-owned.
>
> It was to address this market failure that the need for statutory backing to the Reserve Bank to direct reference

of cases under IBC was considered necessary. The Banking Regulation (Amendment) Ordinance, 2017 empowers the RBI to issue directions to banking companies to initiate an insolvency resolution process in respect of a default, under the provisions of the IBC. It also enables the Reserve Bank to issue directions with respect to stressed assets and specify one or more authorities or committees with such members as the Bank may appoint or approve for appointment to advise banking companies on resolution of stressed assets.

With the RBI directive on twelve large accounts and a second list of twenty-five accounts, the Insolvency Framework took off in a big way. This rendered most of the schemes introduced during and prior to Rajan's tenure redundant.

On 12 February 2018, the RBI issued a circular mandating that all large accounts, where the aggregate exposure was over ₹2,000 crore, be referred for resolution under the Insolvency and Bankruptcy Code. It also wrapped up all other existing restructuring schemes in one fell swoop:

> The extant instructions on resolution of stressed assets such as Framework for Revitalising Distressed Assets, Corporate Debt Restructuring Scheme, Flexible Structuring of Existing Long Term Project Loans, Strategic Debt Restructuring Scheme (SDR), Change in Ownership outside SDR, and Scheme for Sustainable Structuring of Stressed Assets (S4A) stand withdrawn with immediate effect.[11]

Even the Joint Lenders' Forum as an institutional mechanism for resolution was wound up. 'All accounts, including such accounts where any of the schemes have been invoked but not yet implemented, shall be governed by the revised framework,' the circular added.

Seventeen years after faithfully serving Indian lenders and debtors, shutters were downed on the CDR Cell. Staying true to the RBI's penchant for confidentiality, the entire website of *CDRindia.org*, which had become a repository of considerable data about the process over the years, vanished from the internet one fine morning. The URL was then taken over by a pornographic website.

In reply to a parliament query in March 2020, Nirmala Sitharaman listed measures taken by the government.

> A number of steps have been taken by the Government to recover loans advanced, which include, inter-alia, the following: (1) Change in credit culture has been effected, with the Insolvency and Bankruptcy Code (IBC) fundamentally changing the creditor–borrower relationship, taking away control of the defaulting company from promoters/owners and debarring wilful defaulters from the resolution process and debarring them from raising funds from the market. (2) The Securitisation and Reconstruction of Financial Assets and Enforcement of Security Interest Act, 2002 has been amended to make it more effective, with provision for three months' imprisonment in case the borrower does not provide asset details, and for the lender to get possession of mortgaged property within 30 days. (3) Suits for recovery of dues are also filed by banks before Debts Recovery Tribunals (DRTs). Six new DRTs have been established to expedite recovery. (4) Key reforms have been instituted as part of the Public Sector Banks Reforms Agenda, including, inter-alia, the following: (i) Monitoring has been strictly segregated from sanctioning

roles in high-value loans, and specialised monitoring agencies combining financial and domain knowledge have been deployed for effective monitoring of loans above ₹250 crore. (ii) To ensure timely and better realisation in one-time settlements (OTSs), online end-to-end OTS platforms have been setup.[12]

The central bank is constantly improving rules for big loans, tracking their use and repayment. It has also helped set up new organizations to handle specific needs. But there are two main changes that will have significant influence in the long term.

First, the decades-old idea of a bad bank suggested by the Narasimham Committee is now a reality. To tackle this, the government formed two entities, National Asset Reconstruction Company Ltd (NARCL) and India Debt Resolution Company Ltd (IDRCL). Introduced in the 2021 Union Budget, their goal is to handle and resolve NPAs in the banking industry. The NARCL, a government body created in July 2021, which is mainly controlled by public sector banks, and by some private banks, with Canara Bank as the sponsor. It is registered with the RBI as an asset reconstruction company.

Second, the government formed the National Bank for Financing Infrastructure and Development (NABFID) to support long-term infrastructure financing needs. This specialized bank can understand the sector's unique needs, create the right tools and build project monitoring skills to ease pressure on the banking sector. The RBI, in its letter dated 8 March 2022, stated that NABFID will operate as an AIFI under its regulation and supervision.[13]

19

The Sell-off Struggle

M. S. Sahoo, the lean, bespectacled first chief of IBBI was fond of quoting the American author Ernest Hemingway. In his 1926 novel *The Sun Also Rises*, one of the characters asks, 'How did you go bankrupt?' The other one answers, 'Two ways. Gradually, then suddenly.'[1]

Sahoo believed that this was how the bankruptcy reforms also unfolded in our country – gradually and then suddenly. Though discussions and proposals began in the early 1990s, the new regime suddenly came into being on an October morning in 2016.

One limitation of several committees that came before the latest Bankruptcy Law Committee headed by former bureaucrat T. K. Vishwanathan was that they were not accompanied by a draft law. Vishwanathan himself once quipped that it surely wasn't an esoteric or overly complicated exercise. The committee under him identified fourteen laws that needed to be repealed and pointed out the Companies Act provisions that were necessary to amend and manage to draft a bill, with some 214 clauses, which was passed by the Parliament in May 2016.

Within a few months, Vishwanathan's old colleague and partner-in-crime in developing the dematerialization framework for the stock markets, Sahoo, was handpicked to lead this similar reform. When things happen suddenly, the ecosystem is often caught unawares. Sahoo was appointed in October 2016 as the first chairman of IBBI. However, he was the only person to be appointed. He did not even have a personal assistant or an office to work from. Initially, he worked out of a room in the office of the Institute of Cost and Management Accountants of India (ICMAI) on Lodhi Road in New Delhi. On occasional visits, one could see some young law students helping him out. But he had a deadline to meet. By the next two months, he was supposed to prepare out the entire set of regulations that would govern the insolvency and bankruptcy regime. Sahoo sought help from the law ministry, but they were tied up with their own problems and did not have resources to spare. Even as Sahoo went about hiring his team, he served as an adviser on two high-profile committees addressing key finance issues.

The advisory committees of this new board had economists as well as industry professionals, banking, securities market, professional bodies and legal experts. Under the leadership of former Infosys executive Mohandas Pai and Kotak Mahindra Bank's Vice Chairman and Managing Director, Uday Kotak, the panels quickly got to work.

Pai, formerly the Infosys chief financial officer and chairman of Manipal Global Education, headed the nine-member advisory panel on service providers. In marathon meetings in the capital in November 2016, the panel deliberated on key issues and helped the regulator finalize regulation to govern the various aspects concerning it and service providers who would manage the process. The committees spent two full days in the city in order to chisel out the final structure. The draft regulation that ran into 15,000 words was brought down to less than a third of its size, improving clarity. In the process, the new regulator IBBI set a record of sorts. Less than two months into its life, it had already notified several salient rules governing the corporate insolvency framework. Most other regulators in the country did not even come close, with some old timers claiming that none of them managed to notify their first regulation before completing two years.

Vidhi Centre for Legal Policy – a Delhi-based think-tank run by lawyer Arghya Sengupta, which has gained prominence in the policy circles under the NDA government – contributed to the drafting of the regulations. Vidhi had former bureaucrats, businessmen and prominent lawyers among its patrons and board members. It received funding from Tata Trusts, Pirojsha Godrej Foundation, Rohini Nilekani, Arvind Datar and Kiran Mazumdar Shaw, among others.

You can lead a horse to the water, but you can't make it drink. For nearly six months, the public sector banks, the biggest horses of the insolvency market, were not drinking from the code. Between January and May 2017, most cases under the new law were initiated by operational creditors, usually people who had traded with the defaulting company. Asset reconstruction companies, such as Edelweiss, brought forth one or two large cases, but the public sector banks were largely quiet.

The Government of India amended the Banking Regulation Act of 1949 and empowered the central bank to give directions to other banks in order to refer cases to the NCLT. Following this, the RBI issued a directive asking banks to move the twelve large NPAs to insolvency and bankruptcy proceedings.

The Many Battles of Essar

Almost immediately, the move by the RBI faced a challenge. Essar Steel filed a Special Civil Application in the Gujarat high court. It challenged the proceedings initiated by Standard Chartered in the Ahmedabad bench, arguing that the company was discriminated against by the RBI and lenders since they had given other defaulters six months to come up with a restructuring plan. The high court stayed NCLT hearings at on the matter pending disposal of the case.

The loss caused to the company as a result of reduction in gas supply was one of the chief reasons for reduction in production and resultant inability to make payment to the lenders, Essar contended, describing the RBI action as 'hostile, arbitrary and unreasonable'.

The central bank had to amend a portion of its circular, where it said that these twelve cases would be accorded priority in the NCLT proceedings, but the proceedings themselves were allowed to continue. In July, the NCLT duly admitted the proceedings against Essar Steel.

When the time for inviting bids came, the Ruia family did something interesting. A Mauritius-based company called Numetal submitted a resolution plan for Essar Steel:

> Numetal was incorporated on 13.10.2017 by Shri Rewant Ruia, son of Ravi Ruia (who was a promoter of the corporate debtor of ESIL), with the specific objective of trying to acquire ESIL. At the time of its incorporation, one 'Aurora Enterprises Limited' (hereinafter referred to as 'AEL'), a Ruia Group Company, held 100 % shareholding of Numetal. In turn AEL's 100 % shareholding was held by one 'Aurora Holdings Limited' (hereinafter referred to as 'AHL'), 100 % of whose shareholding was held by Shri Rewant Ruia, who was a former director of the corporate debtor, i.e., ESIL. On 18.10.2017, AEL transferred 26.1 % of its shares in Numetal

to one 'Essar Communications Limited' (hereinafter referred to as 'ECL'), a group company. On 19.10.2017 Shri Rewant Ruia settled an irrevocable discretionary trust, called the 'Crescent Trust', which purchased the shares of AHL at par value. On 20.10.2017, when Numetal submitted its expression of interest, it had two shareholders, i.e., AEL (holding 73.9%) and ECL (holding 26.1%).[2]

This was just a few weeks before the crucial state assembly elections in Gujarat in 2018. The Opposition had been turning the heat on the Narendra Modi government for its closeness to business houses, with jibes like *'suit boot ki sarkar'* gaining popularity.

The First Amendment to the Code

On 22 November 2017, the finance minister made a statement that the code would be amended in order to prevent unscrupulous individuals from submitting resolution plans. Section 29A was introduced into the IBC.[3] Many thought that Essar was the primary trigger and the target of this hurried amendment brought in through an ordinance, as the Parliament was not in session, but the section covered a wider array of cases. It listed persons who would not be eligible to submit a resolution plan:

> 29A. A person shall not be eligible to submit a resolution plan, if such person, or any other person acting jointly or in concert with such person
> (a) is an undischarged insolvent;
> (b) is a wilful defaulter in accordance with the guidelines of the Reserve Bank of India issued under the Banking Regulation Act, 1949;

(c) has an account, or an account of a corporate debtor under the management or control of such person or of whom such person is a promoter, classified as non-performing asset in accordance with the guidelines of the Reserve Bank of India issued under the Banking Regulation Act, 1949 and at least a period of one year has lapsed from the date of such classification till the date of commencement of the corporate insolvency resolution process of the corporate debtor: Provided that the person shall be eligible to submit a resolution plan if such person makes payment of all overdue amounts with interest thereon and charges relating to non-performing asset accounts before submission of resolution plan;
(d) has been convicted for any offence punishable with imprisonment for two years or more;
(e) is disqualified to act as a director under the Companies Act, 2013;
(f) is prohibited by the Securities and Exchange Board of India from trading in securities or accessing the securities markets;
(g) has been a promoter or in the management or control of a corporate debtor in which a preferential transaction, undervalued transaction, extortionate credit transaction or fraudulent transaction has taken place and in respect of which an order has been made by the Adjudicating Authority under this Code;
(h) has executed an enforceable guarantee in favour of a creditor in respect of a corporate debtor against which an application for insolvency resolution made by such creditor has been admitted under this Code;

(i) has been subject to any disability, corresponding to clauses (a) to (h), under any law in a jurisdiction outside India; or

(j) has a connected person not eligible under clauses (a) to (i).

Connected person has been defined as:

(i) any person who is the promoter or in the management or control of the resolution applicant; or

(ii) any person who shall be the promoter or in management or control of the business of the corporate debtor during the implementation of the resolution plan; or

(iii) the holding company, subsidiary company, associate company or related party of a person referred to in clauses (i) and (ii). Provided that nothing in clause (iii) of this Explanation shall apply to (A) a scheduled bank; or (B) an asset reconstruction company registered with the Reserve Bank of India under section 3 of the Securitisation and Reconstruction of Financial Assets and Enforcement of Security Interest Act, 2002; or (C) an Alternate Investment Fund registered with the Securities and Exchange Board of India.

One of the core objectives of Section 29A was to ensure that the promoter of the corporate debtor should not, directly or through circular means, come back in order to regain the company that he himself had run to the ground. This was further emphasized in the finance minister's statement on 29 December 2017, while introducing the Bill to amend the code by adding Section 29A, together with the statements of objects and reasons, to the Bill.

There was not much consultation that preceded the introduction of this section, and several lawyers who were a part of the drafting of the law were aghast at its draconian nature.

But Some Bankers Were Not Complaining

The subsection (c) of the new amended section seemed to give new teeth to the bankers. When read with the definition of connected persons and clause on persons acting in concert, it cast a very wide net. In a closely knit community like the promoters of Indian steel companies, it proved to be a double-edged sword for the bidders. For example, ArcelorMittal, which was bidding for Essar Steel, had to shell out over ₹7,000 crore to settle the dues of Uttam Galva Steel, which had been declared an NPA by the lenders. There were several other pitfalls, too.

Perhaps the wide sweep of these provisions was not fully realized when the ordinance was hurriedly pushed through. Several smaller resolution plans where the promoter was often the only person interested in getting the company back on its feet were affected.

One senior lawyer described 29A as a prescription for a 'bloodbath' as it went against the fundamental tenets of the law that was intended to release the assets and stick funds back into the economy for productive uses.

Numetal Goes Russian

On the same day of Finance Minister Jaitley's announcement on 22 November 2017, AEL sold 13.9 per cent of its shares in Numetal, while ECL transferred its entire 26.1 per cent shareholding to a company called Crinium Bay Holdings Ltd. It is a subsidiary of VTB Bank, a Russian company majority-owned by the Russian government.[4]

Essar Group had a previous relationship with VTB. When Essar Oil, the group's oil refinery venture, was sold to Rosneft, the Russian bank had a key role to play. Not only did it finance the deal, it also helped Essar with a $330 million credit line so that it could delist its shares from the stock market.

Crinium Bay Holdings acquired a 40 per cent shareholding in Numetal. AEL later transferred 25.1 per cent of its shares to Indo International Trading FZCO, a Dubai-based company, and 9.9 per cent of its shares to JSC VO Tyazhpromexport, a Russian company. As a result, AEL's shareholding in Numetal decreased to 25 per cent. Eventually, on 29 March 2018, AEL completely divested its remaining 25 per cent shareholding, leaving Crinium Bay with 40 per cent, TPE with 25.9 per cent and Indo with 34.1 per cent ownership in Numetal, while AEL's stake reduced to zero. After disputes in the tribunals, the matter reached the bench of Rohinton Nariman and Indu Malhotra of the Supreme Court.

Rival lawyers argued before the SC:

Numetal was impacted by Section 29A of the code due to the restrictions on VTB Bank's access to securities markets. This affected Numetal's eligibility under various sub-sections of Section 29A. Additionally, Crinium Bay, as a subsidiary of VTB Bank, qualified as a 'connected person' under 29A. The financial contribution made by AEL to Numetal raised concerns about the ongoing involvement of Shri Rewant Ruia in the resolution plan. Based on these factors, the eligibility of AMIPL and Numetal was called into question. However, the Supreme

Court order said Numetal would become eligible if it settled its NPAs with the banking system. Following this, the committee of creditors approved a plan submitted by ArcelorMittal, which included an upfront payment of ₹39,500 crore.

But the Ruias were not done yet. They sprang a surprise by offering to pay over ₹54,000 crore, paying creditors in full. The matter was now back before NCLT Ahmedabad to decide whether this offer would be considered. Bankers working on the case felt that the matter would take months to be resolved as it would go all the way to the Supreme Court again. Finally, in April 2021, ArcelorMittal's resolution plan was approved by the apex court.

Homebuyers of Jaypee Infratech

The Jaypee Infratech (JIL) case brought to the fore a lacuna in the code, which did not define the creditors' status as financial or operational. In fact, there was not even any clarity on whether they could file their claims as creditors.

Until 16 August 2017, the IBC recognized three categories of creditors for the purposes of an IRP – financial creditors, operational creditors and employees and workmen of the corporate debtor. Under the IBC, financial creditors included banks or other financial institutions or persons who had been provided loans or other form of debts to the corporate debtor. Operational creditors were entities that provided goods or services to a corporate debtor. In other words, the term 'operational debt' was held under the IBC to not include any advance paid by a purchaser of goods or recipient of services. Such a purchaser was therefore precluded from initiating IRP against the corporate debtor.

On 16 August 2017, a fourth category of 'other creditors', that is those who were neither financial nor operational creditors, was introduced by the Insolvency and Bankruptcy Board. However, this did not help matters much, as there were concerns about the position of homebuyers vis-à-vis bankers. So Chitra Sharma, the former air hostess from Gurgaon moved the Supreme Court,[5] questioning the constitutional validity of the law. As other homebuyers jumped on to implead themselves, the establishment got into a tizzy.

The Second Amendment to the Code

The Supreme Court initially stayed the insolvency resolution proceedings of JIL to protect the interests of the homebuyers. It subsequently allowed the process to continue, subject to the condition that an interim resolution professional would submit an interim resolution plan within forty-five days, incorporating all necessary measures for protecting the interests of the homebuyers. The Supreme Court issued this order under Article 142, which vests in it the power to pass any order as is necessary for doing complete justice in any cause or matter pending before it. The matter was referred back to the Insolvency Law Committee, which proposed that the homebuyers be classified as financial creditors. This led to a second amendment to the code in 2019. With this, even a single homebuyer could trigger the code and drag errant realtors to the NCLT.

Jaypee's case continued to take bizarre twists and turns. After nearly a year in the Supreme Court, the matter was referred back to the NCLT with instructions that the committee of creditors be formed afresh and include the homebuyers. But there was no clarity on the mechanism to adequately represent the interests of homebuyers in a Committee of Creditors set-up. The matter was further complicated by 'ghost homebuyers', who did not come forward to disclose their identities before the resolution professionals, leading to a lingering doubt that many of them could be influential people or their associates, who had either received these flats as kickbacks or had used them to park unaccounted money.

Meanwhile, Sharma had moved a petition to modify the SC order, citing that it did not provide clarity on whether the homebuyers were 'secured' or 'unsecured' creditors. This would be key in a liquidation scenario, as the secured creditors would be positioned ahead in the sequence of payments.

Two rounds of resolution plans were considered, but after several rounds of legal battles, the Supreme Court finally said that a plan had to be chosen from the ones offered by National Building Construction Corp (NBCC) or Suraksha Realty. In March 2020, over thirty months after it was admitted to the insolvency process, the NCLT gave its nod to a resolution plan submitted by state-owned NBCC. It also directed that the ₹750 crore submitted to the Supreme Court registry by Jaypee Infratech's parent group be included in the resolution plan, thus bringing relief to the homebuyers. However, it allowed certain modifications sought by ICICI Bank and Yamuna Expressway Industrial Development Authority.

Now, these modifications became an issue of contention as the NBCC moved the appellate tribunal, challenging the NCLT powers to alter the resolution plan approved by a Committee of Creditors. After almost two years, the Suraksha Group's offer was approved by the NCLT in March 2023. Nearly 20,000 homebuyers received closure after close to six years of struggle.

Cases Going into Liquidation

While Jaypee has a fresh hope resolution from the state-owned NBCC's resolution plan, the sword of liquidation hangs on ABG Shipyard and Lanco infratech.

By December 2019, three years since the IBC came into force, 3,312 resolution plans had commenced. Of these, 246 have been closed on appeal or review or settled, 135 have been withdrawn, 190 have resulted in approval of resolution plans and 780 have ended in liquidation. In FY2023, the NCLT approved 180 resolution plans out of 1,255 applications from creditors for initiating CIRP. So far, the tribunal has approved a total of 678 resolution plans.[6] From the perspective of the insolvency framework, liquidation is seen as the worst outcome. In a liquidation scenario, jobs are lost and assets are usually purchased for their scrap value, sometime only for the land holdings.

Officials say the high number of liquidation has to be taken with a pinch of salt, as several of these were age-old cases pending in the DRT itself and were transferred to the NCLT for closure.

Even among the 'dirty dozen', for Alok industries, which was picked up by a consortium of JM and Reliance Industries, the amount recovered was barely above the liquidation value. Some of the private lenders on the Committee of Creditors were not agreeable to this proposal, rendering it stuck as it could not get the mandatory 75 per cent nod.

Against the liquidation value of ₹4,200 crore, the Reliance alliance had initially offered ₹4,950 crore on 11 April 2018 and then slightly increased the offer to ₹5,050 crore in the second round on 13 April. The resolution plans failed to manage the mandatory 75 per cent support.

The offer of ₹5,050 crore translated into an 83 per cent haircut on dues of ₹29,500 crore. After the deadline of 270 days was over, the resolution professional of the textile company filed the petition for liquidation with the tribunal. However, the second amendment to the Insolvency Code brought down the threshold for approval to 66 per cent from the earlier 75 per cent. The tribunal asked the CoC to consider the issue afresh, taking into account the change in law. With 72 per cent of the lenders approving the plan, Alok went to Reliance. But the proceedings were not over as two of the dissenting lenders, Kotak Mahindra and the debt-ridden McNally Sayaji Engineering Ltd's director moved the appellate tribunal out of fear that they would not be given equal treatment in the resolution process because they had dissented.

In the matter of Jyoti Structures, a group of 800 employees and a group of investors led by Sharad Sanghi challenged the liquidation plan ordered by the NCLT for the Mumbai-based tower contractor that owed over ₹7,000 crore. Sanghi had initially submitted a resolution plan that offered an upfront payment of ₹170 crore and a loan repayment spread over a fifteen-year timeframe. But the plan did not find any favour with the lenders.

Later, an application was filed stating that some of the bidders who could not participate due to some technical glitches wanted to bid again. Though the creditors were ready to reconsider, the matter had already gone to the NCLT, which ordered the liquidation. The appellate body allowed Sanghi's plan and it was eventually cleared by the Supreme Court in 2019.

Adjudication Infrastructure

This never-ending sequence of appeals and arguments placed the adjudication infrastructure comprising eleven benches of the NCLT and the appellate body in Delhi under severe stress. In fact, in one of its orders in the Binani Cements case – a landmark NCLAT case from 2018 that contributed to the jurisprudence under IBC – the NCLT criticized the RP and CoC for not exercising their judgement by using various resources available at their disposal.[7] It has been often noticed that in cases where high stakes are involved with deep-pocketed bidders and promoters facing off, the RP tries to play safe by seeking the NCLT stamp of approval on each decision. This in turn creates further litigation, as each interlocutory order then becomes a cause of action for the aggrieved party and is taken through the entire appeals process up to the Supreme Court.

With large cases running against time taking up the limited capacity of the tribunals, company law cases and other regular admissions of bankruptcy matters have been held up. According to bankers, as many as 300 cases are awaiting admission across various benches.

In other instances, there were scores of cases where resolution plans have been approved by the NCLT but have been pending in the NCLAT for hearing. A situation similar to that of the DRT or DRAT process is emerging and a plan for more benches of the NCLAT is also under implementation.

In a statement to the Parliamentary Estimates Committee on bank NPAs in September 2018, Raghuram Rajan wrote:

> The Bankruptcy Code is being tested by the large promoters, with continuous and sometimes frivolous appeals. It is very important that the integrity of the process be maintained, and bankruptcy resolution be speedy, without the promoter inserting a bid by an associate at the auction, and acquiring

the firm at a bargain-basement price. Given our conditions, the promoter should have every chance of concluding a deal before the firm goes to auction, but not after. Higher courts must resist the temptation to intervene routinely in these cases, and appeals must be limited once points of law are settled.[8]

This view was echoed in the judiciary as well. During the hearing of the Essar Steel matter, the bench constituted by Nariman and Malhotra observed that the role of the NCLT and NCLAT should come only after the resolution process is finalized and their 'jumping in' when the proceedings are going on before the resolution professional and CoC is like halting the process. 'They are not supervisory authority to see what is happening, who was invited, who was not. The adjudicating authorities can look into the whole thing including if it is in accordance with the law after the resolution process is finalised,' the bench said.

During the discussion over the Appellate Tribunal asking ArcelorMittal to clear the ₹7,000 crore liability towards Uttam Galva and KSS Petron under the provisions of Section 29A (c), 'Here everything is wrong, from top to bottom. Adjudication is wrong,' the bench observed.[9]

Operational Creditors

One of the fallouts of such a significant resolution is its impact on the ecosystem in which these companies operate. Of late, concerns have been raised by this ecosystem, often represented in the form of operational creditors in the insolvency process, that the CoC does not take their interests into account while deciding the resolution plan.

In Bhushan Steel's case, engineering and construction major L&T failed to recover its dues of over ₹900 crore, despite several attempts at the tribunals. In the matter of the landmark Binani Cements case, the operational creditors even served legal notice to Vijaykumar Iyer, the RP, for discriminating against them. However, the RP himself had limited say and was guided by the committee of creditors, who were essentially bankers.

The conduct of the bankers on these committees have been a cause for concern for regulators and policymakers. The lawmakers' rationale for handing over the steering wheel to these financial creditors was that they were in a better position to appraise the business of the company and could arrive at a solution keeping in mind the interests of all stakeholders. But bankers have fallen short of these expectations by miles in the first years. Emphasizing this in an IBBI newsletter, M. S. Sahoo wrote:

> The CoC has a statutory role. It discharges a public function. It can even write off dues of the stakeholders. It must, therefore, apply the highest standards of duty of care. It must not only follow the due process, but also be fair towards all the stakeholders and transparent in discharge of its responsibilities.[10]

He further added that the resolution plan is affected due to the CoC using an assessment system. When the system disregards the claims of operational creditors, the resolution applicant won't provide any value for them. Likewise, if it disregards the importance of improved operations, the resolution applicant won't offer better technology. The CoC needs to create the assessment system in a way that enables resolution plans that take into account the interests of all stakeholders of the company in a fair and equitable manner, while maximizing the firm's asset value. Several operational creditors also moved the Supreme Court challenging the way the CoC was structured. The court was sympathetic to their pleas and observed that some of the provisions in the code were arbitrary and needed a review. But there is a fear that this could open a Pandora's box and affect the ability of the bankers to guide the resolution process effectively. Further, there are some arguments based on principles of risk, claiming that unsecured and operational creditors have knowingly taken a higher degree of risk than the secured creditors and they should not try to alter this and seek a level playing field after things have turned bad.

Another concern voiced by bankers is that many of the operational creditors happen to be parties related to the promoter or key executives of the defaulting company. If a blanket provision is introduced to allow voting rights for operational creditors, this could amount to allowing a backdoor entry for the erstwhile promoters.

For example, over 1,900 entities submitted claims totalling over ₹27,000 crore as claims under the operational creditors category. There were claims ranging from a few lakh rupees to thousands of crores. The largest claim came from Essar Steel Jharkhand, which said Essar Steel owed it ₹2,498 crore.

But the RP rejected the claims on account of insufficient stamp duty. Several other large claims have been admitted, though. These include Essar Bulk Terminal (₹703 crore), Essar Project India (₹639 crore), Essar Bulk Terminal Paradip (₹335 crore) and Essar Power Hazira (₹126 crore). It is not clear how many of the other operational creditors, who do not have Essar in their names, are related to the Ruias. Many of them rushed to the Appellate Tribunal when ArcelorMittal's proposal was cleared by the NCLAT.

Winning Bidders Unable to Pay

While many bidders negotiate legal hurdles before being able to acquire new assets, one successful bidder set a new record of not paying up after winning the bid. Liberty House, a London-based group led by mercurial investor Sanjeev Gupta, placed a ₹4,400 crore plan for Amtek Auto. Though this was only slightly better than the liquidation value of ₹4,119 crore, the offer was preferred by lenders over the one proposed by American hedge fund Deccan Value Investors LP.

Gupta, whose company is associated with the broader GFG Alliance, has spoken about the so-called green metal model. A *Financial Times* article explains it as follows:

> The model advocates using renewable energy to power furnaces and smelters that recycle locally-sourced scrap, with the finished metal then fed to manufacturing businesses that produce high-value components and goods. The idea is to make the entire process environmentally and economically sustainable, by creating a virtuous loop that reduces waste, pollution and costs.[11]

To this end, Gupta had placed bids for the firm Adhunik Metaliks* (which also he won but was unable to pay), ABG Shipyard and Bhushan Power & Steel. It was during the evaluation of the ₹18,500 crore bid made to Bhushan Power that Gupta's funding plans came under a closer scrutiny and he was eventually thrown out.

---

* An alloy, special and construction steel manufacturing company based in Odisha, that was ordered for liquidation by the NCLT in 2019.

Subsequently, it turned out that Liberty was unable to pay for Amtek, for which it had bid successfull. The debacle created a new headache for the regulators and the resolution applicants to deal with. The little-tested penal provisions of the IBC were put to test in Liberty's case. In March 2019, the winning bidder was allowed to withdraw its bid and the next approval was received in December 2021 by Deccan Value Investor LP-based hedge fund, giving them a four-week deadline to bring the RP to fruition and complete the payments.[12]

Disappearing Funds and Other Irregularities

Over the course of the 180 days with the company, the resolution professional gets a fair sense what the earlier promoter had done with the books of accounts. According to different accounts, nine or ten of the 'dirty dozen' saw their RPs smelling a rat. The RPs then recommended forensic audit or reported irregularities to the tribunals.

Here is a sample from a forensic audit of one of large companies, which showed various ways in which promoters siphon funds from their companies:

1. Sales to potentially related or connected parties without adequate collection of receivables, resulting in diversion of funds
2. End use of funds for loans and advances given and the interest foregone
3. Diversion of funds through sales at preferential prices
4. Netting off customer receivables through various accounting charges
5. Raw material procured at higher rates

6. Preferential freight to related party
7. No fixed assets created against prior capital advances
8. Inadequate documentation for expenses and write offs.

In the case referred to above, hundreds of crores were diverted under each of these heads. Similar irregularities have been reported across several companies which have been under resolution for the past few years. It is widely believed that many of the companies where the resolution is at an early stage, more such cases will be detected. Already, the value of fraudulent transactions reported amounts to over ₹50,000 crore. In fact, in May 2023, RBI reported ₹1,750 crores in payment frauds in just seven months during the April–September period of 2022–23.[13] The look-back period ranges between one and two years for these companies, depending on their nature. One can imagine the kind of amounts that could be dug up if the investigators decided to go further back in time.

In a disturbing trend, either these matters have not come up before tribunals or other adjudicating authorities, such as special courts, or have been deliberately kept pending. One reason being cited is that the focus is on resolution and proceedings against the errant promoters could disturb the proceedings. However, there is also a conflict of interest which could be coming in the way of effective pursuance of these matters. The RP reports to a committee of creditors dominated by bankers. There is an apprehension that investigations could lead back to the bank itself regarding failure to follow banking rules and faulty due diligence. Hence, the lack of action against the promoters.

The government is said to be preparing standard operating procedures for reporting and handling of these cases.

Foreign Concerns

As stated earlier, the NCLT approved 180 resolution plans out of 1,255 applications in FY 2023. So far, the NCLT has approved a total of 678 resolution plans. But, there are concerns that there is not much interest from large distress funds and private equity investors from abroad in these assets. The government and regulators have conducted a couple of roadshows in the US and Europe. Feedback from foreign investors has revealed that they believe the process needs to be more certain. Lawyers who have been a part of the process say that the investors are seeking the kind of specificity one would see in a bilateral deal. For example, the investors do not want to have uncertainties such as the cancellation of concession agreement. In an infrastructure company, the only real asset is the concession agreement. If this gets cancelled after the fund takes over the company, then the investor would be left with nothing.

Another insufficiency in the code is the lack of framework in the cross-border insolvency. A committee has put up the proposal, which needs to be taken to the Parliament in the form of a bill, following which bilateral or multilateral agreements have to be entered into with different countries.

Twin Blows of the Supreme Court

IBC, since its inception, has gone repeatedly through legislative scrutiny and various significant amendments have been made to the code. Two judgments of the apex court in 2019 were keenly watched and turned out to be game changers for the young code. The year was a critical period for testing its constitutionality. A total of ten writ petitions and one special leave petition were filed, challenging its constitutional validity. Several issues were raised and on 25 January 2019, the Supreme Court delivered a verdict on this group of petitions in the case of *Swiss Ribbons Private Limited & Anr. vs Union of India*.[14] The Supreme Court bench of Rohinton Nariman and Navin Sinha gave a big boost to the code, upholding its constitutional validity. The judges also gave a glowing report of its performance in the closing paragraph of the judgment: 'We are happy to note that in the working of the Code, the flow of financial resource to the commercial sector in India has increased exponentially as a result of financial debts being repaid.'[15]

This judgment provided clarity on several contentious issues, such as the treatment of operational creditors, validity of Section 29 and the functioning of adjudicating authorities of NCLT and NCLAT.

'The defaulter's paradise is lost. In its place, the economy's rightful position has been regained,' the bench observed.

However, the paradise regained was only short-lived, at least for the bankers and the RBI.

In a separate judgment, on 2 April 2019, the bench of Nariman set aside the 12 February 2018 circular of the RBI, calling it unconstitutional. In its 12 February circular, the central bank had asked lenders to institute a board-approved policy for the resolution of stressed assets of ₹2,000 crore or more.

Under previous guidelines, lenders had the freedom to initiate the resolution process after sixty days of default. However, this circular mandated action on T+1 (the day after the default).

The circular had cancelled all other resolution mechanisms available such as CDR, SDR and S4A. It became a serious weapon in the banks' armour, which was used for over a year to bring promoters to the negotiation table. Thousands of cases were being settled outside the NCLT framework, as promoters rushed to pay up before they lost grip over their companies.

While the judgment came as a relief to several businesses, particularly the power, sugar and fertilizer companies that were distressed largely because of government policies, it evoked fears that the entire resolution process would be thrown into disarray.

Questions were also raised about the cases which had been initiated on the basis of these circulars. Even as the RBI was toying with the idea of a new circular, the IBBI clarified that the cases already admitted to the resolution process based on the order would continue, as the NCLT accepted cases only if it was sure of the default, irrespective of any circular.

'I think the proceedings are admitted by the NCLT on being satisfied of default, not whether it was initiated by the direction of somebody. The test is whether there is default or not. IBC proceeding is admitted if there is a default,' M. S. Sahoo, told IANS, implying that the cases admitted due to the RBI order would continue as the NCLT found default.[16]

'IBC proceeding is admitted if there is a default. NCLT would have satisfied itself that there was a default … NCLT does not consider whether SBI came and applied on its own or on the direction of somebody else,' he added.

The Road Ahead

Despite these roadblocks and difficulties, five of the 'dirty dozen' cases – Essar Steel, Bhushan Steel, Monnet Ispat, Electrosteel and Alok Industries – have been resolved, which has led to the recovery of about ₹96,000 crore for the banking system. Senior bankers say they have not seen such a recovery in a long time. This is, perhaps, the largest haul since the Sick Industrial Companies Act (SICA)* in 1986.

By 2020, three years since the process was kickstarted with the move to amend the RBI Act, the banks were expected to have seen ₹1.25 lakh crore of recovery.

The 2018 *Swiss Ribbons Pvt. Ltd. and Anr. vs the Union of India and Ors* judgment dealt with the constitutional validity of the IBC that had been challenged through ten writ petitions to the apex court in 2019. The landmark judgment gave one of the most detailed assessments of the code as follows:[17]

> Approximately 3300 cases have been disposed of by the Adjudicating Authority based on out-of-court settlements between corporate debtors and creditors which themselves involved claims amounting to over INR 1,20,390 crores. Eighty cases have since been resolved by resolution plans being accepted. Of these eighty cases, the liquidation value of sixty-three such cases is INR 29,788.07 crores. However, the amount realized from the resolution process is in the region of INR 60,000 crores, which is over 202% of the liquidation value. As a result of this, the Reserve Bank of India has come out with figures which reflect these results. Thus, credit that has been given by banks and financial institutions to the commercial sector (other than food) has jumped up from INR 4,952.24 crores in 2016–2017, to INR 9,161.09 crores in 2017–150 2018, and to INR 13,195.20 crores for the first six months of 2018–2019. Equally, credit flow from non-banks has gone up

---

*An Indian law enacted to detect unviable ('sick') companies that could pose systematic financial risk.

from INR 6819.93 crores in 2016–2017, to INR 4,718 crores for the first six months of 2018–2019. Ultimately, the total flow of resources to the commercial sector in India, both bank and non-bank, and domestic and foreign (relatable to the non-food sector) has gone up from a total of INR 14,530.47 crores in 2016–2017, to INR 18,469.25 crores in 2017–2018, and to INR 18,798.20 crores in the first six months of 2018–2019. These figures show that the experiment conducted in enacting the Code is proving to be largely successful.

There are certain concerns around seventy-eight cases, where the plan has been approved but delays have persisted, as with Amtek Auto. The government has been pointing out an equal amount has been realized as companies have approached banks to settle dues.

In an update in March 2020 to the parliamentary standing committee on finance, the Ministry of Corporate Affairs said:[18]

As on 30th November 2019 around 13,210 cases have been disposed under IBC. Around 190 cases involving claims around ₹3.67 lakh crore were resolved with a realizable amount of around of around ₹1.57 lakh crore. Around 11,366 cases involving claims around ₹4.74 lakh crore were disposed prior to admission. The realizable amount with respect to ₹4.74 lakh crore is not available but even if we make a conservative estimate it would be around ₹2 lakh crore. In other words, out of claims of around ₹8.4 lakh crore (₹4.74 lakh crore + ₹3.67 lakh crore), the realizable amount is around ₹3.57 lakh crore (around 43%). Also, the average time taken for resolution has now come to about 394 days.

In August 2021, Corporate Affairs Secretary Rajesh Verma stated that the pre-admission stage of the insolvency law had resulted in the resolution of over 17,800 cases involving an amount of ₹5.5 lakh crore until July that year.[19] Emphasizing the data regarding the number of cases and their status under the IBC, he also highlighted that the disposal of 17,837 cases at the pre-admission stage demonstrates the positive impact and shift in behaviour brought about by the code.

'We have a tendency in past, while searching for a solution we create a problem. We create a further problem in search of half-baked solutions,' then Finance Minister Arun Jaitley had said in 2018.[20] He added that the government was looking to make further changes to the code as the provisions related to related parties were not taking into account cases where people might be related but had parted ways, with the businesses operating separately for years.

Jaitley took ill soon after and passed away in August 2019. His protégé and successor, Nirmala Sitharaman, has since brought in the necessary changes, including the latest amendments in March 2020, which protect successful bidders of insolvent companies from risk of criminal offences committed by previous promoters.

As the code becomes increasingly complex with judicial pronouncements and new areas coming in, Sahoo says the road to success is always under construction. Though things will keep evolving, he feels that the IBC has turned what was a hopeless end for the bankers and companies into one of endless hope.

That, of course, was before a deadly virus from the wet markets of Wuhan began its globe-altering journey.

Epilogue

Three years have flown by from the point where the book ends. Much of the first two were wiped out because of the debilitating Covid-19 pandemic. The third has been spent in rebuilding the economy. However, this process has been disrupted by the war in Ukraine and inflationary pressures it put on the global economy. As countries struggled to keep prices low, interest rates went up, triggering a sluggishness in economic activities.

The post-Covid surge in demand had led to a favourable commodity cycle for many players in the metal segment. Those who utilized it well were able to pay off their debts and regain health. But others who continued to expand aggressively, fuelled by debt, seemed to have lost the plot, as the commodity cycle has quickly turned for the worse.

Two examples from these opposite ends of the spectrum are currently playing out in the IBC space itself.

Jindal Power, a company controlled by Naveen Jindal, has filed its expression of interest to participate in the resolution process of troubled airline GoFirst. The airliner, originally promoted by the Wadia Group, had flown into trouble with lenders initiating the resolution process for debts of over ₹6,500 crore.

As late as 2017, the group had accumulated debt of over ₹46,500 crore, the majority of which was spent in building capacities in Angul Steel operations. It had also collected debt of more than ₹14,000 crore on the books of its overseas subsidiaries. The steel upcycle was utilized by the group in repaying overseas loans, and a smaller portion of debt remains on the local arms, allowing it room to bid for the airline assets of GoFirst.

On the other hand, life has come full circle for the Vedanta Group, which was the first successful resolution applicant among the group of companies listed under the House of Debt. The group had gone on an aggressive expansion spree spurred by debt at the end of which it bought Electrosteel through the IBC process in 2018. Its attempts to monetize some of the earlier investments in government companies, such as Hindustan Zinc and BALCO, have faced resistance from the government, affecting its long-term plans.

Following the downgrade by rating agencies last September, the Anil Agarwal-led group has been trying to deleverage by selling assets and exiting businesses like steel to focus on its core areas. Thus, Electrsteel Steels, one of the 'Big 12', is again on the block.

Meanwhile, some of the defaulting companies are still struggling to complete the first cycle of resolution.

Jaypee Infratech, whose resolution involved delivering flats to some 20,000 homebuyers, finally saw its resolution plan by Suraksha Realty get the NCLT approval in March 2023. However, even this fourth attempt resolution, that involved the infusion of ₹250 crore and a loan of ₹3,000 crore, which will help ensure the delivery of the apartment over a period of four years, has found resistance.

The Yamuna Expressway Industrial Development Authority (YEIDA) has made this conditional upon the resolution applicant paying close to ₹1,700 crore in compensation to farmers who were affected by the projects.

Another troubled resolution that continues to drag on is that of Era Infra Engineering. The process was interrupted as the enforcement directorate froze several accounts of the company after the resolution process began in 2018. The company has admitted claims of over ₹22,216 crore as of July 2023, of which over ₹17,100 crore are from secured financial creditors. Though the CoC had shortlisted some four resolution applications as early as December 2022, the final decision still seems elusive. About 99 per cent of assenting creditors have approved a resolution plan submitted by SA Infrastructure Consultation promoted by Saurav Shekhar. The highlight of the plan is that its total value is around ₹2,000 crore, which is ten times the liquidation value. Yet it amounts to less than 10 per cent of total admitted claims. The plan is awaiting approval from the NCLT.

In at least two cases, though the resolution process seems complete, investigations are ongoing after allegations of fraud and siphoning of funds surfaced.

In the matter of ABG Shipyard, which has gone into liquidation, the consortium of banks led by SBI filed a complaint with CBI. It has been alleged that the promoters and directors misused loan funds of over ₹28,000 crore borrowed from some twenty-eight banks for purposes other than stated objectives.

In November 2022, the Serious Fraud Investigation Office discovered that funds lent to Amtek Auto (which has been sold to Deccan Value Investors for ₹500 crore), valued at over

₹12,000 crore, had found their way to some entities linked to erstwhile promoters.[1] As many as 500 related party entities are said to be under the scanner for having received these funds.

Even as these investigations go on, the IBC process continues to evolve. The arrival of GoFirst into the insolvency process saw announcements of fresh tweaks to the code, wherein lessors were exempted from the moratorium applicable after an insolvency case is admitted in the NCLT. This allows taking back leased aircrafts from the airline.[2]

Similarly, in September in 2023, the Reserve Bank of India tweaked provisions around wilful defaulters. In a new draft master direction on treatment of wilful and large defaulters, the central bank proposed broadening the definition of wilful default and expanded the scope of entities that can classify borrowers as wilful defaulters. Provisions have also been added for the entire process to be completed in a span of six months. Moreover, the draft contains provisions for banks to report errant auditors to regulators such as the National Financial Reporting Authority.

These developments augur well for the lending industry and raise hopes for better management of bad debts and errant borrowers.

Notes

Foreword

1. Caricature by Ravikanth, 13 February 2024, *Hindu BusinessLine*. Available: https://www.thehindubusinessline.com/opinion/cartoons/pocket/article67842508.ece.

2. Insolvency and Bankruptcy Board of India, Discussion Paper, 27 August 2021. Available: https://ibbi.gov.in/Discussionpaper-CIRP-27Aug2021.pdf.

3. Economic Survey of India 2016–17. Available: https://www.indiabudget.gov.in/budget2017-2018/es2016-17/echapter.pdf.

Introduction

1. N. Sundaresha Subramanian, 'The mystery of PNB's vanishing loans', *Business Standard*, 8 March 2016. Available: https://www.business-standard.com/article/finance/the-mystery-of-pnb-s-vanishing-loans-116030801266_1.html.

Chapter 1: The Origins

1. 'Non-Performing Asset', Corporate Finance Institute, 14 March 2023. Available: https://corporatefinanceinstitute.com/resources/accounting/non-performing-asset/; Trupti Jalan, 'Non Performing Assets (NPA)', *Scripbox*, 28 November 2022. Available: https://scripbox.com/pf/non-performing-assets/#provisions-for-non-performing-assets.

2. Report of the Committee on Industrial Sickness and Corporate Restructuring (New Delhi: July 1993). Available: http://reports.mca.gov.in/Reports/31-Goswami%20committee%20of%20the%20industriai%20sickness%20and%20corporate%20restructuring,%201993.pdf.

3. 'Union Finance Minister Nirmala Sitharaman's reply to #Budget2019 debate in Rajya Sabha,' PIB India, 2019. Available: https://www.youtube.com/watch?v=wg-qfnNiNX4.

4. Financial Stability Report, Issue No. 16, RBI, December 2017. Available: https://rbidocs.rbi.org.in/rdocs/PublicationReport/Pdfs/0FSR201730210986ADDA44E2A946A3F6C4408581.PDF.

5. Adverse Impact of NPAs on Economy, Unstarred Question No.†2462, Rajya Sabha, Ministry of Finance, Government of India. Available: https://sansad.in/getFile/annex/250/AU2462.doc?source=pqars.

6. Atul Thakur, 'Bad Loans: India's Wilful Defaulters Owe More than Rs 1 Lakh Crore to Banks', *Times of India*, 23 February 2018. Available: https://timesofindia.indiatimes.com/business/india-business/indias-wilful-defaulters-owe-more-than-rs-1-lakh-crore-to-banks/articleshow/63035851.cms.

7. Report of the Committee on Industrial Sickness, Submitted to the Union Minister of Finance, Government of India, July 1993, 53. Available: https://ibbi.gov.in/uploads/resources/31Goswamicommitte oftheindustriaisicknessand corporaterestructuring1993.pdf.

8. Ibid, 96.

9. 'Of the dirty dozen, eight large NPAs yield 51% recovery at IBC', *ET BFSI (indiatimes.com)*, 18 March 2022. Available: https://bfsi.economictimes.indiatimes.com/news/industry/of-the-dirty-dozen-eight-large-npas-yield-51-recovery-at-ibc/90302848.

Chapter 2: Companies Cry, But Owners Party

1. 'NPAs driven by big corporates; small firms have better record: RBI's Chakrabarty', *KNN*, 3 December 2013. Available: https://knnindia.co.in/news/newsdetails/economy/npas-driven-by-big-corporates-small-firms-have-better-record-rbis-chakrabarty.

2. PTI, 'Banks' improving financial performance supports intrinsic creditworthiness: Fitch', *Times of India (indiatimes.com)*, 21 February 2023. Available: https://timesofindia.indiatimes.com/business/india-business/banks-improving-financial-performance-supports-intrinsic-creditworthiness-fitch/articleshow/98118456.cms?from=mdr.

3. 'Gross NPAs of banks to improve to 3.3% in FY24, says India Ratings', *Moneycontrol*, 2 March, 2023. Available: https://www.moneycontrol.com/news/business/gross-npas-of-banks-to-improve-to-3-3-in-fy24-says-india-ratings-10181701.html.

4. RBI, notification dated 15 July 2014, 'Flexible Structuring of Long-Term Project Loans to Infrastructure and Core Industries.' Available: https://www.rbi.org.in/scripts/NotificationUser.aspx?Id=9101.

5. RBI, notification dated 23 August 2001, 'Corporate Debt Restructuring (CDR)'. Available: https://www.rbi.org.in/Scripts/NotificationUser.aspx?Id=440&Mode=0.

6. G. Arun Kumar and Dheeraj Tiwari, 'Ex-deputy Governor of RBI, K. C. Chakrabarty, under Lens in Kingfisher Debt, Airworth Cases,' *Economic Times*, 17

September 2018. Available: https://economictimes.indiatimes.com/news/politics-and-nation/ex-deputy-governor-of-rbi-kc-chakrabarty-under-lens-in-kingfisher-debt-airworth-cases/articleshow/65835493.cms?from=mdr.

7. Charan Singh and Jagvinder Brar, 'Stressed Assets and Banking in India', *SSRN*, 7 April 2016. Available: https://papers.ssrn.com/sol3/papers.cfm?abstract_id=2760198.

8. Scope for Insolvency Professional, CA Bhawani Shankar Rathi. Available: https://www.wirc-icai.org/images/material/Sumedha-IBC-Presentation-scope-professionals-9082017.pdf.

9. Bankruptcy Law Reforms Committee, 'The report of the Bankruptcy Law Reforms Committee Volume I: Rationale and Design', November 2015. Available: https://ibbi.gov.in/BLRCReportVol1_04112015.pdf.

Chapter 3: Corruption and Political Involvement

1. PTI, 'CBI charge sheet against ex-Canara Bank CMD R K Dubey in loan default case', *Economic Times*, 19 March 2018. Available: https://economictimes.indiatimes.com/news/politics-and-nation/cbi-charge-sheet-against-ex-canara-bank-cmd-r-k-dubey-in-loan-default-case/articleshow/63367732.cms?from=mdr.

2. PTI, 'CBI arrests Syndicate Bank CMD SK Jain for taking bribe', *Times of India*, 2 Aug 2014. Available: https://timesofindia.indiatimes.com/business/india-business/cbi-arrests-syndicate-bank-cmd-sk-jain-for-taking-bribe/articleshow/39492335.cms.

3. PTI, 'CBI Case Against UCO Bank Former Top Officer In 621 Crore Fraud Case', *NDTV*, 14 April 2018. Available: https://www.ndtv.com/india-news/cbi-case-against-former-uco-bank-top-officer-arun-kaul-in-rs-621-cr-fraud-case-1837652.

4. N. Sundaresha Subramanian, 'What's so special in officers of govt-run Dena Bank?', *Rediff.com*, 8 October 2014. Available: https://www.rediff.com/money/special/special-whats-so-special-in-officers-of-govt-run-dena-bank/20141008.htm.

5. Report of the Committee on HR Issues of Public Sector Banks, June 2010. Available: https://financialservices.gov.in/sites/default/files/HRIssuesOfPSBs.pdf.

6. Report of The Committee to Review Governance of Boards of Banks in India, May 2014. Available: https://rbidocs.rbi.org.in/rdocs/PublicationReport/Pdfs/BCF090514FR.pdf.

7. Banks Board Bureau, Wikipedia. Available: https://en.wikipedia.org/wiki/Banks_Board_Bureau.

8. N. Sundaresha Subramanian, 'When it comes to PSB appointments, 'BJP flavour' is the strongest,' *Rediff.com,* 20 September 2016. Available: https://www.rediff.com/business/report/when-it-comes-to-psb-appointments-bjp-flavour-is-the-strongest/20160920.htm.

9. 'Syndicate Bank elects Kamal Kishore Singhal as director', *Moneycontrol*, 30 October 2015. Available: https://www.moneycontrol.com/news/business/announcements/syndicate-bank-elects-kamal-kishore-singhal-as-director-1484229.html.

10. 'H N Sinor withdraws resignation, decides to re-engage with BBB', *Moneycontrol*, 22 May 2017. Available: https://www.moneycontrol.com/news/trends/current-affairs-trends/h-n-sinor-withdraws-resignation-decides-to-re-engage-with-bbb-2284977.html.

11. 'Bank union AIBEA demands action against top executives in bank fraud cases, *Moneylife*, 22 February 2018. Available: https://moneylife.in/article/bank-union-aibea-demands-action-against-top-executives-in-bank-fraud-cases/53173.html.

12. Department of Financial Services. Available: https://financialservices.gov.in/banking-divisions/public-sector-banks.

13. 'More Than One-third Posts on Public Sector Banks Boards Vacant; Only One in Ten Directors a Woman: CHRI Study', *Moneylife*, 13 January 2023. Available: https://www.moneylife.in/article/more-than-one-third-posts-on-public-sector-banks-boards-vacant-only-one-in-ten-directors-a-woman-chri-study/69492.html.

14. PTI, 'CBI arrests ex-ICICI Bank CEO Chanda Kochhar, husband Deepak Kochhar in Videocon loan case', *Business Today*, 23 December 2022. Available: https://www.businesstoday.in/latest/corporate/story/cbi-arrests-ex-icici-bank-ceo-chanda-kochhar-and-her-husband-in-loan-fraud-case-357623-2022-12-23.

Chapter 4: Mallya and the Art of Leaving

1. Vijay Mallya Interview (1998), *ZNN TV*, 24 March 2016. Available: https://www.youtube.com/watch?v=vlwvtX4rbQ8.

2. 'Who is Vijay Mallya', *Business Standard*. Available: https://www.business-standard.com/about/who-is-vijay-mallya.

3. Neeraj Chauhan, 'Expedite Vijay Mallya and Nirav Modi's extradition: India to UK officials', *Hindustan Times*, 22 October 2022. Available: https://www.hindustantimes.com/india-news/expedite-mallya-and-nirav-s-extradition-india-to-uk-officials-101666373521897.html.

4. 'In 2016, Vijay Mallya left India with 300 bags and a cargo, lawyer says it was "for a meeting"', *Times Now*, 12 December 2018. Available: https://www.timesnownews.com/india/article/vijay-mallya-extradition-kingfisher-airlines-owner-left-india-with-300-bags-and-a-cargo-lawyer-says-it-was-for-a-meeting-enforcement-directorate/330118.

5. 'Did SBI's Delay in Moving Court despite Top Lawyer's Advice Help Mallya Leave?' *Times of India*, 10 March 2016, Available: https://timesofindia.indiatimes.com/india/did-sbis-delay-in-moving-court-despite-top-lawyers-advice-help-

mallya-leave/articleshow/51336391.cms?utm_source=contentofinterest&utm_medium=text&utm_campaign=cppst.

6. PTI, 'PM's blue-eyed boy in CBI weakened notice against Mallya, allowed him to flee: Rahul Gandhi', *Economic Times*, 15 September 2018. Available: https://economictimes.indiatimes.com/news/politics-and-nation/pms-blue-eyed-boy-in-cbi-weakened-notice-against-mallya-allowed-him-to-flee-rahul-gandhi/articleshow/65820842.cms?from=mdr.

7. 'Staring at extradition, Vijay Mallya drags in FM Arun Jaitley; Jaitley rubbishes claim', *Economic Times*, 13 September 2018. Available: https://economictimes.indiatimes.com/news/politics-and-nation/met-arun-jaitley-before-i-left-india-vijay-mallya/articleshow/65785235.cms?from=mdr.

8. Shaswati Das, 'Arun Jaitley Denies Meeting Vijay Mallya before He Left India,' *Mint*, 12 September 2018. Available: https://www.livemint.com/Politics/0L5o3iRS82tWEs4STfjvmL/Jaitley-denies-Mallyas-claim-that-he-met-FM-before-leaving.html.

9. 'Swamy says order to downgrade Mallya notice came from finance ministry', *India Today*, 13 September 2018. Available: https://www.indiatoday.in/india/story/subramanian-swamy-undeniable-fact-mallya-told-jaitley-he-was-leaving-for-london-1338734-2018-09-13.

10. *Dr Subramaniam Swamy vs Ramakrishna Hegde on 18 October, 1989*, 1990 AIR 113, 1989 SCR Supl. (1) 469. Available: https://indiankanoon.org/doc/1559770/.

11. 'Follow the Leader with Dr Vijay Mallya' (Aired: April 2004), *NDTV*, 20 July 2013. Available: https://www.ndtv.com/video/shows/follow-the-leader/follow-the-leader-with-dr-vijay-mallya-aired-april-2004-283789.

12. Kingshuk Nag, 'The Rise, Fall and Escape of Vijay Mallya,' *Hindu BusinessLine*, 25 September 2018. Available: https://www.thehindubusinessline.com/opinion/columns/the-rise-fall-and-escape-of-vijay-mallya/article25040919.ece.

13. 'Defaulters Must Not Flaunt Money: Raghuram Rajan,' *Economic Times*, 23 January 2016. Available: https://economictimes.indiatimes.com/news/economy/policy/defaulters-must-not-flaunt-money-raghuram-rajan/articleshow/50693200.cms?from=mdr.

14. K. Giriprakash, *The Vijay Mallya Story* (New Delhi: Portfolio by Penguin Books, 2014).

15. Mihir Dalal and P. R. Sanjai, 'How Vijay Mallya Inherited an Empire and Proceeded to Lose It,' *Mint*, 26 February 2016. Available: https://www.livemint.com/Companies/1YrLuntaxmNyeNoYFbUX1L/How-Vijay-Mallya-inherited-an-empire-and-then-proceeded-to-l.html.

16. Ibid.

17. Sindhu Bhattacharya, 'The inside story of Vijay Mallya's tumble: He bought Deccan with eyes closed', *Firstpost*, 16 April 2014. Available: https://www.firstpost.

com/business/corporate-business/the-inside-story-of-vijay-mallyas-tumble-he-bought-deccan-with-eyes-closed-1967877.html.

18. TNN, 'SFIO cites violations, takes Vijay Mallya to court', *Times of India*, 10 January 2018. Available: https://timesofindia.indiatimes.com/city/bengaluru/sakala-services-only-4-mobile-numbers-registered-for-366-citizens/articleshow/62435112.cms.

19. *Mallya vs Government of India*, England and Wales High Court, 20 April 2020. Available: https://www.casemine.com/judgement/uk/5e9e77d92c94e067e627e8b2.

20. Munish Pandey, 'Attached Vijay Mallya shares were part of unpaid Yes Bank loan', *India Today*, 27 March 2019. Available: https://www.indiatoday.in/india/story/attached-vijay-mallya-shares-were-part-of-unpaid-yes-bank-loan-1487846-2019-03-27.

21. 'Kingfisher Airlines owes Rs 785 crore to oil firms', *India Today*, 6 May 2009. Available: https://www.indiatoday.in/latest-headlines/story/kingfisher-airlines-owes-rs-785-crore-to-oil-firms-46676-2009-05-05.

22. PTI, 'Vijay Mallya resigns from Rajya Sabha, says I will not get fair trial or justice', *Times of India*, 2 May 2016. Available: https://timesofindia.indiatimes.com/india/vijay-mallya-resigns-from-rajya-sabha-says-i-will-not-get-fair-trial-or-justice/articleshow/52079729.cms.

23. 'Between: Vijay Mallya and Government of India and National Crime Agency', 20 April 2020. Available: https://www.judiciary.uk/wp-content/uploads/2020/04/Mallya.APPROVED.pdf.

24. 'Vijay Mallya: The HC (Queen's Bench) while dismissing the appeal against Extradition, has found prima facie case of – conspiracy, false representation, dishonest intention & negative net worth at time of availing loans', *Advocate Retainer*, 20 April 2020. Available: https://www.advocateretainer.com/blogs/top-stories/vijay-mallya-the-hc-queens-bench-while-dismissing-the-appeal-against-extradition-has-found-prima-facie-case-of-conspiracy-false-representation-dishonest-intention-negative-net-worth-at-time-of-availing-loans.

25. 'Vijay Mallya loses leave to appeal against extradition in UK Supreme Court', *Indian Express*, 14 May 2020. Available: https://indianexpress.com/article/india/vijay-mallya-kingfisher-extradition-uk-court-6410008/.

26. Vijay Mallya (@TheVijayMallya), 14 May 2020. Available: https://twitter.com/TheVijayMallya/status/1260722248060735489?lang=en.

Chapter 5: The Point of No Return?

1. 'Urjit R Patel: Resolution of stressed assets – towards the endgame', Bank for International Settlements, 30 August 2017. Available: https://www.bis.org/review/r170830a.htm.

2. Urjit R. Patel, 'Resolution of Stressed Assets: Towards the Endgame,' (speech) at the Inaugural Session of the 'National Conference on Insolvency and Bankruptcy: Changing Paradigm,' Reserve Bank of India, Mumbai, on 19 August 2017. Available: https://m.rbi.org.in/Scripts/BS_SpeechesView.aspx?Id=1044.

3. Bhuvan Bagga, 'What makes NDA's 'India Shining' campaign the 'worst' poll strategy in Indian history', *India Today*, 14 May 2013. Available: https://www.indiatoday.in/india/story/nda-india-shining-worst-poll-strategy-162922-2013-05-13.

4. ETBFSI Research, 'Debt recovery from top corporates under IBC at dismal 17%', BFSI, *Economic Times*, 16 May 2023. Available: https://bfsi.economictimes.indiatimes.com/news/financial-services/debt-recovery-from-top-corporates-under-ibc-at-dismal-17/100269322.

5. Status Note on Corporate Insolvency Resolution Process, Insolvency and Bankruptcy Board of India. Available: https://ibbi.gov.in/uploads/meetings/b7fe220b5301841670a6e36b7719bfa2.pdf.

Chapter 6: Lanco Infratech

1. 'History', Lanco Infratech Limited. Available: http://www.lancogroup.com/.

2. 'Lanco MD Held with Rs 34 lakh', *Business Standard*, 5 February 2013. Available: https://www.business-standard.com/article/companies/lanco-md-held-with-rs-34-lakh-107032601016_1.html.

3. 'Lanco's Sasan Bid Annulled,' *Business Standard*, 14 June 2013. Available: https://www.business-standard.com/article/economy-policy/lanco-s-sasan-bid-annulled-107072501082_1.html.

4. Utpal Bhaskar 'The Lessons of Lanco Infratech,' *Mint*, 4 August 2015. Available: https://www.livemint.com/Companies/3MJwTroXN1TQEvQyKPesNL/The-lessons-of-Lanco-Infratech.html.

5. Sangita Mehta, 'Crisil Downgrades Rs 8207 Crore Bank Facilities of Lanco Power,' *Economic Times*, 30 May 2012. Available: https://m.economictimes.com/markets/stocks/news/crisil-downgrades-rs-8207-crore-bank-facilities-of-lanco-power/articleshow/13671990.cms.

Chapter 7: Amtek Auto

1. Ashish Gupta, 'Amtek Auto – the Pacman way', *Fortune India*, 5 February 2015. Available: https://www.fortuneindia.com/ideas/amtek-auto---the-pacman-way/100438.

2. 'Welcome to AMTEK'. Available: https://www.amtek.com/.

3. Gupta, 'Amtek Auto – the Pacman Way'.

4. 'Amtek Auto to buy Japan-based Asahi Tec's iron casting, forging & machining business', *Business Standard*, 29 April 2015. Available: https://www.business-standard.com/content/b2b-manufacturing-industry/amtek-auto-to-buy-japan-based-asahi-tec-s-iron-casting-forging-machining-business-115042900706_1.html.

5. 'Castex Technologies in Focus after Issuing Clarification Regarding FCCBs,' *Business Standard*, 19 June 2015. Available: https://www.business-standard.com/article/news-cm/castex-technologies-in-focus-after-issuing-clarification-regarding-fccbs-115061900139_1.html.

6. PTI, 'Amtek Auto, Castex Technologies Plunge on Sebi Probe', *NDTV Profit*, 10 September 2015. Available: https://www.ndtvprofit.com/business/amtek-auto-castex-technologies-plunge-on-sebi-probe-1216128.

7. Russell Hotten, 'Volkswagen: The scandal explained', *BBC*, 10 December 2015. Available: https://www.bbc.com/news/business-34324772.

8. Partha Sinha, 'Amtek fund crunch hits JP Morgan MF', *Times of India*, 29 August 2015. Available: https://timesofindia.indiatimes.com/business/india-business/amtek-fund-crunch-hits-jp-morgan-mf/articleshow/48718237.cmss.

9. 'We Will Never Again Enter Non Auto Business, Says Arvind Dham, Amtek Auto Group Promoter', *ETAuto.com*, 21 September 2015. Available: https://auto.economictimes.indiatimes.com/news/auto-components/we-will-never-enter-non-auto-business-says-arvind-dham-amtek-auto-group-promoter/48949439.

10. Gupta, 'Amtek Auto – the Pacman Way'.

11. Shruti Mahajan, 'The long and tumultuous journey of Amtek Auto's insolvency process', *Moneycontrol*, 7 December 2019. Available: https://www.moneycontrol.com/news/trends/legal-trends/the-long-and-tumultuous-journey-of-amtek-autos-insolvency-process-7801321.html.

Chapter 8: Jaypee Infratech

1. N. Sundaresha Subramanian, Karan Choudhury and Shreya Jai, 'Homebuyers caught between banks and builders,' *Rediff.com*, 16 September 2017. Available: https://www.rediff.com/money/special/homebuyers-caught-between-banks-and-builders/20170916.htm.

2. Disclosure Document prepared in conformity with Securities and Exchange Board of India (Issue and Listing of Debt Securities) Regulations, 2008 issued vide circular No. LAD-NRO/GN/2008/13/127878 dated June 06, 2008) and SEBI (Issue and Listing of Debt Securities) Regulations, Amendments, 2012. Available: https://www.bseindia.com/downloads/ipo/201512014933im%20jaypee.pdf.

3. Ravi Teja Sharma, 'How Manoj Gaur's leadership helped Jaypee Group clock a turnover of over Rs 20k crore in 2011-12', *Economic Times*, 23 August 2012.

Available: https://economictimes.indiatimes.com/news/company/corporate-trends/how-manoj-gaurs-leadership-helped-jaypee-group-clock-a-turnover-of-over-rs-20k-crore-in-2011-12/articleshow/15610235.cms?from=mdr.

4. N. Sundaresha Subramanian, Karan Choudhury and Shreya Jai, 'Realty Check: Homebuyers Caught between Banks and Builders,' *Business Standard*, 3 September 2017. Available: https://www.business-standard.com/article/current-affairs/noida-homebuyers-caught-between-banks-and-builders-117090200899_1.html.

5. Jaypee Infratech, Annual Report 2015–16. Available: http://www.jaypeeinfratech.com/annual_report/Annual-Report-for-the-Year-2015-16.pdf.

6. TNN, 'Buyers bunch together to ask SC what their rights are', *Times of India*, 5 September 2017. Available: https://timesofindia.indiatimes.com/city/noida/buyers-bunch-together-to-ask-sc-what-their-rights-are/articleshow/60369198.cms.

7. N. Sundaresha Subramanian and M. J. Antony, 'In Relief to over 30,000 Homebuyers, SC Stays Jaypee Insolvency Proceedings,' *Business Standard*, 4 September 2017. Available: https://www.business-standard.com/article/companies/in-relief-to-over-30-000-homebuyers-sc-stays-jaypee-insolvency-proceedings-117090400472_1.html.

8. *Anuj Jain Interim Resolution ... vs Axis Bank Limited*, Supreme Court of India, 26 February 2020. Available: https://indiankanoon.org/doc/15033988/.

9. Jeevan Prakash Sharma, 'Five Years of Jaypee Infratech Insolvency Case: Why do Homebuyers End Up As The Biggest Losers?', *Outlook*, 26 August 2022. Available: https://www.outlookindia.com/business/five-years-of-jaypee-infratech-insolvency-case-why-do-homebuyers-end-up-as-the-biggest-losers--news-218988.

10. Vandana Ramnani, 'Jaypee Infratech insolvency case: Relief for homebuyers who fought a decade-long legal battle', *Moneycontrol*. Available: https://www.moneycontrol.com/news/business/real-estate/jaypee-infratech-insolvency-case-relief-for-homebuyers-who-fought-a-decade-long-legal-battle-10217221.html.

Chapter 9: Alok Industries

1. Partners' Speak, Celebrating 25 Years 1986–2011. Available: https://www.alokind.com/Uploaded_Files/watsnewspeak.pdf.

2. Sugata Ghosh, 'SBI-led banks in search of Rs 20,000 crore borrowed by Alok Industries', *Economic Times*, 9 May 2016. Available: https://economictimes.indiatimes.com/industry/banking/finance/banking/sbi-led-banks-in-search-of-rs-20000-crore-borrowed-by-alok-industries/articleshow/52180569.cms?from=mdr.

3. 'Indian Textile & Apparel Industry: Brightest Future Ever,' Alok Industries Limited – ™Integrated Textile Solutions. Available: https://www.alokind.com/events.aspx.

4. 'Letter of Offer', Alok Industries Limited, 20 March 2013. Available: https://www.sebi.gov.in/sebidata/attachdocs/1364280936793.pdf.

5. 'Milestones', Alok Industries Limited. Available: https://www.alokind.com/milestones.html.

6. Draft Letter of Offer, Alok Industries Limited, page 16. https://idbicapital.com/pdf/Alok_Industries_Limited_DLoF.pdf

7. Madhurima Nandy, 'Alok sells office space in Mumbai for Rs 425 cr', *Mint*, 21 May 2012. Available: https://www.livemint.com/Companies/tPHZrYhQJR6RkWjqyEDsCO/Alok-sells-office-space-in-Mumbai-for-Rs425-cr.html.

8. Sharleen D'Souza, 'Alok Industries to shut 45 retail stores', *Business Standard*, 25 January 2013. Available: https://www.business-standard.com/article/companies/alok-industries-to-shut-45-retail-stores-1120817000251.html.

9. Luke Tugby, 'Store Twenty One collapses into compulsory liquidation', *Retail Week*, 11 July 2017. Available: https://www.retail-week.com/fashion/store-twenty-one-collapses-into-liquidation/7023438.article.

10. Shayan Ghosh, 'Alok Industries: Debtors were not 'locatable', says RP', *Financial Express*, 26 April 2018. Available: https://www.financialexpress.com/industry/alok-industries-debtors-were-not-locatable-says-rp/1146052/.

11. PTI, 'CB1 files corruption case against senior Mumbai I-T officer', *Hindu*, 28 July 2017. Available: https://www.thehindu.com/news/national/cbi-files-corruption-case-against-senior-mumbai-i-t-officer/article19379839.ece.

12. Anupam Dasgupta, 'I-T officer Vivek Batra, wife 'made 21 foreign trips in 6 years'', *Mumbai Mirror*, 18 August 2017. Available: https://mumbaimirror.indiatimes.com/mumbai/crime/i-t-officer-wife-made-21-foreign-trips-in-6-years/articleshow/60111524.cms.

13. Deb P. Samaddar, 'Alok industries and the Story of its Revival', *Insider*, 19 October 2020. Available: https://insider.finology.in/success-stories/alok-industries-and-its-revival-story#:~:text=As%20in%20the%20case%20of,the%20minimum%20requirement%20of%2075%25.

Chapter 10: Era Infra Engineering

1. PTI, 'Rs 621 crore UCO Bank loan fraud: Enforcement Directorate registers money laundering case', *Financial Express*, 6 May 2018. Available: https://www.financialexpress.com/industry/banking-finance/rs-621-crore-uco-bank-loan-fraud-enforcement-directorate-registers-money-laundering-case/1157555/.

2. Dipu Rai, 'How 18 banks ignored auditor red flags in Era Infra's CDR', *DNA*, 18 July 2018. Available: https://www.dnaindia.com/business/report-dna-money-exclusive-how-18-banks-ignored-auditor-red-flags-in-era-infra-s-cdr-2638503.

3. 'Era Infra Engineering Profit and Loss', *Economic Times* Available: https://economictimes.indiatimes.com/era-infra-engineering-ltd/profitandlose/companyid-7936.cms.

4. Era Infra Engineering, 24th Annual Report 2013–14, *Moneycontrol*. Available: https://www.moneycontrol.com/download-annual-report/erainfraengineering/EIE01/2014.

5. SEBI Order, WTM/PS/61/IMD-CIS/NRO/OCT/2015, Before the Securities and Exchange Board of India Coram: Prashant Saran, Whole Time Member. Available: https://www.sebi.gov.in/sebi_data/attachdocs/1444217970874.pdf.

6. PTI, 'Sebi directs Adel Landmarks to refund investors within 3 months', *Economic Times*, 8 October 2015. Available: https://realty.economictimes.indiatimes.com/news/regulatory/sebi-directs-adel-landmarks-to-refund-investors-within-3-months/49266270.

7. 'The Curious Case of Era Infra', *Insolvency Tracker*, 8 August 2020. Available: https://insolvencytracker.in/2020/08/08/the-curious-case-of-era-infra/.

8. NCLT New Delhi Special Bench, 3 June 2019. Available (https://ibbi.gov.in/en/claims/order-process/L74899DL1990PLC041350). Available: https://ibbi.gov.in//webadmin/pdf/order/2019/Jun/3rd%20May%202019%20in%20the%20matter%20of%20Era%20Infra%20Engineering%20Limited%20IB-190(PB0-2017_2019-06-06%2016:20:13.pdf.

Chapter 11: Jyoti Structures

1. Jyoti Structures Ltd., Financials. Available: https://www.moneycontrol.com/financials/jyotistructures/profit-lossVI/JS03/4#JS03.

2. 'Electrification of Villages', Ministry of Power, 27 April 2012. Available: https://pib.gov.in/newsite/erelcontent.aspx?relid=82717.

3. JSL, Annual Report 2008–09. Available: https://www.bseindia.com/HIS_ANN_RPT/HISTANNR/2009/JYOTI_STRUCTURES_LTD-513250-MARCH-2009.PDF

4. Jyoti Structures Limited, 26 September 2014. Available: https://www.bseindia.com/downloads/ipo/ 2014926211310JSL%20PPD.pdf.

5. JSL, Annual Report 2018–19. Available: http://www.jyoti structures.in/download/JSL_Annaul%20Report%202018-19.pdf.s.

6. JSL, Annual Report, 2015–2016. Available: http://www.jyotistructures.in/download/Annual%20Report_16.pdf.

7. Ibid.

8. Sandeep Bamzai, 'SBI Stuck with Yet Another Lemon?,' *Pioneer*, 8 April 2016. Available: https://www.dailypioneer.com/2016/page1/sbi-stuck-with-yet-another-lemon.html.

9. Maulik Vyas, 'NCLT clears Sharad Sanghi's revised resolution proposal for Jyoti Structures', *Economic Times*, 27 March 2019. Available: https://economictimes.

indiatimes.com/news/company/corporate-trends/jyoti-structures-goes-to-netmagics-sanghi-as-nclt-approves-new-bid/articleshow/68599648.cms?from=mdr.

10. Indu Bhan, 'Supreme Court clears Rs 4,000-crore resolution plan for Jyoti Structures', *Indian Express*, 16 April 2019. Available: https://indianexpress.com/article/business/companies/supreme-court-clears-rs-4000-crore-resolution-plan-for-jyoti-structures-5677436/.

11. 'Jyoti Structures road to recovery', *Insolvency Tracker*, 11 July 2021. Available: https://insolvencytracker.in/2021/07/11/jyoti-structures-road-to-recovery/#:~:text=Jyoti%20Structures%2C%20which%20was%20acquired,this%20on%2025%20June%202021.

Chapter 12: ABG Shipyard

1. 'The rise & rise of Sensex: Journey from 7,000 to 20,000!', *Economic Times*, 19 September 2007. Available: https://economictimes.indiatimes.com/the-rise-rise-of-sensex-journey-from-7000-to-20000/articleshow/2382766.cms?from=mdr.

2. Team M&A, 'Great Offshore Takeover Saga – Bharati Shipyard v/s ABG Shipyard', M&A Lab, 16 December 2009. Available: https://www.nishithdesai.com/fileadmin/user_upload/pdfs/Ma%20Lab/Great%20Offshore%20Lab.pdf.

3. Saikat Das, 'ABG Shipyard faces criminal proceedings', *Economic Times*, 24 October 2017. Available: https://economictimes.indiatimes.com/industry/transportation/shipping-/-transport/abg-shipyard-faces-criminal-proceedings/articleshow/61209186.cms?from=mdr.

4. Bruhadeeswaran R., 'Religare Finvest In Big One-Time Bad Loans Write-Off', *VCCircle*, 15 November 2016. Available: https://www.vccircle.com/religare-finvest-resorts-big-write-bad-loans-mount.

5. Ibid.

6. *W.P.(C) 1180/2017& C.M.No.5358/2017, Strategic Credit Capital Pvt. vs Ratnakar Bank Ltd. & Anr, Indian Kanoon*, 29 May 2017. Available: https://indiankanoon.org/doc/159296171/?type=print.

7. Sam Chambers, 'Liberty House plans to convert ABG Shipyard into a ship recycling site', *Splash 247*, 27 August 2018. Available: https://splash247.com/liberty-house-plans-to-convert-abg-shipyard-into-a-ship-recycling-site/.

8. Jyotindra Dubey, 'IBBI suspends resolution professional in the ABG Shipyard case. What went wrong?', *Economic Times*, 30 September 2022. Available: https://economictimes.indiatimes.com/prime/corporate-governance/ibbi-suspends-resolution-professional-in-the-abg-shipyard-case-what-went-wrong/primearticleshow/94543468.cms.

Chapter 13: Essar Steel

1. 'Aegis Launches Delivery Centre in Sivaganga, Tamil Nadu', Aegis Facebook account. Available: https://www.facebook.com/Aegisglobal/videos/aegis-launches-delivery-centre-in-sivaganga-tamil-nadu/517259308334881/.

2. Manojit Saha, 'HDFC Bank sells Rs 550 crore Essar Steel loans at 40% discount', *Business Standard*, 30 April 2015. Available: https://www.business-standard.com/article/finance/hdfc-bank-sells-rs-550-crore-essar-steel-loans-at-40-discount-115042900916_1.html.

3. 'Bank of India classifies Essar Steel as bad loan', *Economic Times*, 30 May 2015. Available: https://economictimes.indiatimes.com/industry/banking/finance/banking/bank-of-india-classifies-essar-steel-as-bad-loan/articleshow/47473212.cms?from=mdr.

4. 'Essar Steel – Defaulting on Debt Payment', ICMR, IBS Center for Management Research, 2002. Available: https://www.icmrindia.org/casestudies/catalogue/Finance/Finance%20-%20Essar%20Steel%20-%20Defaulting%20on%20Debt%20Payment.htm.

5. 'Essar Steel – Defaulting on Debt Payment', ICMR, IBS Center for Management Research, 2002. Available: https://www.icmrindia.org/casestudies/catalogue/Finance/Finance%20-%20Essar%20Steel%20-%20Defaulting%20on%20Debt%20Payment.htm.

6. Krishn Kaushik and Atul Dev, 'How Essar Handed Out 195 iPads as Diwali Gifts to Top Politicians, Bureaucrats and Journalists in 2010', *Caravan*, 20 July 2015. Available: https://caravanmagazine.in/vantage/how-essar-handed-out-ipads-diwali-gifts-top-politicians-bureaucrats-and-journalists-2010-list1.

7. PTI, 'Whistleblower levels fresh allegations against Kochhar', *Economic Times*, 2 June 2018. Available: https://epaper.indiatimes.com/news/whistleblower-levels-fresh-allegations-against-kochhar/articleshow/64424146.cms.

8. PTI, 'Sebi penalises erstwhile Essar Steel India for disclosure lapses', *Economic Times*, 28 March 2022. Available: https://economictimes.indiatimes.com/markets/stocks/news/sebi-penalises-erstwhile-essar-steel-india-for-disclosure-lapses/articleshow/90502632.cms.

Chapter 14: The Bhushan Twins: Bhushan Steel and Bhushan Power & Steel

1. PTI, 'Syndicate Bank bribery scandal: CBI arrests Bhushan Steel vice chairman', *Times of India*, 7 August 2014. Available: https://timesofindia.indiatimes.com/india/syndicate-bank-bribery-scandal-cbi-arrests-bhushan-steel-vice-chairman/articleshow/39827434.cms.

2. Megha Mandavia, 'Bhushan Steel sees sharp credit ratings downgrade by CARE, Brickwork in 2014', *Economic Times*, 18 August 2014. Available: https://economictimes.indiatimes.com/industry/indl-goods/svs/steel/bhushan-steel-sees-sharp-credit-ratings-downgrade-by-care-brickwork-in-2014/articleshow/40352643.cms?from=mdr.

3. Deepak Shenoy, 'All You Wanted to Know About The Bhushan Steel Situation', *Capitalmind*, 22 August 2014. Available: https://www.capitalmind.in/2014/08/all-you-wanted-to-know-about-the-bhushan-steel-situation/.

4. N. Sundaresha Subramaniam, 'Friends in law', *Business Standard*, 21 January 2013. Available: https://www.business-standard.com/article/beyond-business/friends-in-law-112110300045_1.html.

5. PTI, 'Family feud plagues Bhushan group', *Telegraph*, 2 September 2016. Available: https://www.telegraphindia.com/business/family-feud-plagues-bhushan-group/cid/961865.

6. Meera Mohanty, 'Brij Bhushan Singal business group splits to end family dispute', *Economic Times*, 16 November 2011. Available: https://economictimes.indiatimes.com/industry/indl-goods/svs/steel/brij-bhushan-singal-business-group-splits-to-end-family-dispute/articleshow/10748995.cms.

7. Draft Letter of Offer, Bhushan Steel Limited, 21 February 2012. Available: https://idbicapital.com/pdf/BhushanSteelLimitedDraftLetterofOffer.pdf.

8. Ministry of Coal, Comptroller and Auditor General of India, Report No. 7 of 2012-13 – Performance Audit of Allocation of Coal Blocks and Augmentation of Coal Production, 17 August 2012. Available: https://cag.gov.in/en/audit-report/details/1837.

9. PTI, 'Inter-Ministerial Group recommends cancellation of three more coal blocks', *Economic Times*, 15 September 2012. Available: https://economictimes.indiatimes.com/industry/indl-goods/svs/metals-mining/inter-ministerial-group-recommends-cancellation-of-three-more-coal-blocks/articleshow/16413432.cms?from=mdr.

10. 'CBI arrests Bhushan Steel vice-chairman in bribery case', *India Today*, 15 August 2014. Available: https://www.indiatoday.in/business/story/cbi-arrests-bhushan-steel-vice-chairman-in-bribery-case-203214-2014-08-07.

11. *Uma Singal, New Delhi vs Acit, Centrl Circle-3*, New Delhi, 7 December 2018. Available: https://indiankanoon.org/doc/57630964/

12. PTI, 'Sebi bars Bhushan Steel promoters, 256 others for money laundering and tax evasion', *Business Today*, 23 December 2014. Available: https://www.businesstoday.in/latest/corporate/story/bhushan-steel-promoters-among-260-entities-barred-by-sebi-138601-2014-12-23.

13. *Brij Bhushan Singal, New Delhi vs Acit, Central Circle-3, New Delhi, Indian Kanoon*, 7 April, 2019. Available: https://indiankanoon.org/doc/9709826/?type=print.

14. 'Settlement Order in respect of 1) Mr. Neeraj Singal, 2) Mr. Brij Bhushan Singal and 3) Ms. Ritu Singal in the matter of Rander Corporation Limited', Securities and Exchange Board of India, 8 February 2019. Available: https://www.sebi.gov.in/enforcement/orders/feb-2019/settlement-order-in-respect-of-1-mr-neeraj-singal-2-mr-brij-bhushan-singal-and-3-ms-ritu-singal-in-the-matter-of-rander-corporation-limited-_42031.html.

15. Tribune News Service, 'Bhushan Industries' MD, 6 others held guilty', *Tribune*, 3 September 2016. Available: https://www.tribuneindia.com/news/archive/features/bhushan-industries-md-6-others-held-guilty-289616.

16. 'ED arrests former MD of Bhushan Steel in bank fraud case of Rs 56,000 cr', *Economic Times*, 11 June 2023. Available: https://economictimes.indiatimes.com/industry/indl-goods/svs/steel/ed-arrests-former-md-of-bhushan-steel-in-bank-fraud-case-of-rs-56000-cr/articleshow/100910332.cms.

Chapter 15: Monnet Ispat & Energy

1. CMD's Profile: Mr. Sandeep Jajodia, Monnet Group. Available: http://www.monnetgroup.com/cmd-profile.php.

2. 'Orissa Sponge: A mini Satyam?', DNA, 16 March 2018. Available: https://www.dnaindia.com/business/report-orissa-sponge-a-mini-satyam-1242684.

3. Sarita Singh, 'There's no investigation against Monnet Ispat: Sandeep Jajodia, MD, Monnet Ispat & Energy', *Economic Times*, 19 November 2011. Available: https://economictimes.indiatimes.com/opinion/interviews/theres-no-investigation-against-monnet-ispat-sandeep-jajodia-md-monnet-ispat-energy/articleshow/10788285.cms?from=mdr.

4. PTI, 'Fresh CBI case in coal scam investigation; FIR against Monnet Ispat', *Economic Times*, 19 July 2017. Available: https://energy.economictimes.indiatimes.com/news/coal/fresh-cbi-case-in-coal-scam-investigation-fir-against-monnet-ispat/59666752.

5. Srestha Banerjee, 'Supreme Court cancels allotment of 214 coal blocks', *Down To Earth*, 24 September 2014. Available: https://www.downtoearth.org.in/news/supreme-court-cancels-allotment-of-214-coal-blocks-46561.

6. 'Coal Concern for Monnet', *Coaljunction*, 16 September 2014. Available: https://www.coaljunction.in/news/n_newsdetail/Coal-concern-for-Monnet_1/6140#sthash.lEFTwDrD.dpbs.

7. Monnet Ispat & Energy Limited. Available: http://www.monnetgroup.com/pdfs/may17/31/Regulation30(6).pdf.

8. Monnet Industries Limited, 36th Annual Report 2018–2019. Available: http://www.monnetgroup.com/pdfs/aug19/mil/MINDAnnualreport2018-19.pdf.

9. 27th Annual Report 2016–2017, Monnet Ispat & Energy Limited. Available: http://www.monnetgroup.com/pdfs/sep2017/Annual_Report-2017.pdf.

Chapter 16: Electrosteel Steels

1. Electrosteel Steels Limited, Draft Red Herring Prospectus, 25 March 2010. Available: https://www.sebi.gov.in/sebi_data/attachdocs/1288346613150.pdf.

2. Electrosteel Steels Limited, Red Herring Prospectus, 11 September 2010. Available: https://www.sebi.gov.in/sebi_data/attachdocs/1287809559308.pdf?QUERY.

3. Electrosteel Steels Limited, Red Herring Prospectus, 11 September 2010. Available: https://www.sebi.gov.in/sebi_data/attachdocs/1287809559308.pdf?QUERY.

4. 'Narendra Modi trying to intimidate me: Jayanthi Natarajan on "tax for clearing files" allegation', *NDTV*, 13 January 2014. Available: https://www.youtube.com/watch?v=9s5jCej5MPM.

5. Electrosteel Steels Limited, 7th Annual Report 2013–2014. Available: https://www.eslsteel.com/investor-relations/pdf/annual-report-2013-14.pdf.

6. Electrosteel Steels Limited, Red Herring Prospectus, 11 September 2010. Available: https://www.capitalmarket.com/pub/dp/dp32039.pdf.

7. Maulik Vyas and Sachin Dave, 'NCLT directs to consider operational creditors dues four years after Electrosteel's resolution', *Economic Times*, 19 August 2022. Available: https://economictimes.indiatimes.com/markets/stocks/news/nclt-directs-lenders-to-consider-other-creditors-dues-four-years-after-electrosteels-resolution/articleshow/93648905.cms?from=mdr.

Chapter 17: Conquerors, Survivors and Hindustan Leavers

1. Ahmad Abbas, 'Antigua High Court Rules Choksi Allowed to Remain Despite Govt's Wish to Deport Him', *IMI Daily*, 19 April 2023. Available: https://www.imidaily.com/caribbean/antigua-high-court-rules-choksi-allowed-to-remain-despite-govts-wish-to-deport-him/.

2. N. Sundaresha Subramanian, 'Sterling Biotech's FCCB holders file liquidation petition', *Business Standard*, 25 January 2013. Available: https://www.business-standard.com/article/markets/sterling-biotech-s-fccb-holders-file-liquidation-petition-1121018000321.html.

3. 'Sandesara Brothers: Wanted in India, flourishing with state-backed support in Nigeria', *Wion News*, 7 June 2023. Available: https://www.wionews.com/world/

sandesara-brothers-wanted-in-india-flourishing-with-state-backed-support-in-nigeria-601543.

4. Ira Dugal, '39% Of Debt With Companies That Don't Earn Enough To Cover Interest Payments', *BQ Prime*, 11 October 2016. Available: https://www.bqprime.com/business/corporate-balancesheets-from-eight-feet-under-to-four-feet-under.

5. House of Debt, Credit Suisse, 21 October 2015. Available: https://research-doc.credit-suisse.com/docView?language=ENG&format=PDF&sourceid=csplusresearchcp&document_id=1054415551&serialid= %2FEOOR9XE%2F3qd5FUva3g KCECkykSM0oe3%2BxTPm74mNLc% 3D&cspId= null.

6. Maryam Nawaz Sharif (@MaryamNSharif), 27 April 2017. Available: https://twitter.com/MaryamNSharif/status/857597261362188288.

7. Saurav Anand, 'JSW Steel's crude steel production up 7% YoY in April', *Mint*, 10 May 2023. Available: https://www.livemint.com/news/india/jsw-steel-reports-7-yoy-growth-in-april-2023-crude-steel-production-targets-38-5-mtpa-capacity-by-fy25-11683709579438.html.

8. PTI, 'JSW Steel plans to add 6 mtpa steel capacity at Bellary plant', *The Economic Times*, 27 October 2014. Available: https://economictimes.indiatimes.com/industry/indl-goods/svs/steel/jsw-steel-plans-to-add-6-mtpa-steel-capacity-at-bellary-plant/articleshow/44949685.cms?from=mdr.

9. House of Debt, Credit Suisse, 21 October 2015. Available: https://research-doc.credit-suisse.com/docView?language=ENG&format=PDF&sourceid=csplusresearchcp&document_id=1054415551& serialid=%2FEOOR9XE%2F3qd5FUva3gKCECkyk SM0oe3%2BxTPm74m NLc%3D&cspId=null.

10. JSW Steel, Corporate Presentation May 2023. Available: https://www.jsw.in/sites/default/files/assets/industry/steel/IR/JSW_Steel_Investor_Presentation/JSW%20Steel_Corporate%20Presentation_May-23_vF-2.pdf.

11. Nikita Periwal and Nehal Chaliawala, 'JSW Steel to use entire Rs 18,000 crore fundraise to refinance debt in FY24', *Economic Times*, 22 May 2023. Available: https://economictimes.indiatimes.com/industry/indl-goods/svs/steel/jsw-steel-to-use-entire-rs-18000-crore-fundraise-to-refinance-debt-in-fy24/articleshow/100402648.cms?from=mdr.

12. 'About Power', Adani Power Limited. Available: https://www.adanipower.com/about-us.

13. 'With 339 MMT, Adani Ports End FY23 On A New High'. Available: https://www.adaniports.com/newsroom/media-releases/with-339-mmt-adani-ports-end-fy23-on-a-new-high.

14. K. Bharat Kumar, 'What is the Adani-Hindenburg saga all about?', *Hindu*, 4 February 2023. Available: https://www.thehindu.com/business/watch-what-is-the-adani-hindenburg-saga-all-about/article66470266.ece.

15. Rohit Chandock, 'Complete Analysis of Hindenburg's report on Adani Group', *TaxGuru*, 4 February 2023. Available: https://taxguru.in/finance/complete-analysis-hindenburgs-report-adani-group.html.

16. Mayur Shetty, 'Adani Group raises ₹19,235 crore debt since Hindenburg report', *Times of India*, 8 June 2023. Available: https://timesofindia.indiatimes.com/business/india-business/adani-group-raises-19235-crore-debt-since-hindenburg-report/articleshow/100834317.cms.

17. Mahim Pratap Singh, 'Vedanta-Owned Company Evaded Thousands of Crores of Mining Royalties Owed to Rajasthan Govt', *Wire*, 26 July 2021. Available: https://thewire.in/business/rajasthan-mining-royalties-vedanta-hzl.

18. Divya Patil, 'Spotlight still on Vedanta $3 billion debt despite spinoff plan', *Economic Times*, 5 October 2023. Available: https://economictimes.indiatimes.com/markets/stocks/news/spotlight-still-on-vedanta-3-billion-debt-despite-spinoff-plan/articleshow/104174152.cms.

19. Sucheta Dalal and Debashis Basu, '"Once we decide to get into something, we get into it with the assumption that we don't know anything" – Grandhi Mallikarjuna Rao', *Moneylife*, 24 April 2010. Available: https://www.moneylife.in/article/once-we-decide-to-get-into-something-we-get-into-it-with-the-assumption-that-we-dont-know-anything-grandhi-mallikarjuna-rao/4979.html.

20. Arindam Majumder, 'GMR inks pact with Andhra govt to develop greenfield airport near Vizag', *Business Standard,* 14 June 2020. Available: https://www.business-standard.com/article/companies/gmr-inks-pact-with-andhra-govt-to-develop-greenfield-airport-near-vizag-1200614000191.html.

21. 'Company History – GMR Airports Infrastructure', *Moneycontrol*. Available: https://www.moneycontrol.com/company-facts/gmrinfrastructure/history/GI27.

22. 'Our main focus is to strengthen our balance sheet: Saurabh Chawla, GMR Infra', *Economic Times*, 6 April 2023. Available: https://economictimes.indiatimes.com/markets/expert-view/our-main-focus-is-to-strengthen-our-balance-sheet-saurabh-chawla-gmr-infra/articleshow/99287296.cms?from=mdr.

23. GVK Power & Infrastructure Limited, 24th Annual Report 2017–18. Available: https://www.gvk.com/files/investorrelations/financialinformation/annualreports/2017__18_86ec57ac81bb494bb3f554b4a09a7286.pdf.

24. GVK Power & Infrastructure Limited, 28th Annual Report 2021–22. Available: https://www.gvk.com/files/investorrelations/financialinformation/annualreports/2021__22_7226 fca12eff4b2599baa961173c7bcd.pdf.

25. Sangita Mehta, 'GVK Power (Goindwal Sahib) admitted for insolvency', *Economic Times*, 11 October 2022. Available: https://economictimes.indiatimes.com/industry/energy/power/nclt-admits-gvk-power-goindwal-sahib-for-corporate-resolution-on-axis-banks-petition/articleshow/94769689.cms?from=mdrs.

26. 'Adani Group takes control of the Mumbai Airport', *5paisa*, 12 December 2022. Available: https://www.5paisa.com/blog/adani-group-takes-control-of-the-mumbai-airport.

27. Anirban Chowdhury & Saloni Shukla, 'GVK agrees to cede control of airport business to Adani Group', *Economic Times*, 1 September 2020. Available: https://economictimes.indiatimes.com/industry/indl-goods/svs/construction/gvk-agrees-to-cede-control-of-airport-business-to-adani-group/articleshow/77844759.cms?from=mdr.

28. 'Anil Ambani to continue clearing dues, next debt repayment to be worth $2.1 billion', *Business Today*, 30 September 2019. Available: https://www.businesstoday.in/latest/corporate/story/anil-ambani-continue-clearing-dues-next-debt-repayment-21-bn-rcap-agm-229557-2019-09-30.

29. Niharika Sharma, 'Tata and Adani are queueing up to take over Anil Ambani's debt-laden company', *Quartz*, 28 March 2022. Available: https://qz.com/india/2147413/tata-and-adani-queue-up-to-buy-anil-ambanis-reliance-capital#:~:text=In%20September%202021%2C%20the%20Anil,the%20quarter%20ended%20December%202021.

30. 'Torrent Wins Race To Acquire Anil Ambani's Reliance Capital For Rs 8,640 Crore: Report', *ABP Live*, 22 December 2022. Available: https://news.abplive.com/business/torrent-wins-race-to-acquire-anil-ambani-s-reliance-capital-for-rs-8-640-crore-report-1571150.

31. Madhura Karnik, 'Debt trap: Videocon is a classic case of what overborrowing can do to a company', *Scroll.in*, 16 February 2017. Available: https://scroll.in/article/829428/debt-trap-videocon-is-a-classic-case-of-what-overborrowing-can-do-to-a-company.

32. Dipak Mondal, 'Videocon's Dhoot offers to settle Rs 31,289 crore debt; creditors say 10-15 years plan no good', *Business Today*, 9 December 2020. Available: https://www.businesstoday.in/latest/corporate/story/videocon-dhoot-offers-to-settle-rs-31289-crore-debt-creditors-10-15-yrs-plan-goo-280926-2020-12-09.

33. PTI, 'Videocon insolvency: Creditors to take 96% haircut on loans; NCLT says bidder "paying almost nothing"', *India Today*, 16 June 2021. Available: https://www.indiatoday.in/business/story/videocon-insolvency-creditors-to-take-96-haircut-on-loans-nclt-says-bidder-paying-almost-nothing-1815646-2021-06-16.

Chapter 18: The Central Bank's Response

1. RBI, notification, 'Revised Guidelines on Corporate Debt Restructuring (CDR) Mechanism'. Available: https://www.rbi.org.in/upload/notification/pdfs/67158.pdf.

2. Raghuram G. Rajan, 'Why have bad loans been made?': Full text of Raghuram Rajan's speech to Assocham', *Scroll.in*, 22 June 2016. Available: https://scroll.in/article/810450/why-have-bad-loans-been-made-full-text-of-raghuram-rajans-speech-to-assocham.

3. Raghuram G. Rajan, 'The Greenspan Era: Lessons for the Future, Speech by Raghuram G. Rajan, Economic Counsellor and Director of the IMF's Research Department,' International Monetary Fund, 27 August 2005. Available: https://www.imf.org/en/News/Articles/2015/09/28/04/53/sp082705.

4. RBI, notification dated 21 March 2014, 'Early Recognition of Financial Distress, Prompt Steps for Resolution and Fair Recovery for Lenders: Framework for Revitalising Distressed Assets in the Economy'. Available: https://rbidocs.rbi.org.in/rdocs/Notification/PDFs/DNBSF21032014.pdf.

5. Ministry of Finance (Budget Division), Annual Report 2014–15. Available: https://financialservices.gov.in/sites/default/files/AnnualReport2014-15%20DFS.pdf.

6. RBI, notification dated 1 July 2014, 'Master Circular – Prudential norms on Income Recognition, Asset Classification and Provisioning pertaining to Advances'. Available: https://www.rbi.org.in/commonman/English/Scripts/Notification.aspx?Id=1459.

7. Sangita Mehta, 'SDR won't solve sticky loan issue, will result in big NPAs', *Economic Times*, 5 January 2016. Available: https://economictimes.indiatimes.com/news/economy/finance/sdr-wont-solve-sticky-loan-issue-will-result-in-big-npas/articleshow/50446213.cms?from=mdr.

8. 'Corporate Debt Restructuring Cases, Unstarred Question No. 1731, Rajya Sabha, Department of Financial Services, Ministry of Finance, Government of India. Available: https://sansad.in/getFile/annex/244/Au1731.doc?source=pqars.

9. 'Raghuram Rajan Explains the Origins of India's NPA Crisis', *Wire*, 12 September 2018. Available: https://thewire.in/banking/raghuram-rajan-npa-parliamentary-committee-modi-government.

10. Raghavanathan V., 'Data Displays Descent, Decay and Decline of Banking Sector over Past 2 Decades', *Moneylife*, 13 September 2021. Available: https://www.moneylife.in/article/data-displays-descent-decay-and-decline-of-banking-sector-over-past-3-decades/65112.html.

11. RBI, notification dated 12 February 2018, 'Resolution of Stressed Assets – Revised Framework'. Available: https://www.rbi.org.in/scripts/NotificationUser.aspx?Id=11218&M.

12. 'Wilful Defaulters', Starred Question no. *305, Lok Sabha, Ministry of Finance, Government of India. Available: https://sansad.in/getFile/loksabhaquestions/annex/173/AS305.pdf?source=pqals.

13. National Bank for Financing Infrastructure and Development. Available: https://www.nabfid.org/history.

Chapter 19: The Sell-off Struggle

1. Ernest Hemingway, *The Sun Also Rises*. New York: Scribner, 1926.
2. Arcelormittal India Private vs Satish Kumar Gupta, *Indian Kanoon*, 4 October 2018. Available: https://indiankanoon.org/doc/161012846/.
3. Ministry of Law and Justice, The Gazette of India, The Insolvency and Bankruptcy Code (Amendment) Act, 2017. Available: https://ibbi.gov.in/webadmin/pdf/legalframwork/2018/Jan/182066_2018-01-20%2023:35:29.pdf.
4. *Arcelormittal India Private Limited vs Satish Kumar Gupta & ORS.*, *Indian Kanoon*, 4 October 2018. Available: https://indiankanoon.org/doc/178724787/?type=print.
5. *Chitra Sharma and ors vs Union of India and ors*. Available: https://ibbi.gov.in/webadmin/pdf/whatsnew/2018/Aug/9th%20Aug%202018%20in%20the%20matter%20of%20Chitra%20Sharma%20and%20Ors.%20Vs.%20Union%20of%20India%20and%20Ors.%20WP%20(C)%20No.%20744-2017%20&%20Connected%20WPs%20&%20SLPs_2018-08-09%2018:02:42.pdf.
6. PTI, 'NCLT Approves 180 Resolution Plans Involving Realisation Amount Of Rs 51,424 Cr In FY23', *Outlook*, 4 June 2023. Available: https://www.outlookindia.com/business/nclt-approves-180-resolution-plans-involving-realisation-amount-of-rs-51424-cr-in-fy23-news-291978.
7. Noor Mohammad, 'India's Operational Creditors May No Longer Be Discriminated Against in Bankruptcy Cases', *Wire*, 15 November 2018. Available: https://thewire.in/business/binani-cement-nclat-operational-creditors.
8. 'Raghuram Rajan Explains the Origins of India's NPA Crisis', *Wire*, 12 September 2018. Available: https://thewire.in/banking/raghuram-rajan-npa-parliamentary-committee-modi-government.
9. *Arcelormittal India Private Limited vs Satish Kumar Gupta & Ors*. Available: https://ibbi.gov.in/webadmin/pdf/whatsnew/2018/Oct/33945_2018_Judgement_04-Oct-2018_2018-10-04%2018:02:45.pdf.
10. 'COC Dharma', Quarterly Newsletter of the Insolvency and Bankruptcy Board of India, vol. 7, April–June 2018. Available: https://ibbi.gov.in/uploads/publication/Newsletter_IBBI_April_jun2018.pdf.
11. Michael Pooler, 'Sanjeev Gupta: is the steel magnate spinning too many plates?', *Financial Times*, 12 November 2018. Available: https://www.ft.com/content/ce33912c-e1f1-11e8-a6e5-792428919cee.
12. Gaurav Noronha, 'NCLT approves Amtek Auto resolution plan', *Economic Times*, 10 July 2020. Available: https://economictimes.indiatimes.com/news/politics-and-nation/nclt-approves-amtek-auto-resolution-plan/articleshow/76882571.cms?from=mdr.
13. George Mathew, 'Banks, payment operators report Rs 1,750 crore payment frauds in 7 months: RBI', *Indian Express*, 3 May 2023. Available: https://indianexpress.com/article/business/banking-and-finance/banks-payment-operators-report-rs-1750-crore-payment-frauds-in-7-months-rbi-8586237/.

14. Sudipta Routh and Pooja Dadoo, 'Swiss Ribbons And Its Implications – The Supreme Court On The Constitutionality And Key Provisions Of The Insolvency & Bankruptcy Code', *mondaq*, 12 February 2019. Available: https://www.mondaq.com/india/insolvencybankruptcy/781154/swiss-ribbons-and-its-implications---the-supreme-court-on-the-constitutionality-and-key-provisions-of-the-insolvency--bankruptcy-code.

15. Ashok Kini, '"Defaulter's Paradise Lost; Economy's Rightful Position Regained"; IBC Code Passes Constitutional Muster: SC', *LiveLaw*, 25 January 2019. Available: https://www.livelaw.in/top-stories/ibc-code-constitutional-142385.

16. 'IBC cases admitted over RBI circular to continue, says IBBI chief', *Mint*, 15 April 2019. Available: https://www.livemint.com/companies/news/ibc-cases-admitted-over-rbi-circular-to-continue-says-ibbi-chief-1555344091566.html.

17. *Swiss Ribbons Pvt. Ltd. & Anr. vs Union of India & Ors.* Available: https://ibbi.gov.in/webadmin/pdf/order/2019/Jan/25th-Jan-2019-in-the-matter-of-Swiss-Ribbons-Pvt.-Ltd.-and-Anr-Writ-Petition-Civil-No.37-99-100-115-459-598-775-822-849-and-1221-2018-In-Special-Leave-Petition-Civil-No.28623-of-2018_2019-01-25-13-58.pdf.

18. Sixth Report Standing Committee on Finance (2019-2020) (Seventeenth Lok Sabha) The Insolvency and Bankruptcy (Second Amendment) Bill, 2019 (Ministry of Corporate Affairs) Presented To Lok Sabha On 4 March, 2020. Available: https://ibbi.gov.in/uploads/whatsnew/20ef77b3a1200f12ad19cee1c2c3dba9.pdf.

19. PTI, 'Over 17,800 cases involving Rs 5.5 lakh cr disposed of at pre-admission stage under IBC: Official', *Economic Times*, 27 August 2021. Available: https://economictimes.indiatimes.com/news/economy/policy/over-17800-cases-involving-rs-5-5-lakh-cr-disposed-of-at-pre-admission-stage-under-ibc-official/articleshow/85689286.cms?from=mdr.

20. Speech by Arun Jaitley at the Conference on 'Insolvency and Bankruptcy Code, 2016: A Roadmap for the Next Two Years' at New Delhi on 18 December 2018. Available: https://ibbi.gov.in/uploads/resources/Vidhi_Speech_FM.pdf.

Epilogue

1. PTI, 'SC seeks report from SFIO, CBI on plea alleging laundering of over Rs 12,000 crore', *Economic Times*, 3 November 2022. Available: https://economictimes.indiatimes.com/news/india/sc-seeks-report-from-sfio-cbi-on-plea-alleging-laundering-of-over-rs-12000-crore/articleshow/95284187.cms.

2. 'Breather for aircraft lessors: Centre exempts aircraft, engines from moratorium under IBC', *Business Today*, 5 October 2022. Available: https://www.businesstoday.in/industry/aviation/story/breather-for-aircraft-lessors-centre-exempts-aircraft-engines-from-moratorium-under-ibc-400823-2023-10-05.

Abbreviations

ABG	Aditya Birla Group
ADAG	Anil Dhirubhai Ambani Group
ADB	Asian Development Bank
AEL	Adani Enterprises Limited
AHL	Affordable Housing Loan
AIBEA	All India Bank Employees Association
AIBOA	All India Bank Officers' Association
AIFI	All India Financial Institution
AIMPL	ArcelorMittal India Private Limited
ALL	Adel Landmarks Limited
AQR	Asset Quality Review
ARC	Asset Reconstruction Company
ARF	Asset Reconstruction Fund
ATR	Action Taken Report
ATV	Average Transaction Value
BBB	Banks Board Bureau
BBMB	Bhakra Beas Management Board
BG	Bank Guarantees
BHEL	Bharat Heavy Electricals Limited
BIFR	Board for Industrial and Financial Reconstruction
BIS	Bank for International Settlements
BJP	Bharatiya Janata Party
BKC	Bandra Kurla Complex
BPCL	Bharat Petroleum Corporation Limited
BPO	Business Process Outsourcing
BPSL	Bhushan Power & Steel Limited
BSE	Bombay Stock Exchange
BSL	Bhushan Steel Limited

BSSL	Bhushan Steel and Strips Limited
CAG	Comptroller and Auditor General
CAGR	Compound Annual Growth Rate
CAP	Corrective Action Plan
CARE	Credit Analysis and Research Limited
CDR	Corporate Debt Restructuring
CHRI	Commonwealth Human Rights Initiative
CIC	Credit Information Corporation
CIRP	Corporate Insolvency Resolution Process
CIS	Collective Investment Scheme
CLB	Company Law Board
CoC	Committee of Creditors
CoF	Cost of Fund
CPIL	Centre for Public Interest Litigation
CRA	Credit Rating Agency
CRILC	Central Repository of Information on Large Credits
CRISIL	Credit Rating Information Services of India Limited
CS	Credit Suisse
CVC	Central Vigilance Commission
DBS	Development Bank of Singapore
DCA	Debtor-Creditor Agreement
DBG	Dalmia Bharat Group
DRAT	Debts Recovery Appellate Tribunal
DRHP	Draft Red Herring Prospectus
DRT	Debt Recovery Tribunal
DSCR	Debt Service Coverage Ratio
DVC	Damodar Valley Corporation
DVI	Deccan Value Investors
EBIT	Earnings Before Interest and Taxes
EBITDA	Earnings Before Interest, Taxes, Depreciation and Amortization
ECL	Electrosteel Castings Limited
ED	Directorate of Enforcement
EFERL	Exsto Foundation Enterprises and Reserves
EGoM	Empowered Group of Ministers
EoI	Expression of Interest
EPC	Engineering, Procurement and Construction
ERP	Enterprise Resource Planning
ESIL	Essar Steel India Limited
EY	Ernst & Young Global Limited

ABBREVIATIONS

FAC	Forest Advisory Committee
FCCB	Foreign Currency Convertible Bond
FEMA	Foreign Exchange Management Act
FERA	Foreign Exchange Regulation Act
FFSL	First Financial Services Limited
FI	Financial Institution
FM	Financial Management
FRN	Floating Rate Notes
FZCO	Free Zone Company
GDR	Global Depository Receipt
GE Shipping	Greater Eastern Shipping
GFC	Global Financial Crisis
GFG Alliance	Gupta Family Group Alliance
GNPA	Gross Non-Performing Assets
GOL	Great Offshore Limited
GSPCL	Gujarat State Petroleum Corporation Limited
HAL	Hindustan Aeronautics Limited
HDFC	Housing Development Finance Corporation
HRD	Human Resource Development
HSBC	Hongkong and Shanghai Banking Corporation
HZL	Hindustan Zinc Limited
IANS	Indo-Asian News Service
IBBI	Insolvency and Bankruptcy Board of India
IBC	Insolvency and Bankruptcy Code
ICA	Inter-Creditor Agreement
ICD	Inter-Corporate Deposit
ICICI	Industrial Credit and Investment Corporation of India
ICMAI	Institute of Cost and Management Accountants of India
ICMR	IBS Center for Management Research
IDBI	Industrial Development Bank of India
IDRCL	India Debt Resolution Company Limited
IFCI	Industrial Finance Corporation of India
IL&FS	Infrastructure Leasing and Financial Services
IOCL	Indian Oil Corporation Limited
IPCL	Indian Petrochemicals Corporation Limited
IPO	Initial Public Offering
IRACP	Income Recognition, Asset Classification and Provisioning
IRP	Insolvency Resolution Professional
IRR	Internal Rate of Return

ABBREVIATIONS

JAL	Jaiprakash Associates Limited
JDU	Janata Dal United
JII	Jyoti International
JIL	Jaypee Infratech Limited
JISCO	Jindal Iron and Steel Company
JLF	Joint Lenders' Forum
JLM	Joint Lenders' Meeting
JSAPL	Jyoti Structures Africa (Pty) Limited
JSL	Jyoti Structures Limited
JSW	Jindal South West
JV	Joint Ventures
KFA	Kingfisher Airlines
KPMG	Klynveld Peat Marwick Goerdeler
L&T	Larsen & Toubro
LC	Letter of Credit
LIC	Life Insurance Corporation
LJPL	Lauren Jyoti Private Limited
LKPL	Lanco Kondapalli Power Limited
LoU	Letter of Undertaking
LTCG	Long-Term Capital Gains
MBA	Multiple Banking Accounts
MCA	Model Concession Agreements
MDRA	Master Debt Recast Agreement
MIAL	Mumbai International Airport Limited
MIS	Management Information System
MMT	Million Metric Ton
MoU	Memorandum of Understanding
MP	Member of Parliament
MTPA	Millions of Tonnes Per Annum
NABFID	National Bank for Financing Infrastructure and Development
NARCL	National Asset Reconstruction Company Limited
NBCC	National Buildings Construction Corporation
NCD	Non-Convertible Debentures
NCLAT	National Company Law Appellate Tribunal
NCLT	National Company Law Tribunal
NDA	National Democratic Alliance
NDDB	National Dairy Development Board
NNPA	Net Non-Performing Assets
NPA	Non-Performing Asset

NSE	National Stock Exchange
OC	Over-Collateralization
OEM	Original Equipment Manufacturer
OTS	Operator Training Simulator
PA	Procuring Authority/ Project Authority
PAT	Profit After Tax
PBT	Profit Before Tax
PE	Private Equity
PFS	Pyramids Freight Services
PIB	Press Information Bureau
PIL	Public Interest Litigation
PNB	Punjab National Bank
PPA	Power Purchase Agreement
PPP	Public-Private Partnership
PSB	Public Sector Banks
PSU	Public Sector Undertaking
PTI	Press Trust of India
PVB	Private Sector Banks
RBI	Reserve Bank of India
RCOM	Reliance Communications
REGE	Regulation E.
RFL	Reliance Financial Limited
RGG	Resurgent Group of Gujarat
RICS	Royal Institution of Chartered Surveyors
RoC	Registrar of Companies
ROCE	Return on Capital Employed
RoFR	Right of First Refusal
RP	Resolution Professional
RSA	Restructured Standard Assets
RTI	Right to Information
S4A	Scheme for Sustainable Structuring of Stressed Assets
SA	Stressed Assets
SAP	Statutory Accounting Principles
SARFAESI Act	Securitisation and Reconstruction of Financial Assets and Enforcement of Security Interest Act, 2000
SAT	Securities Appellate Tribunal
SBI	State Bank of India
SBLC	Standby Letter of Credit
SCB	Scheduled Commercial Banks

SCN	Show Cause Notice
SDR	Strategic Debt Restructuring
SDRI	State Directorate of Revenue Intelligence
SEBI	Securities and Exchange Board of India
SFIO	Serious Fraud Investigation Office
SIA	Special Investigative Auditor
SICA	Sick Industrial Companies Act
SLBC	State Level Bankers' Committee
SMA	Special Mention Account
SOP	Standard Operating Procedure
SOTP	Sum of the Parts
SPV	Special-Purpose Vehicle
SWIFT	Society for Worldwide Interbank Financial Telecommunication
TEV	Techno-Economic Viability
TISCO	Tata Iron and Steel Company
TMT	Thermo Mechanical Treatment
TPC	Total Project Cost
TPE	Total Potential Exposure
TUFS	Technology Upgradation Funds Scheme
UB/UBHL	United Breweries Holdings Limited
UCO	United Commercial Bank
UPA	United Progressive Alliance
UT	Unit Trust
VOVL	Videocon Oil and Ventures Limited
VW	Volkswagen
WACA	Western Australian Cricket Association
YEIDA	Yamuna Expressway Industrial Development Authority

Acknowledgements

Foremost thanks are due to my agent, Kanishka Gupta, who first saw the idea of this book in me and convinced me to work on it. I am grateful to my publisher, Pan Macmillan India, led by Rajdeep Mukherjee, for keeping their faith in the book despite my own doubts. I am indebted to the team and my editors, Shreya Gupta and Teesta Guha Sarkar, for giving the book the shape it has today and going out of their way to tie up all the loose ends. I must also thank the editors Sushmita Chatterjee, Avneet Kaur, Elizabeth James and Sanjiv Sarin who worked on earlier versions and added value.

My friends Vivek and R. Anand who patiently read the drafts and gave inputs – I owe them teetotallers a few mocktails. Above all, this book would have not been possible without the guidance and motivation received from Founder-Chairman of the IBBI, M. S. Sahoo, who was kind enough to go through the manuscript and provide valuable inputs, even though I could not incorporate them entirely. I must also thank the many bankers, insolvency professionals, investigators and consultants who shared important revelations with me while choosing to remain anonymous.